Spinsters and Lesbians

D1447228

THE CUTTING EDGE
Lesbian Life and Literature

THE CUTTING EDGE
Lesbian Life and Literature

Series Editor: Karla Jay
Professor of English and Women's Studies
PACE UNIVERSITY

EDITORIAL BOARD

THE CUTTING EDGE:
Lesbian Life and Literature

Series Editor: Karla Jay

The Cook and the Carpenter: A Novel by the Carpenter
by June Arnold
with an introduction by Bonnie Zimmerman

Ladies Almanack
by Djuna Barnes
with an introduction by Susan Sniader Lanser

Adventures of the Mind:
The Memoirs of Natalie Clifford Barney
translated by John Spalding Gatton
with an introduction by Karla Jay

Sophia Parnok: The Life and Work of Russia's Sappho
by Diana Burgin

Paint It Today
by H.D. (Hilda Doolittle)
edited and with an introduction by
Cassandra Laity

The Angel and the Perverts
by Lucie Delarue-Mardrus
translated and with an introduction by Anna Livia

Heterosexual Plots and Lesbian Narratives
Marilyn R. Farwell

*Spinsters and Lesbians: Independent Womanhood
in the United States*
by Trisha Franzen

Diana: A Strange Autobiography
by Diana Frederics
with an introduction by Julie L. Abraham

Lover
by Bertha Harris

Elizabeth Bowen: A Reputation in Writing
by renée c. hoogland

Lesbian Erotics
edited by Karla Jay

*Changing Our Minds: Lesbian Feminism and
Psychology*
by Celia Kitzinger and Rachel Perkins

(Sem)Erotics: Theorizing Lesbian : Writing
by Elizabeth A. Meese

*Bisexuality and the Challenge to Lesbian Politics:
Sex, Loyalty, and Revolution*
by Paula C. Rust

The Search for a Woman-Centered Spirituality
by Annette J. Van Dyke

I Know My Own Heart: The Diaries of Anne Lister,
1791-1840
edited by Helena Whitbread

No Priest but Love: The Journals of Anne Lister,
1824-26
edited by Helena Whitbread

Spinsters and Lesbians

Independent Womanhood
in the United States

Trisha Franzen

NEW YORK UNIVERSITY PRESS
New York and London

NEW YORK UNIVERSITY PRESS
New York and London

Copyright © 1996 by New York University

Library of Congress Cataloging-in-Publication Data
Franzen, Trisha, 1951–
     Spinsters and lesbians : independent womanhood in the United
States / Trisha Franzen.
        p.   cm. — (The cutting edge)
     Includes bibliographical references and index.
     ISBN 0-8147-2641-0. — ISBN 0-8147-2642-9 (pbk.)
      1. Lesbianism—United States.   2. Single women—United States.
   3. Feminism—United States.   4. Women—United States—Biography.
   I. Title.   II. Series: Cutting edge (New York, N.Y.)
   HQ75.6.U5F73   1996
   306.76'63—dc20   95-32464
                              CIP

New York University Press books are printed on acid-free
paper, and their binding materials are chosen for strength
and durability.

Manufactured in the United States of America

10 9 8 7 6 5 4 3 2 1

Contents

Foreword by Karla Jay   *xiii*

Acknowledgments   *xix*

Progressive Era Spinsters   *xxi*

Contemporary Lesbians   *xxv*

Introduction: Spinsters and Lesbians   1

1. "What Are You Going to Be?"   11
   Families and Childhoods in the Progressive Era
2. "I Knew I Was Odd"   25
   Growing Up Female, 1936-1965
3. "O, the Glorious Privilege of Being Independent"   47
   Defining Independent Womanhood in the Progressive Era
4. "I Was Going to Have to Do It All on My Own"   79
   Toward Independent Womanhood after World War II
5. "Such Beautiful Lives Together"   107
   Community and Companions among Progressive Era Women
6. "We're Not the Only Ones"   133
   Lesbian Identities and Communities after World War II
7. Spinsters and Lesbians   159
   Resisting and Surviving as Independent Women

On Methodology   *179*

Appendix: Tables   *185*

Notes   *191*

References   *209*

Index   *225*

Foreword

Despite the efforts of lesbian and feminist publishing houses and a few university presses, the bulk of the most important lesbian works has traditionally been available only from rare-book dealers, in a few university libraries, or in gay and lesbian archives. This series intends, in the first place, to make representative examples of this neglected and insufficiently known literature available to a broader audience by reissuing selected classics and by putting into print for the first time lesbian novels, diaries, letters, and memoirs that are of special interest and significance, but which have moldered in libraries and private collections for decades or even for centuries, known only to the few scholars who had the courage and financial wherewithal to track them down.

Their names have been known for a long time—Sappho, the Amazons of North Africa, the Beguines, Aphra Behn, Queen Christina, Emily Dickinson, the Ladies of Llangollen, Radclyffe Hall, Natalie Clifford Barney, H.D., and so many others from every nation, race, and era. But government and religious officials burned their writings, historians and literary scholars denied they were lesbians, powerful men kept their books out of print, and influential archivists locked up their ideas far from sympathetic eyes. Yet some dedicated scholars and readers still knew who they were, made pilgrimages to the cities and villages where they had lived and to the graveyards where they rested. They passed around tattered volumes of letters, diaries, and biographies, in which they had underlined what seemed to be telltale hints of a secret or different kind of life. Where no hard facts existed, legends were invented. The few precious and often available pre-Stonewall lesbian classics, such as *The Well of Loneliness* by Radclyffe Hall, *The Price of Salt* by Claire Morgan (Patricia Highsmith), and *Desert of the Heart* by Jane Rule, were cherished. Lesbian pulp was devoured. One of the primary goals of this series is to give the more neglected works, which constitute the vast majority of lesbian writing, the attention they deserve.

A second but no less important aim of this series is to present the "cutting edge" of contemporary lesbian scholarship and theory across a wide range of disciplines. Practitioners of lesbian studies have not adopted a uniform approach to literary theory, history, sociology, or any other discipline, nor should they. This series intends to present an array of voices that truly reflects the diversity of the lesbian community. To help me in this task, I am lucky enough to be assisted by a distinguished editorial board that reflects various professional, class, racial, ethnic, and religious backgrounds as well as a spectrum of interests and sexual preferences.

At present the field of lesbian studies occupies a small, precarious, and somewhat contested pied-à-terre between gay studies and women's studies. The former is still in its infancy, especially if one compares it to other disciplines that have been part of the core curriculum of every child and adolescent for several decades or even centuries. However, although it is one of the newest disciplines, gay studies may also be the fastest-growing one—at least in North America. Lesbian, gay, and bisexual studies conferences are doubling and tripling their attendance. Although only a handful of degree-granting programs currently exists, that number is also apt to multiply quickly during the next decade.

In comparison, women's studies is a well-established and burgeoning discipline with hundreds of minors, majors, and graduate programs throughout the United States. Lesbian studies occupies a peripheral place in the discourse in such programs, characteristically restricted to one lesbian-centered course, usually literary or historical in nature. In the many women's studies series that are now offered by university presses, generally only one or two books on a lesbian subject or issue are included, and lesbian voices are restricted to writing on those topics considered of special interest to gay people. We are not called upon to offer opinions on motherhood, war, education, or on the lives of women not publicly identified as lesbians. As a result, lesbian experience is too often marginalized and restricted.

In contrast, this series will prioritize, centralize, and celebrate lesbian visions of literature, art, philosophy, love, religion, ethics, history, and a myriad of other topics. In "The Cutting Edge," readers can find authoritative versions of important lesbian texts that have been carefully prepared and introduced by scholars. Readers can also find the work of academics and independent scholars who write about other aspects of life from a distinctly lesbian viewpoint. These visions are not only various but intentionally contradictory, for lesbians speak from differing class, racial, ethnic, and religious perspectives. Each author also speaks from and about a certain moment of time, and few would argue that being a lesbian today is the same as it was for Sappho or Anne Lister. Thus no attempt has been made to homogenize that diversity, and no agenda exists to attempt to carve out a "politically correct" lesbian studies perspective at this juncture in history or to pinpoint the "real" lesbians in history. It seems more important for all the voices to be heard before those with the blessings of aftersight lay the mantle of authenticity on any one vision of the world, or on any particular set of women.

What each work in this series does share, however, is a common realization that gay women are the "Other" and that one's perception of culture and literature is filtered by sexual behaviors and preferences. Those perceptions are not the same as those of gay men or of nongay women, whether the writers speak of gay or feminist issues or whether the writers choose to look at nongay figures from a lesbian perspective. The role of this series is to create space and give a voice to those interested in lesbian studies. This series speaks to any person who is interested in gender studies, literary criticism, biography, or important literary works, whether she or he is a student, professor, or serious reader, for the series is neither for lesbians only nor even by lesbians only. Instead, "The Cutting Edge" attempts to share some of the best of lesbian literature and lesbian studies with anyone willing to look at the world through lesbians' eyes. The series is proactive in that it will help to formulate and foreground the very discipline on which it focuses. Finally, this series has answered the call to make lesbian theory, lesbian experience, lesbian lives, lesbian literature, and lesbian visions the heart and nucleus, the weighty planet around which for once other viewpoints will swirl as moons to our earth. We invite readers of all persuasions to join us by venturing into this and other books in the series.

In the early years of lesbian and gay studies, the vast majority of efforts focused on researching and recasting important literary and historical figures whose reputation as lesbians had been obscured or denied. Broader historical studies tended to focus on the place of difference in historical events ranging from the impact of the Inquisition on rebellious communities of nuns to the fate of homosexuals during the Holocaust. In the 1990s, however, in the wake of Elizabeth Lapovsky Kennedy's and Madeline Davis's groundbreaking *Boots of Leather, Slippers of Gold,* lesbian historians, sociologists, and anthropologists, as well as independent scholars, have turned their attention to the lives of ordinary lesbians in various communities around the world during the twentieth century. Trisha Franzen's *Spinsters and Lesbians* represents the best of this trend. By investigating two sets of women, markedly different yet on the same continuum, Franzen is able to explore both the richness of similarity and the complexity of difference in a book that is both fascinating and enlightening.

KARLA JAY

Acknowledgments

Over the many years of this book's gestation, I have been privileged to have the support and assistance of many wonderful people. My words of appreciation will be inadequate. At the University of New Mexico, Jane Slaughter supported me and my work throughout my graduate career. Jane kept me on track, always supportive but always demanding. Her broad knowledge of history, especially women's history and the history of sexuality, and her skills as a teacher ensured that my work was built on a solid foundation. I could have asked no more from a dissertation committee chair, but she always was more—a friend, a mentor, and a colleague. Since my undergraduate years in Women's Studies at SUNY Buffalo I have been fortunate to work with Liz Kennedy. Her research on lesbian history constantly informed my studies. Through long-distance phone calls and express mail, Liz pushed me to be clearer and stronger in my writing and analysis. Louise Lamphere provided a steady stream of questions, suggestions, and encouragements which I appreciated. Jane Caputi and Ann Nihlen each contributed from her area of expertise. I was fortunate to have such a strong group of feminists and scholars with whom to work.

xx • Acknowledgments

The staff of the Schlesinger Library of Radcliffe College were consistently helpful and encouraging with my research there. That research was supported by both the Office of Graduate Studies and the Women's Studies Program of the University of New Mexico. My colleagues in Women's Studies at the University of New Mexico, especially Tey Diana Rebolledo and Helen Bannan (now at West Virginia University), provided an intellectual home for me.

Niko Pfund of New York University Press has been most patient and encouraging throughout the long revision process. The Faculty and Staff Research Group at Albion College gave me very helpful suggestions on the Introduction.

Over the final years of getting this material in shape, Jeanne-Marie Hémond has not only held our household together so I could focus on this work, but she has read and reread drafts of this book, patiently correcting grammar and spelling, suggesting clarification, and providing enthusiasm for my work when my energy flagged. My daughter, Emiliana Franzen, has always been a trooper and understanding of my need to work.

Finally I need to dedicate this book to the lesbians who shared their stories with me. This book has been a long time coming, but I hope in some way it acknowledges your struggles and your courage.

Progressive Era Spinsters

EDITH HAMILTON, born 1867, was the oldest child of a wealthy Fort Wayne, Indiana, family. Educated at Bryn Mawr College, she was headmistress of the Bryn Mawr School in Baltimore before she became famous as a classicist. From 1922 until her death in 1967, she lived with Doris Reid and helped raise four of Reid's nieces and nephews.

ALICE HAMILTON, born 1869, was the next Hamilton sister. After completing her medical degree at the University of Michigan and additional training in the United States and Europe, Alice became a resident of Hull House, the Chicago settlement house. She pioneered the field of industrial medicine and was the first woman appointed to the faculty of Harvard University.

LEONORA O'REILLY, born 1870 in New York City, was among the best known of the turn-of-the-century female labor activists. O'Reilly entered factory work at age twelve. A founder of both the Working Women's Society and the National Association for the Advancement of Colored People (NAACP), she was a member of the Knights of Labor and an outspoken leader within the Women's Trade Union League (WTUL).

MARY ANDERSON, born 1872 in Sweden, was a factory worker and union organizer when she became involved with the Women's Trade Union League. She was hired in 1917 as a staff member of the Women in Industry Service. In 1920, when this office became the Women's Bureau of the Department of Labor, Anderson was appointed director.

SARA JOSEPHINE "JO" BAKER, born 1873 in Pough-keepsie, New York, graduated from the medical school of the New York Infirmary for Women and Children. Her success in reducing infant mortality fostered the creation of the Bureau of Child Hygiene and her appointment as its director. Her life included several women companions.

FRANCES KELLOR was born in Columbus, Ohio, in 1873. Her father abandoned her family when Frances was quite young and she was raised in poverty. Through the patronage of two wealthy sisters, she was able to attend Cornell Law School. She also studied at the University of Chicago. Her work first focused on working women and African American urban immigrants. She later was a leading expert on arbitration. Her partner was Mary Elisabeth Dreier.

MARY "MOLLY" DEWSON, born 1874 in Massachusetts to a middle-class family, graduated from Wellesley College. She was involved in social welfare and suffrage work, the Red Cross (in Europe during World War I), and the fight for a minimum wage. She is best known as the first woman political "boss," from her work as head of the Women's Division of the Democratic National Party during the New Deal. Her life partner was Polly Porter.

MARY ELISABETH DREIER, born 1875, the fourth child of wealthy German immigrants, was raised in New York City and privately educated. Though from an elite background, Mary Elisabeth earned the respect of many women workers as a leader of the New York chapter of the WTUL. She remained politically active in progressive and women's causes throughout her life, using her wealth to support the struggles to which she was committed.

MARY ELLICOTT ARNOLD, born 1876 on Staten Island, lost her father when she was six. After attending Drexel Institute of Technology in Philadelphia, she traveled extensively, holding down various jobs including serving as an Indian Matron in Northern California and managing a cooperative apartment building for the Consumer Corporation of New York City.[1] From the time they were both sixteen, Mary Ellicott Arnold and Mabel Reed were companions.

CONNIE GUION was born in 1883 in North Carolina on a 10,000-acre farm. She majored in chemistry at Wellesley and graduated from Cornell Medical School at the age of thirty-four. She was especially dedicated to the advancement of women in the medical field.

LURA BEAM was born in 1887 in the seacoast town of Marshfield, Maine. After graduating from Barnard College, she went south, teaching in schools for African Americans. She co-wrote two books with Dr. Robert Latou Dickinson under the auspices of the National Committee on Maternal Health. There is some evidence that she also had a long-term partnership with another woman.

EDITH STEDMAN, born in 1888 in Cambridge, Massachusetts, graduated from Radcliffe College. She left her family's candy business to work for the YWCA in France during World

War I. From 1920 to 1927, she was a medical social worker in China and completed her working career with Radcliffe College.

FRIEDA MILLER was born in La Crosse, Wisconsin, in 1889. Though she was from a wealthy family, her childhood was marked by the deaths of her mother when she was five, and her grandfather (with whom she lived) and father when she was thirteen. After graduating from Milwaukee-Downer College and doing graduate work, she joined the WTUL in 1918 as an organizer. Through this work she met her life partner, Pauline Newman. Miller had one child, Elisabeth, born in 1923. Frieda eventually became director of the Women's Bureau.

PAULINE NEWMAN, the only Jewish member of this group, was born in Lithuania in about 1890.[2] Her father, a Talmudic scholar, died when she was young and her mother brought her and her young siblings to New York City. A factory worker from the age of twelve, including working at the Triangle Shirtwaist Factory until a week before the deadly fire, Pauline was a gifted organizer. She was involved in the Socialist Party, the International Ladies Garment Workers' Union (ILGWU), and the Women's Trade Union League (WTUL).)

MARTHA MAY ELIOT, born 1891 in Dorchester, Massachusetts, graduated from Radcliffe College and Johns Hopkins Medical School. At Johns Hopkins, she met her life partner, Ethel Durham. While on the faculty of Yale Medical School, she served as director of the Division of Child Hygiene of the Children's Bureau. She eventually served as director of the Children's Bureau and as consultant for the United Nations' agencies.

Contemporary Lesbians

AUDREY STREIG, born 1936, is the only child of a wealthy family. She was raised in the New York City area. She earned B.A. and M.S.W. degrees. She has worked as a social worker, rancher, and businesswoman. With her longtime lover, she adopted three children. She is a grandmother.

JO MARTINEZ, a Chicana, was born in 1936 in a small town in central New Mexico. She was the older of two children, and has earned B.A. and M.A. degrees. She has worked primarily as an educator but also has a long history of community activism.

JAMIE HENSON, born 1938, is the oldest child of a working-class, German-American family. Raised in the Northeast, she entered the medical field after high school. She settled in New Mexico with her partner, Bobbi Denova, in the 1970s. She is an independent health-care provider.

BOBBI DENOVA, born 1941, is also the oldest child of a working-class Euro-American family. She has a number of years in postsecondary health-care training and is an independent health-care provider. She worked overseas before settling in New Mexico with her partner, Jamie Henson.

JEAN LABOV is the older of two daughters of a Jewish family. She was born in 1943 in New York City. Her father died when she was young. She earned a B.A. and lived and worked in Europe for several years. She is a self-employed professional.

CARRIE STERN, born 1943, was the second child and only daughter adopted by a wealthy New Mexican couple. Carrie has a B.A. from a small, private women's college. She started her own business several years after college, and now has a second business career.

PAULA MITCHELL, born 1944, is the older of two daughters born to a middle-class, Euro-American family. Raised in the Midwest, she moved to New Mexico for college. She earned a B.A. and teaching certification. After teaching for over a decade, she now works in a wholesale business.

ANNE MCCONNELL, born 1945, was raised in the South. She is the oldest daughter of a large Irish-American family. She was raised in "genteel poverty." She earned B.A. and M.A. degrees, is a prize-winning author, and co-owns a women's business.

AMY ADAMS was born in 1946 and raised in southern California. She is the oldest daughter and second child of an upper-middle-class WASP family. She also earned B.A. and M.A. degrees and taught before moving to New Mexico. She owned a women's business before returning to school. She is now an accountant.

GLORIA WHELAN, born 1947, was raised in the New York City area in a large Irish-American family. She has several advanced degrees. She moved to New Mexico to take a teaching position and is an active athlete.

ROBIN EDWARDS was born in 1947 in Albuquerque, New Mexico. An only child of a WASP family, her father was ill when she was young and died when she was in college. She graduated from the University of New Mexico. She is an educator.

YOLANDA PEÑA, a New Mexican Chicana, was born in 1948. Raised in a poor family, she attended the local technical/vocational school before she joined the armed forces. She has also earned a B.A., is working on her M.A., and is a published poet. She works for a large corporation in a nontraditional field.

TRUDY HARDIN was born in 1949 in New York City. An African American, she is the eldest child in her family. After putting herself through college, she moved to New Mexico. She has worked in several fields and attended professional school.

LEE POWELL, born in 1949, is African American. She was raised in a large, southern city by a foster mother who was employed as a domestic worker. After earning her B.A., she worked in the performing arts. She has earned an M.A. in education and works in higher education. She has a foster daughter.

IRIS MILLER, born 1951, is the only child born to her Cherokee mother and Anglo father. After her mother died when Iris was nine, Iris was raised by her paternal relatives. A southerner, she has worked for the same large corporation since shortly after graduating from a private girls' high school. She settled in Albuquerque in the 1970s.

Introduction
Spinsters and Lesbians

Spinsters and lesbians—the images associated with these words are seldom positive. We have no simple, nonjudgmental terms for the women who are this book's focus—never-married Progressive Era women and contemporary lesbians. Introducing these women and titling this book has been a challenge because our language offers no expressions that easily position these women to be viewed in a positive light. There are no quick phrases that capture the energy of their full, creative, often amazing lives. The culture's vocabulary for never-married women forces us to start from characterizations of them as negative, inherently deficient, or even perverted.

The problem is not just with language. As I struggled to name these women, I found they were also without an adequate place in history. Even women's historians who acknowledge the existence of never-married women—spinsters or lesbians (and many continue simply to ignore them)—tend to relegate them to the margins of women's experience. Noted, they are then compartmentalized as anomalies whose lives have little to do with the mainstream of women's history.[1] The developing lesbian history that inspired and grounds this study remains segregated from too much of women's history.

While this study cannot resolve the problem of naming these women, it does identify the battle over labels, especially of independent women—women who have rejected heterosexual marriage and/or chosen other women as their intimate partners—as a persistent and important theme in the last century of U.S. women's history. Further, it disputes their current status in women's history, arguing that the problems of naming and placing never-married women reflect the limitations all women faced and are connected with many historical issues that need to be explored and understood.

Independent Women

While the title of this volume includes the words "spinsters," "lesbians," and "independent," none of these terms alone captures clearly the essence of this research. Among the "spinsters" in this study are women who were truly single as well as women who partnered with other women. The "lesbians" in this study are not a clear-cut category either. These lesbians are women who never married, while in the larger population many lesbians are, or have been, married. Both groups therefore are never-married independent women, some of whom partnered with other women while others remained single. These two groups of women themselves claim, and history has given them, different labels. Nevertheless, I remain conscious that I defined these individuals as independent women on the basis of these shared characteristics.

While this study certainly grew out of issues raised in feminist theory, women's history, and lesbian history, its immediate inspiration came from women's own stories.[2] The clearest single directive I had for the questions I wanted to research came from a friend, one of the women who came to be included in this research. "When did you know you were a lesbian?" was a question often asked among lesbians, especially newly "out" lesbians, in the 1970s and 1980s. Robin, who had been "out" before the reemergence of the Women's Movement and therefore qualified as a lesbian elder, never responded directly to that question. When asked, she always joked that her first conscious thought was, "I'm never getting married!" She explained that she always knew she would be independent and self-supporting. Issues of sexual identity came much later. Her response argued that long before feminist, lesbian or queer histories and theory, she knew that what she wanted for her life involved more than just sexual desire. Embracing an outlawed sexual identity, which was difficult enough, was only part of building independent women-centered lives—lives in opposition to many aspects of male dominance. Robin's answer and her discussion of her decisions informed this study and were key to framing this research's comparison of spinsters and lesbians. She expanded the discussion and brought other gender-related sources of dependence and oppression into view.

This research centers on women who constructed lives that seemed to be in opposition to rather persistent norms of womanhood. It asks if these independent women grew up with the expectation of economic, legal, social, and sexual autonomy. With or without conscious dreams of self-sufficiency, how did they forge such lives? What did autonomy give them? What did it demand of them? For all the growth in women's history, such women have hardly been studied.[3]

Thirty women are included in this study: fifteen never-married women of the Progressive Era and fifteen never-married lesbians of the post-World War II era. Their lives demand that we deconstruct questions of autonomy that focus only on sexual or economic issues, and develop a more holistic view of all the concerns, challenges, and opportunities that spinsters and lesbians confronted. It was easy to see that never-married women who earned their own way and paid their own bills faced particular barriers in a world that still expects men to head households and be the wage earners, and envisions women primarily as dependents or secondary earners. But these single women were not lonely or isolated individuals. They led full lives outside the usual and validated options this culture had presented to women. These spinsters and lesbians gathered each other into families in a culture where families continue to be named through the males and defined by marriage and birth. They created communities, found meaningful work, were politically involved, loved, disagreed with each other, and had fun. Both groups of women established women-centered lives within a male-dominant culture, but they did so from very different bases and at very different times.

From Spinsters to Lesbians

Fifteen spinsters—independent, never-married, socially and politically active women—make up the first group of this study. In their time, social commentators might have called them "new women," perhaps without major comment or judgment about their marital status, intimate relationships, or sexuality.[4] These spinsters lived in a time when the definition of womanhood was broad enough to easily include the women who were challenging its parameters in both action and theory. Only the revised gender and sexuality ideologies of the intervening years produced the equation between "real" womanhood and married, reproducing women only.

This cohort enjoyed as close to a golden age for independent women as can be found in United States history. Unmarried women have emerged as leading players in the Women's Movement, as well as in other movements, of the Progressive Era. They were leaders in women's education and were overrepresented among the women pioneers in other professions. While most scholarly attention has focused on middle-class, Euro-American, never-married women, some working-class women and women of color also chose to remain single.[5]

At the most basic demographic level, the generations of women born between 1865 and 1895 had the highest proportion of single women in U.S. history.[6] Yet we cannot assume that a high percentage of single women, in and of itself, explains the prominent roles they played in American life during the late nineteenth and early twentieth centuries. In the last two decades of the nineteenth century, Susan B. Anthony, leader of the suffrage movement, and Frances Willard, president of the increasingly powerful Women's Christian Temperance Union, were two of the most visible and valued women in the United States. For the first two decades of the twentieth century, Jane Addams was among the most admired of this nation's women. These models for young American females were single women dedicated to public service, including the cause of women's rights. Certainly the message their lives provided was the possibility of female agency and autonomy, coupled with a dedication to social welfare and justice. The unmarried state was respectable for both working-class and middle-class women. In the public's view, less privileged women were objects of concern as "women adrift," while they viewed middle-class, educated women as "social housekeepers." In addition, among feminists and progressives, turn-of-the-century independent women had been seen as the vanguard of women's struggle for equality.

In the opening decades of the twentieth century there lurked concerns that would undermine this acceptance and threaten the status of independent women. From President Theodore Roosevelt down, leaders sounded alarms about the low birthrate of middle-class white women and the resulting "race suicide."[7] Male leaders accused the educated woman who was not reproducing at her mother's rate of undermining the culture. On another front, the sex radicals of the turn of the century, whose earliest causes were clearly political rebellions, eventually became part of the modern celebration of individual sexual freedom and pleasure. Assisted by the new theories of Freud and other sexologists, they ushered in a new sexuality system that denigrated as abnormal the assumed asexuality of genteel women and made dangerous the "mannish" lesbian. They established a female sexual need that was defined by, and deeply grounded in, heterosexuality. Even as these activists struggled for a more enlightened view of sexuality, they contributed to the creation of a stigmatized homosexual minority (D'Emilio and Freedman 1988).

By the late 1920s, the unmarried, autonomous woman had disappeared as an alternative model of American womanhood. According to Nancy Cott (1987), "Just when individual wage-earning made it more possible than ever before for women to escape the economic necessity to marry, the model of companionate marriage with its emphasis on female heterosexual desires made marriage a sexual necessity for 'normal' satisfaction." Women's participation in waged work continued to increase, though they faced a more rigidly sex-segregated labor force. Even the career options of college-educated women shifted; positions as department store buyers or executive secretaries, along with work in the women's professions of nursing, teaching, social work, and library science, hardly presented the challenge or allowed the creativity professional women of the earlier generation had enjoyed in paid employment. Dedication to politics and a sense of civic duty paled as admirable traits; modern values celebrated individualism, leisure, and consumerism. The independent working woman was not only no longer on the cutting edge, she had become marginal—the "frigid" spinster or suspected lesbian. The conditions of the following decades did not foster her reemergence, especially not as a positive model.

The fall from grace of these independent, educated, and active women of the early twentieth century reflects changes in feminism and societal attitudes toward women generally. Based on the assumption that the major barriers to equality had been dismantled, the solidarity of female separatism gave way to a spirit of integration where women were not a disadvantaged group with specific interests. Under the new, supposedly egalitarian gender order, this society no longer saw women as having different qualities or restricted options. Ideologically, women, single or married, were no longer oppressed, and the popular media and sociologists presented the unmarried, urban woman as dangerous to men. The image of the 1920s flapper who wanted the same freedoms as men captured these changes.

From the 1920s on, psychologists and psychoanalysts were major contributors to the debate over gender roles in the United States. Freudian views of women and how a woman came to maturity centered on the resolution of the female Oedipus complex and the production of the male child. It followed that a woman was not a complete being or a "normal" woman if she was not partnered with a male and reproductively successful. Such a definition of womanhood meant that the single woman was suspect because she was unmarried, an "unnatural" state for females. Furthermore, in an era of greater public recognition of women's sexuality and growing condemnation of homosexuality, the possibility that these independent women might be lesbians added greater stigma.

By the 1930s, when the American woman was considered at all, it was within her roles as wife and mother. If she was not a wife or mother, working hard to become a wife and mother, or not happily a wife and mother, she was a problem. This ideological placement of women within the family had a strong material base. In spite of the changes of the previous decades, most women continued to be economically dependent on men and were held responsible for child care and the home. With few

opportunities in the sex-segregated labor force and the continuing family demands, the greatest number of females had no
chance for the realization of equality and independence. Although more women and more wives were entering the waged
labor force, these shifts had not seriously challenged the power
structure within the patriarchal family.

Furthermore, single women were declining as a proportion of
the female population. After a consistent rise during the nineteenth century, the percentage of women who never married
had peaked at 11 percent for the generation born between 1865
and 1875. The rate had gone down to 8.7 percent for the cohort
born between 1884 and 1894. Of the women born between
1915 and 1918 only 4.8 percent never married. For the entire
population, the percentage of single individuals consistently declined from 37 percent in 1900 to 21 percent in 1960, while the
percentage married rose from 54 percent to 68 percent during
the same period. The remaining 9 percent and 11 percent, respectively, were divorced or widowed.

In contrast to the Progressive Era when the "new woman"
was in the vanguard of women's struggle for emancipation,
during the post-World War II era, when the lesbians of this
study were coming to maturity, marriage rates were high and
severe ideological constraints were placed on women and their
roles. The family was the national focus, yet these women built
their lives outside the traditional family. Though more women
were working, our popular culture and social policymakers
marginalized the self-supporting women. Woman's sexuality,
though affirmed socially, was also confined to heterosexuality
and endorsed only within monogamous marriages. While many
activists had publicly critiqued gender norms in the earlier period, from the Second World War until the Women's Movement
psychiatrists and sociologists charged that those few voices who
questioned women's "traditional" roles suffered from individual

neurosis at the least (Breines 1992). This second group faced very different barriers, ideologically and materially.

The Progressive Era women tell us their stories with some mix of nonchalance and adventure, in a time when womanhood forged ahead and didn't look back. Those who had regrets had them later, when this society denied them as unpatriotic radicals, meddlesome spinsters, or perverted lesbians. Lesbians raised after World War II tell of adventures too, but their childhoods included complex struggles in which gender trouble was one more unnamed complication. Issues of poverty, racism, and abuse often added burdens and demanded new strengths.

Womanhood was far more problematic during the childhoods of the contemporary women. Heterosexual marriage, complete with motherhood, was such a norm for women raised in the mid-twentieth century, so central to that era's hegemonic definition of womanhood that, as one author noted, "the current of the mainstream was so strong that you only had to step off the bank and float downstream into marriage and motherhood" (Harvey 1993). It was the center around which women built their futures. To not share this expectation cast doubts on one's identity as a woman.

These women's stories illuminate questions and issues hidden when we view the world through the norm of the heterosexual, nuclear family or assume that all women are married or would choose to be. The Progressive Era women joined in strong communities supported by a broad and visible women's movement. They formed lifelong partnerships and were among the first to struggle with the demands of dual careers. They raised children together long before current debates over single-parent adoption and lesbian parenting. The contemporary lesbians, however, planned to be self-supporting at a time when no one validated their plans and goals. They traveled and worked far from home to resist strong heterosexual pressures from their families and communities. They persisted in loving women when they had nothing but negative images of such love.

The emergence of the stigma associated with never-married women, spinsters, and their deviant sisters, lesbians, is an important theme traced through the lives of both groups of women. The Progressive Era women eventually had to struggle, among themselves and against male-controlled evolving sexual discourse, over definitions of womanhood, women's sexuality, and respectability. Dealing, years later, with the resulting restrictive definitions of "normal" gender and sexual behavior for females, the midcentury lesbians individually constructed psychological as well as material paths around their era's barriers to autonomous womanhood and lesbian desire. As a survivor of post-World War II misogyny and homophobia, this group emerges with the women's and gay liberation movements as a role model of strong and independent women.

ONE

"What Are You Going to Be?"

Families and Childhoods in the Progressive Era

Sara Josephine "Jo" Baker, M.D., was born in Poughkeepsie, New York, in 1873, the daughter of a seemingly solid middle-class, Euro-American family. Writing her autobiography, *Fighting for Life,* in the mid-1930s, Jo recalls an idyllic childhood, unexceptional for her class and racial background. She was both a tomboy and an accomplished student of the domestic arts, privately educated at a progressive school and planning to attend college as her mother had before her. Though raised in a strict household, Jo nevertheless found means to adventures, often in the company of her brother. Yet, when her father's death left the family in serious economic straits, this self-described average female child of privilege chose to take the family savings and put herself through medical school to become the family breadwinner. She went on to became a pioneer in the field of public health and child hygiene. Dr. Baker was a suffragist and a never-married lover of women, part of a diverse community of politically and socially active women, many of whom were single and independent.[1] It is a question, then, why this competent, active, humorous woman, whose life was full of professional successes and political accomplishments—full also of friends and lovers—felt the need to "normalize" herself when she wrote her autobiography.[2] Jo Baker writes,

> I know that women of my generation who struck out on their own are supposed to have become rebellious because they felt cramped and suppressed and unhappy as children in an alien environment. It is a convenient formula and no doubt perfectly applicable in many cases. But it does not fit mine. I was reared in a thoroughly conventional tradition and took to it happily. I understood that after I left school I would go to Vassar, and then, I supposed, I would get married and raise a family and that would be that. Until events of the sort that are notoriously beyond one's control forced me to take bewildered thought for the morrow, I had no more purpose in life than a million other American girls being brought up just as I was in the [eighteen] eighties and nineties. (Baker 1939)

Below the surface of Jo Baker's seemingly casual and good-natured dismissal of the clearly psychoanalytically based theories on never-married women is a strong sense of resistance. Her narrative demands to have her childhood acknowledged as normal. Especially through humor, by showing the inconsistencies and contradictions between her life and those analyses developed by male sexologists, she challenges readers to listen to her reflect on her life. She suggests we reconsider those theories that have stigmatized never-married, women-loving women. For her it was not childhood trauma that pushed her toward autonomy, variant or deviant sexuality, and kept her from marriage.[3] These beliefs, which gained popularity during her life, had provided ammunition for those who wished to question her life, the lives of other independent women, and ultimately the lives of any women who had priorities other than husband and children.

To counter these ideas, Jo Baker lays a different foundation in her story of an independent woman. She grounds her decision to pursue a career in economics and family need. Her description of her life and her decisions, her declaration of her ordinariness, is echoed in the voices of many other never-married women of her generation.

Families

Because the theories referred to by Jo Baker, which still influence today's public opinion, focus so on tracing the origins of these women's problematic independence to difficulties from their childhoods, an in-depth consideration of these women's early years is the place to start hearing about their lives. Analyzing their childhoods from their words and their actions may also give very different clues about the connection between their socialization and their life choices.

The scholarship on children's lives in the nineteenth century only hints at the diversity of childhood experiences found among the women in this study.[4] The varied realities of families' lives are reflected in their children's roles and responsibilities. Though this is a predominantly middle-class, Euro-American group, the class backgrounds of these women are varied and the economic environments of their childhoods range from the urban poverty of Leonora O'Reilly to the privilege and security of Mary Elisabeth Dreier. While eleven of these women came from middle-class or elite families and therefore presumedly had secure early years, the second half of the nineteenth century witnessed numerous recessions and depressions that kept even the middle classes from financial stability (Wiebe 1967). While a few of these women came from families that had sufficient wealth to protect them from these economic fluctuations, most did not. In a significant number of cases, illness or death of the male breadwinner exacerbated these economic concerns, producing in these young women an early awareness of financial realities and women's economic vulnerability.

During this period of great immigration and the expansion of industrialization, working-class families often could hold on to a minimally stable existence only with the wages of at least one adult male breadwinner supplemented by the earnings of older children. The childhoods of the working-class women in this set attest to this. Leonora O'Reilly's mother, Winifred, had worked even after she was married while the couple saved to buy a grocery store. With the death of her husband in 1891 when Leonora was only a year old, Winifred O'Reilly was forced to return to the garment industry. Leonora joined her mother in the work force when she was a preadolescent (Shively 1971). Similarly, Pauline Newman's father died when she was young, and she too joined the work force at an early age, working up to thirteen and a half hours a day (Newman Papers SL). Across the Atlantic, Mary Anderson's father lost his farm in Sweden when a severe agricultural depression hit in the late 1880s (James 1980; Anderson 1951). Mary was a teenager then.

> My mother and father could not support us any longer and we knew that we had to get out and do something to earn a living, but we could not think of what to do because there was no opportunity for anything except housework in our neighborhood. The solution came when my sister Anna, who had gone to America the year before, sent for Hilda and me to join her. (Anderson 1951)

Nor were stability and intact nuclear families the norm among the more privileged women in this study. Similar factors disrupted their families, though the consequences were not quite as severe or immediate. While Connie Guion's family lived on a 10,000 acre plantation in North Carolina and her father worked as a civil engineer, she remembers that "we were extremely poor," and "when my two older sisters were 16 years old, they realized that the oncoming generations had to have more support than one could rake out of the plantation soil with a few helpers" (Guion 1958, 1972). These two oldest sisters trained as nurses and then worked to educate the rest of the children.

Jo Baker's father died of typhoid in 1889 when she was sixteen.

> Perhaps it was just as well that financial troubles appeared so soon after Father's funeral to make us all think of something else. We had always had a comfortable home and enough money, and Father had saved too. But when the estate came to be settled, a recent series of losses and bad investments told the inevitable story of practically nothing left. It was immediately evident that somebody would have to get ready to earn a living for all three of us—my mother, my sister, who had always been delicate and a semi-invalid, and myself. I considered myself elected. (Baker 1939)

Three other fathers died when their daughters were still minors: Mary Ellicott Arnold was six; Frieda Miller, thirteen; and Edith Stedman, fourteen. While financial problems do not appear to have accompanied these paternal deaths, these daughters did lose the emotional security and nonmaterial support their fathers appear to have provided. Through these deaths, they experienced the fragility of nineteenth-century ideals of family and the vulnerability and dependence of women and children in this family structure.

For the Hamilton sisters of Fort Wayne, Indiana, the failure of their father's business in 1885 brought to them the realization that they would have to earn their own living. This business failure robbed them of their father's protection in another way as well. Montgomery Hamilton, who had actively directed his children's education, began to withdraw from his family, spending most of his time in his library. He started to drink, and, "His daughters, mortified by his drinking, rarely spoke of it. By the time they reached young adulthood, they viewed their father as an ineffective but disturbing presence who demanded more attention than they wanted to give" (Sicherman 1984). These four sisters closed ranks with their mother, who came to define family for them.

On the seacoast of Maine, in an effort to remain close to his family, Lura Beam's father tried farming for six years. Unsuccessful on land, he returned to seafaring. Beam was conscious at an early age that her father was "earning for four females" (Beam Papers SL).

In spite of these difficulties and disruptions, many of these fathers had close relationships with their daughters. They gave their daughters other gifts, and in their writings these women fondly express the gentle influence their fathers had on their lives. Edith Stedman recalled,

> My father and I were great friends, and as a child he saw to it that I learned to know Boston and all of the historic sites. It was great fun going with him to places like Faneuil Hall and the Market, and one Washington's Birthday he took me to a governor's reception so that I could see the State House. We rode the Swan Boats in the Public Garden, and he took me to my first theater which was Joe Jefferson in "Rip Van Winkle." . . . I think that having a girl was a great comfort to him, but he died suddenly when I was fourteen of an attack of angina and I had to grow up overnight. (Stedman Papers SL)

Susan Ware, Molly Dewson's biographer, concludes that Molly was clearly her father's favorite. Pauline Newman, the youngest daughter of a Lithuanian Jewish family, wrote that her scholarly father, "to the surprise of neighbors and friends, included me in his classes" (Newman Papers SL). Patricia Palmieri, in her research on Wellesley faculty women, uses William James's term "tender-minded" to describe the fathers of her subjects (1983). Similar characteristics were shared by the fathers of this cohort. These men had not become distant, modern fathers who left the home early, returned late, and abdicated childrearing to mothers (Griswold 1993).

In their mothers, and in other important women in their lives, these women found females whose spirits seemed too lively and independent to be contained within what historians have proposed as the nineteenth-century feminine ideals (Bloch 1978; Welter 1978). These mothers and role models do not appear to have claimed the ethical superiority of "moral mothers" nor accepted the submissiveness of the "cult of true womanhood." None could be characterized as fully rebellious, but generally they were practical, competent, and literate women even though their lives were for the most part confined to the domestic sphere. With this characterization of their mothers, these women construct a continuum from their mothers to themselves. To them, their sense of an independent, competent womanhood was honestly inherited. Of her mother, Jo Baker wrote, "She had a touch of the pioneer in her." Baker believed that it was this sense of adventure which inspired her mother who "went to Poughkeepsie and, on the first day of the opening of Vassar College, enrolled herself as a student there" (1939).

In her unpublished tribute to her mother, Molly Dewson listed all the traditional domestic chores her mother fulfilled, but she makes it clear that Mrs. Dewson did these activities without distinguishing talent or consuming interest. She also writes that her mother, a devout Unitarian, loved to dance. It was Dewson's mother who stabilized the family emotionally and managed the money during the periods of Molly's father's illnesses (Dewson Papers SL). Similarly, Connie Guion's mother managed her twelve children and a 10,000-acre plantation during her husband's frequent absences, setting the rules of work and behavior. According to Guion, her mother "made her decisions very quickly and stuck to them" (Guion 1958, 1972).

Alice and Edith Hamilton's grandmother, Emerine Holman Hamilton, was an early supporter of women's rights and hosted Susan B. Anthony when Anthony's travels brought her to Fort Wayne. These sisters, their younger siblings, and their cousins all grew up in a family compound dominated by this matriarchal figure. Their own mother, Gertrude Pond Hamilton, maintained her own priorities within this rather strong-minded and locally powerful family. With Montgomery Hamilton and his brother relinquishing their familial responsibilities in their later years, Alice and Edith, their siblings and cousins, grew to maturity in a world dominated by women both numerically and emotionally. Gertrude Hamilton supported her daughters' efforts for independent lives. It was from her mother that Alice learned that "personal liberty was the most precious thing in life" (Sicherman 1984).

Among the working-class women, the dominant culture's familial and gender ideals had little in common with their realities. As discussed above, both Leonora O'Reilly and Frances Kellor's mothers worked, and these daughters grew up aware that they were economically supported by their mothers' earnings in an era that hardly acknowledged female-headed households. It was Mary Anderson's mother who pushed Mary and her sister to emigrate when it became clear that their native Sweden held no employment prospects for them. In her autobiography, Anderson writes, "I think Mother was really a feminist" (Anderson 1951).

Biographers of other independent women of this generation have found similar economic and emotional characteristics. Sharon O'Brien, in her study of Willa Cather, wrote,

> But the most important gift of all was the discrepancy her female relatives displayed between the Victorian "Cult of true womanhood" and real women's capabilities. . . . And so, even though these women could not grant Willa Cather the public sphere she wanted to occupy, by implicitly exposing the contradictions between ideology and lived experience they gave her an imaginative space within which to redefine womanhood. (O'Brien 1987)

Grace and Edith Abbott, also never-married leaders, had a strong and competent mother, a father whose business was threatened during the depression of 1893, and a family generally supportive of female accomplishments (Costin 1983). Palmieri, in her study of Wellesley women, concurs on the prevalence and significance of this constellation of factors (1983).

Within their families these women experienced something much less sinister and elusive than repression and unhappiness, the alleged causes of their independence and rebellions against women's proper roles. These women grew up seeing the reality of an imperfect world, one with changing economic and social systems in which women and children were especially vulnerable. While the contradictions between real women's lives and ideals may have allowed them the imaginative space in which to redefine womanhood, their families also allowed them to develop strong senses of themselves and their abilities unencumbered by strongly gendered messages.

Childhoods

If the immediate family situations of these women contradict the familial ideal of distant patriarchal breadwinners and pious domestic homemakers, their childhood actions and consciousnesses raised further questions about the form and power of gender messages in these nineteenth-century childhoods. Nowhere is there a sense of passivity, frailty, inferiority, or the need for protection among these daughters, nor such expectations for female children among their parents. They were, in contrast, healthy, active, energetic, and outgoing. While their parents clearly expected different futures for their daughters than for their sons, at least through their childhoods these girls were often allowed to be simply children. Encouraged to a certain degree to prepare for their future domestic roles, they were not restricted in childhood by an all-pervasive dichotomy between female and male attributes, abilities, or even activities, or by anxieties over their femininity, attractiveness, or sexuality.

To a significant extent these young women were not enclosed in a static domestic circle, but exposed to the larger world physically and intellectually. While Mary Anderson was expected to help with her share of the household chores, she tried to escape from the indoor work as much as possible. She loved horses and "never played with dolls" (Anderson 1951). Lura Beam recalled that she was encouraged to read and to consider "What are you going to be?" (Beam Papers SL).

While these women's families appear to have allowed adventurous behavior in their daughters, these women's recollections also indicate that they themselves took an active role in pushing the limits of acceptable behavior. Jo Baker remembered:

> The circus was very important in my life. The night before the circus came to town, my brother and I always went to bed with strings tied to our toes and dangling out of the windows. Our confederate was the local Poughkeepsie bad boy, whom we were forbidden to know, and whom, in consequence, we cultivated on every possible occasion. As soon as the circus arrived, he ran to our house and jerked the strings. We got up, dressed and crept out and went down to the circus lot where they were unloading elephants and erecting tents with shouting and heaving on ropes and hammering in stakes with smashing sledge hammers, all in the weird savage light of kerosene flares. Lots of Poughkeepsie youngsters would be unaccountably drowsy in school on circus day, but they were all boys except me. (Baker 1939)

Edith Stedman combined a sense of adventure with a strong early cynicism about male superiority.

> When I was about five I was given a tricycle and as soon as I could stay on it began venturing afield. Partly I played running away, but it was mostly curiosity to see around the next corner. A horrid little boy named Ray used to perch on his own fence and smugly call out to anyone who might be looking for me "I know where Eduf [sic] is." His only accomplishment was to show me how far he could piddle, a feat that, though I tried to admire, rather bored me. (Stedman Papers SL)

Others shared this celebration of mobility and prided themselves on their physical skills. Molly Dewson was the pitcher on the baseball team with her brothers and male cousins. Like Mary Anderson, Connie Guion loved to ride horses, and the Hamilton sisters took on vigorous, physical chores during their summer camping trips. These women did not hesitate to express their dislike for housework and tell of the various methods they devised for escaping the confines of the kitchen and the sewing room. Childhood experiences gave them a sense of competence and accomplishment or, in Edith Stedman's words, "I think what my childhood gave me was a sense of security and a knowledge of my own basket" (Stedman Papers SL). This sentiment was shared by many of the women.

While for most of these women physical freedom in childhood meant opportunities to explore the outdoors, the countryside, or their urban environments, a significant number also had early experiences with more distant travels. Mary Anderson emigrated from Europe at the age of sixteen with her sister, Hilda. These young women continued on to the Midwest to join their other sister, Anna. While Anderson's only immediate employment opportunities were in domestic work, the same work she had emigrated to escape, she did not resign herself to remaining in such positions. While her sisters married, she continued to travel around the region in search of better jobs. Pauline Newman emigrated with her family from Lithuania. For her, union activism brought mobility; during strikes the union sent this eloquent young speaker on fund-raising tours where she was exposed to the lives of middle-class women. At eighteen, Mary Arnold left New Jersey and went with Mabel Reed and Reed's family to Europe before entering Drexel Institute in Philadelphia. Jo Baker's family had made boat excursions from Poughkeepsie to New York City throughout her childhood. When she decided to enter medical school in New York City, she went to a place she already knew. Lura Beam's father had taken his family on several voyages, so when she left her Maine home to enter Barnard College when she was eighteen she had already seen different shores. For Edith and Alice Hamilton, attendance at Miss Porter's, a boarding school in Connecticut, was the expected culmination of their childhood. These young women had the benefits that travel brought, as well as gaining the knowledge that they could cope somewhere other than home.

Though these girls may have experienced greater freedom and broader exposure than many of their generation, they were not freed from certain cultural silences. Their silence on sexuality is particularly important. Few of these young women leave any discussion of sexual desire or heterosexual pressures from their girlhoods or their adolescent years. Through letters to her cousin, we know that Alice Hamilton felt most ill at ease when cajoled into dating or courtship situations. In a pattern seen throughout her life, she underplayed her social skills, describing herself as a wallflower. She contrasts the ease she feels when relating to young men who are her equals and friends and the discomfort she experiences when a romantic interest is present (Sicherman 1984).

Given the research on women of this generation, we cannot assume that sexual desire was absent from these women's lives. Data from Katherine Bement Davis's 1929 study of unmarried women similar to this group report sexual desires, both heterosexual and same-sex, were experienced by women of this cohort.[5] This study challenged many myths concerning the sexuality of middle-class women born in the nineteenth century. This work, which surveyed one thousand married women and twelve hundred unmarried, college-educated women, discusses in a frank but straightforward manner topics such as same-sex desires/activities and masturbation. There is no reason to believe the women in this study were significantly different from Davis's sample, but without other sources it is impossible to know how aware they were of their own sexuality. This void must leave to speculation whether concerns about love and desire played any part in their early years.

Taken as a whole, these women's early years certainly support Jo Baker's challenge and repudiate psychoanalytical ideas about single, independent women. Overwhelmingly, these women did not leave stories of feeling odd or unhappy or restricted, nor did they have great conflicts with their families. Any basis for rebellion, any restrictions they did experience as females, were not acute in their childhoods.

Their stories suggest a far more materialist evaluation of the importance of their early years on their later choices. These women saw themselves as among strong, competent women, in their families and in society. And the important men in their lives generally supported them in this self-conception. They were accepted as they were, whatever their abilities, interests, and personal attributes. As children, they played hard with boys and girls. These young women traveled, explored, and had adventures. They rose to hard challenges when necessary.

They leave us a strong sense that their shared gender identity was never up for question; it was assumed. Within their families' and communities' social codes, there was a single, ungendered standard of morality. And while female and male roles may have differed, the desired personal attributes of girls and boys did not. Consequently this group was encouraged to do what they could do and be what they could be, with the implied message that whatever they did was all right for girls and young women to be doing on the simple basis that they, as females, were doing it. With their womanhood presented as a biological given, their gender was not questioned on the basis of what they did.

While certain of these women may have pushed the boundaries of acceptable behavior, it is significant that none felt the need to go to the extreme of rejecting her gender role like young Willa Cather, for example, who cropped her hair before it was fashionable and took to signing her name "William" (O'Brien 1987). They found they could push the gender boundaries from within, not even being labeled as odd or nonconformist.

What these women did see were the contradictions between the ideals of family and gender and the realities of the heterosexual, male-dominated, nuclear family. Fathers died. Businesses failed. Women worked, struggling, holding the family together. Children worked and families separated for economic and emotional reasons. They had no romantic visions of marriage or women's lot. These early experiences of dissonance in a context of cultural change, in a period of an active women's movement, were the likely foundations on which these women constructed a different vision of womanhood. If these women ultimately rejected women's traditional roles, it was because they could, having seen the weaknesses and limitations.

TWO

"I Knew I Was Odd"

Growing Up Female, 1936–1965

Robin Edwards, a forty-two-year-old teacher, born and raised in Albuquerque, New Mexico, knew as long as she could remember that she was going to be a teacher. Marriage, along with motherhood, was "something I was not going to do. And I knew that early too and I don't know how . . . that's just what I was going to do. Live with my parents all my life, taking care of my dad and mom."

Robin never did marry, and she did become a teacher. She didn't continue to live with her parents; her father died when she was twenty and she moved out on her own soon afterward. She remains close to her mother. While none of the other women in this group remember being so clear and consistent in their rejections of the heterosexual imperative, none of them married either. They have all become or are becoming professionals, own or have owned homes, and, along with Robin, have come to claim a lesbian identity. According to their accounts they are, on the whole, successful and productive women. How did women of this generation achieve materially

25

and socially autonomous lives in an era when independent women were generally invisible and lesbians were considered mentally ill or sexual psychopaths?

Post-World War II Lesbians

This chapter explores the childhoods and early adult years of fifteen never-married lesbians who came to maturity during the post-World War II era. Recently this period has begun to receive more scholarly reconsideration.[1] While scholars such as Margolis (1984) had analyzed ideals of motherhood and the prescriptive child-rearing literature of this period, these newer works are debating the diversity of lives that existed behind the facade of postwar peace and prosperity.

The fifteen women who participated in this research were all part of the Albuquerque, New Mexico, lesbian community. They were between the ages of thirty-nine and fifty-four at the time of the oral history interviews in 1986–87. These women all came to maturity before the major impact of the Women's and Gay Liberation Movements, as well as before there was significant support for being a lesbian or for being a "career woman." This set includes two Chicanas, two African American women, one Jewish woman, and eleven Euro-American women, including one woman with a physical disability.

Though none of these fifteen women have achieved national prominence, as a significant number of the turn-of-the-century women did, several of them have been important leaders in their communities.[2] All have been part of the diverse Albuquerque lesbian community, and most have been active in feminist organizations (Franzen 1993). An additional difference is that none of these women came from the level of wealth Mary Elisabeth Dreier enjoyed.

Families

During the period of these women's childhoods the popular media, especially television shows such as *Father Knows Best* and *Leave It to Beaver* depicted family life as harmonious, functional, and with few serious problems. In these WASP, middle-class nuclear TV family units, "Dad" went off to work every morning in a suit, "Mom" stayed home with the children, and the biggest problems were "normal" children's pranks. The houses were ample, sturdy, and nicely furnished and the neighborhood was homogeneous and safe. Both parents were attractive, able-bodied and very understanding of their children. There was no poverty, no racism, no divorce, and certainly no child abuse or incest. Such images promoted a single standard of what family, parents, and childhood should be. Such images not only had little to do with reality, but produced self-doubts and discontent among many whose kin groups could not achieve this bland perfection. This era's preoccupation with maintaining appearances may be seen as a perfect breeding ground for denial on many fronts (Harvey 1993).

In contrast to this monolithic ideal, the families of the women in this study show significant individual as well as class, racial/ethnic, and regional differences. The minimal qualifications for a "typical" post-World War II family—breadwinner father, homemaker mother, and no traumas or abuse—were met by only Paula Mitchell's and Jamie Henson's families. Among the other families there were various deviations, ranging from the incest Anne experienced to the necessity of seven of the mothers to take jobs outside the home.

Six of the fifteen women, all Euro-American from nuclear families, described their childhoods in generally positive terms. Another six women used words such as "lonely," "pitiful," "painful," "oppressive," and "awkward" to characterize their earliest years. Five of these women are survivors of childhood physical and/or sexual abuse: Trudy, Lee, and Anne were abused by male relatives; Audrey, by her mother; and Yolanda, by both her mother and her father.[3] The three remaining women described their childhoods as partially good, partially hard.

In contrast to the turn-of-the-century women who portrayed generally positive bonds with their mothers, these postwar daughters described more diverse and complex mother-daughter relationships. The first specific contradiction of the ideal comes from the fact that not all of these women had their biological mothers as their primary caretakers. Both Carrie Stern and Audrey Streig had nannies; Lee Powell was raised by a foster mother; Iris Miller's mother died when she was nine; and Jo Martinez's and Trudy Hardin's parents relied on their extended families for child-care assistance.

Though Audrey's mother did not work outside the home, a succession of nursemaids cared for her only child. Carrie's mother chose to work in the family business from the time her daughter was adopted as an infant. "[My mother] just isn't a very nurturing person. By the time I came along she was thirty-nine years old, and she had had five years of my brother. So I guess she figured she'd go back to work and not deal with it, and so I had this kind of nanny-type person."

While hiring nannies was an option for the wealthiest mothers, economic need forced poorer mothers to make other arrangements. Joanne Powell, from an African American family in the rural South, was only in her mid-teens when she had her daughter, Lee. Her family put her and the baby on a bus heading for the closest city, telling her she was on her own because she was too disruptive a model to have at home. This mother and child were befriended by Mrs. Martin, a domestic worker in her thirties who was raising five sons. Mrs. Martin eventually convinced Joanne that it would be in the child's best interest if she, Mrs. Martin, became Lee's guardian. At various times in

Lee's life, Mrs. Martin actively kept Joanne Powell from contact, hiding presents and letters sent from mother to child.

Trudy Hardin's mother was a single parent and had to work when her daughter was young, relying on her extended family to care for Trudy. Jo Martinez was cared for by her grandparents. This couple intervened because Jo's young mother was very sick after childbirth and Jo's father considered putting her up for adoption. While both elders were important to her, she preferred following her grandfather around the farm, helping him with the chores. Most of her first memories center on her interactions with him and life on the farm, with its hard work and its opportunities for adventures.

Other stresses influenced mother-daughter relationships. Only seven women felt they had good relationships with their mothers, while another six described their relationships with their mothers as neutral, "okay," but somewhat distant. It is in this latter category that four of the five mothers of the large families (five or more children) are found. Their daughters found these women to be "harried," as "not having a lot of time," or "distant from everyone." Two women did not feel their relationships with their mothers were positive at all. The postwar daughters did not as consistently describe their mothers as important role models and sources of support as the turn-of-the-century women did.

The gentle and involved fathers of the earlier women were missing also. There are at least two possible interpretations of this finding. It could be that daughters' expectations and perceptions had changed, since the TV fathers of the fifties were perfect providers and protectors. But it is also true that most of these fathers worked away from the home, keeping them distant from their offspring. Three of these women do describe their relationships with their fathers as positive and close. They were supportive and involved in their daughters' lives but engaged them in their own interests and activities as well. These fathers taught their daughters nontraditional skills. Bobbi Denova, raised outside of a small town in the Northeast, described her father as both "the patriarch" and a loving teacher.

> He was stern, authoritative [sic], strict. . . . But he was also, on the other hand, a good teacher. He taught us well. He helped us with our homework. And when it came to a lot of life's philosophy, he was a teacher. . . . And my dad was all smiles about [her being a tomboy]. He enjoyed having a tomboy around. I helped him with everything since I was the oldest, number one. He taught me to drive this god-awful thing which was neither car nor tractor. My feet couldn't reach the pedals . . . but he taught me to drive that. He had a hand plow he'd chain up behind that, and he and I would plow . . . do all these kinds of things. I was his second hand . . . I mean I was right there with him, we talked a lot. . . . Maybe that's why I got that and my brother and sister didn't. It surprises me how much of an influence my father was.

Six women describe their fathers with mixed feelings, as removed influences on their lives. Their fathers were "nice guys" and their relationships "okay." Several sounded like "fifties dads" who did things with their children but were not emotionally involved with their daughters. Paula Mitchell, raised in the Midwest, said about her father,

> And he'd play catch with us and throw the ball so we could hit it for hours on end. Yeah, he was involved a lot in our upbringing; it wasn't like he would come home from work and do his own thing, like you read about a lot of men doing. He wasn't like that. He would take us places and do things with us. He'd take me with him to the store, and so forth. It's just that there were some problems there, or disagreement, or conflict that wasn't with my mom.

Playing catch with their fathers came up spontaneously in seven of the women's stories. Sharing this activity was independent of the type of relationship the daughters and fathers had.

One wonders if there was some shared instruction book which said, "If all else fails, at least play catch with your children."

Paternal affection and protection was absent for five women who described their fathers' overall influence in negative terms. For Anne McConnell, Trudy Hardin, and Yolanda Peña, the cause was sexual and/or physical abuse. While moderate physical discipline was generally accepted in this era, Yolanda felt her father overstepped the norms.

> Physical abuse was almost accepted where I grew up. Hitting was very much a fundamental part of raising kids. . . . Sometimes they'd go too far. [For example] my mother had to pull my father away. She kept yelling, "You're going to kill her. You're going to kill her." . . . I don't think anybody really knew because we were an isolated unit.

The other two women's fathers manifested emotionally and psychologically undermining behavior toward their daughters. Jo Martinez felt she could never live up to her father's expectations of her in part because she was female. Jean Labov's father was loving as long as she stayed his image of a cute little girl. She was her father's favorite until she was five, when she began to gain weight. This physical change signified a shift in her father's feelings toward her. He would yell that she was "helpless and hopeless," and wonder at her, "Who would ever marry you?" Although Jean was very bright and successful in school, her father never acknowledged her intellectual achievements, but harped instead on her supposed physical shortcomings.

While the turn-of-the-century women recognized the disparities between their own families and the cultural ideals, they were less likely to individualize the blame than the post-World War II daughters. The earlier cohort saw their families as coping, as best they could, with challenges over which they had little control. The daughters of the post-World War II families articulated their families' difficulties in a very different way. Where physical, sexual, or psychological abuse was present, these women held their fathers or mothers responsible. A significant number mourned the absence of a closeness to their parents, especially their mothers. The happiest families had a basic level of material security, and these families resemble Gans's (1967) "child-centered" families. Women from both economic extremes, poverty and significant wealth, had the least happy childhoods, but it was the emotional, more than material, deprivations that disturbed them, producing descriptions of pain and loneliness.

As stated, all but two of these families deviated from the postwar ideal. The extreme cases were among those women who experienced physical and sexual abuse or extreme poverty. Though sexual abuse within the family was not acknowledged as a widespread occurrence during these women's childhoods, recent research suggests that one in four female children experience such incestuous assaults (Hermann 1981; Rush 1980; Bass and Thorton 1984).[4]

While the women who were sexually abused experienced women's sexual vulnerability, others observed women's economic vulnerability. For Robin Edwards and Jean Labov, paternal illness and death caused their families' standard of living to drop and forced their mothers into the breadwinner role. Bobbi Denova's and Gloria Whelan's mothers had to enter the labor force to help provide for the family even though their fathers held steady jobs. Three of the women felt a dissonance that was much harder to identify. Each of this trio stated that she felt her mother was unhappy as a mother.

Were these women's families significantly different than most of this era? Without much more data, it is impossible to tell. This finding of family diversity is important, though, for arguing against theories that trace nontraditional gender or sexual behavior to particular family structures. What these women do share with the Progressive Era women is that they also experienced women's vulnerability in traditional familial roles.

Childhoods

Throughout the post-World War II period, females were permanently assigned to the "ladies auxiliaries." Ideologically at the sidelines of this male-centered era, the perfect female could have no plans or actions of her own. The "real" woman waited, prepared to follow the direction of the man in her life. Her most admired attribute was the ability to respond selflessly to the needs of others. To have one's own desires or abilities made one less of a woman.

In spite of, or perhaps because of this ideal, all of the women in this study developed areas of competence that were core to their self-esteem. Most also identified as "different" from other children, especially other girls. While the bases of these attitudes varied, generally these women named as sources of competence characteristics that fell outside the postwar definition of femininity. These mid-twentieth century daughters liked to do, and did, many of the same things the turn-of-the-century women enjoyed. They were intellectually curious and imaginative. They were physically active, exploring their environments. They resisted the restrictions of the domestic sphere. Generally their families allowed them to do what they wished, but the girls felt they were odd because of what they wanted to do and spoke differently about themselves compared to the earlier generation.

Of course there have always been contradictions of this ideal, so these young women were not completely without role models. Even in the mid-1950s *Life* magazine featured in their special Christmas Eve focus on the American women the story of a woman who had a husband, career, and baby. Class factors made it impossible for many women to fulfill this narrowly defined proper role. In African American communities, women, married or single, had always worked proportionately more than other women and women had always played important roles in their communities, churches, and political struggles

(Jones 1985; Higginbotham 1993). Many Black women were becoming nationally visible through their roles in the Civil Rights Movement (Crawford, Rouse, and Woods 1990).

Importantly in their families, these young women did not have a strict enforcement of dichotomized gender roles in their childhoods, even when their parents were conflicted about these freedoms.[5] They could play what they wished to play, with boys, with girls, or by themselves. They generally did not experience a major emphasis on physical beauty or ladylike behavior, either before or during puberty. As discussed above, Jean Labov's father is an exception here, humiliating Jean about her weight. Other parents sporadically tried to enforce feminine behaviors and appearances. These women were less consistently supported by their parents and other significant mentors in their athletic/physical endeavors and intellectual developments than the earlier group. There is a trend for the nonabusive fathers to be more supportive of athletic/nontraditional physical activities, while the moms gave encouragement to the intellectual/academic achievements.

Again, these women described themselves as busy and active. They spent a lot of time out-of-doors in imaginative play, sometimes by themselves and sometimes with other children. Though Paula was shy with people outside her family, within it she remembers,

> I was kind of independent, really, and I was the oldest sibling and very close to a bunch of first cousins. And I am the oldest of all of them, as well, so I was very independent and . . . was the leader of the cousin group, the boss. . . . We did a lot of sports at that time, and then games like hide-and-seek, cowboys and Indians, and all that stuff.

In their earliest years, while a significant minority hated and never played with dolls and other stereotypical female toys, most combined traditionally male and traditionally female activities. Anne remembers, "I had a Tiny Tears that I loved dearly. I loved my Tiny Tears. I loved it a whole lot [and] . . . I liked cowboys and Indians. I liked cap guns. They were neat. Sometimes my brother would let me shoot his 'bb' gun. That was very exciting."

Jo, raised in a rural New Mexican village in the 1940s and 50s, used these words to describe herself:

> I remember being extremely precocious. I got into everything I could get into . . . I used to play in the ditch, and dig trenches, and build my own private whatevers. Had a little fortress that caved in on me once. Activities which weren't exactly female. I played a lot with boys because there weren't very many . . . there were a lot of girls but I didn't want to play with them. They never seemed to do the things that were fun.

Raised in a middle-class suburb in southern California, Amy describes adventures reminiscent of those of Jo Baker: "It seems through the second half of elementary school I was always the only girl in the pack of boys getting in trouble, leaving the school yard during lunch on our bikes to go to the nearest store to get candy and bring it back to the other kids. I was never afraid of consequences."

All but three of the women clearly identified themselves as "tomboys," with Robin and several others wanting to be boys. When asked how long she had wanted to be a boy, Robin stated, "All my life I guess. I knew I wanted to play sports. I didn't want to do that [female things], I wanted to do this [boys' things]." The world was divided into female and male "things," though these girls were not completely clear who made these demarcations.

Westerns, especially the Lone Ranger, headed the list of favored media influences. Play activities reflected these preferences. Gloria Whelan recalls, "My sisters had dolls and they would try to get me to play with their dolls, but I was just bored. I used to like to get on my bike and go to the woods. And I would just play by myself in the woods. Pretend I was an Indian tracking people and games like that."

Issues of dress and appearance were also much more contested than they were at the turn of the century. Until early in this century, infants of both sexes were dressed alike. Pictures of boys of three in dresses and long curls were not unusual. By the post-World War II era, apparel and grooming was rigidly set by gender. While the modern girls might be allowed to wear "boys' " clothes more than the Progressive Era girls could, it was clear that they were wearing "boys' " clothes. Quite a few of these girls had this preference.

Those occasions when they were forced into stereotypical attire caused resentment and rebellion. Iris Miller recalled, as the only granddaughter out of nine grandchildren, "constantly being dressed up in these obnoxious little dresses with these petticoats and my hair curled and taken to lunch and had . . . great manners." Carrie Stern's mother had wanted a dainty little girl and had dressed her daughter in frilly outfits throughout her infancy. Carrie recalled that such outfits were worthless once she started to walk. In her words, she then "hit the ground running," and didn't stop. "Clothes were a major issue all my life with her typically. She wanted a real debutante person." For others, traditional feminine attire was actually painful. Gloria Whelan recalled sitting in her bedroom crying on those Sundays when her parents made her stay in a dress after church. For several, even getting to wear pants wasn't enough; they wanted boys' pants which had zippers in the front and they insisted upon boys' shoes, high-top sneakers, oxfords, or work boots.

Feeling different, choosing to be special/different, and being treated and labeled as different get intertwined in these women's lives. Sources of difference varied from woman to woman, as did the power they derived from that status. As stated above, several of the women are survivors of incest and other forms of abuse. In a society and an era where sexual abuse of children was denied, or children, especially girl children, were blamed for such abuse, these women struggled for psychic survival. One of Lee Powell's coping strategies was to sit, hiding, in closets, for hours developing fantasies in her imagination, which she would rather do than go outside to play. She connects these times of retreat with the development of her own voice, which later bloomed in her church and creative work.

As discussed above, some describe their being different or being labeled "different" because of gender nonconformity: wanting to be a boy; wanting to dress in boys' clothes; or wanting to do the things boys could do. Gloria's statement best sums up the complex responses these girl children had to gender boundaries.

> I know I was odd because I would be walking down the street . . . people would ask me, "Are you a boy or a girl? They were really confused. And I would always answer, "I'm a boy." I remember wanting to be a boy because I thought my brother had it so much better. And then I could do all the rough and tumble stuff. And then I would have been able to be a doctor.[6]

Gloria and others had gotten clear messages that girls couldn't do certain things, and the fact they even wanted to do those things was problematic.

In contradiction to the societal prescriptions for female dependency and submissiveness, women of this group sought out and enjoyed their opportunities to handle responsibilities and gain adult skills. Jean Labov stated,

> But you know what, when my father died, I did, to some extent, become the man in the family. She [her mother] asked me advice. She was a scared woman. She asked this fourteen-, fifteen-, sixteen-year-old girl what to do. . . . So in some ways my mother built me up to be very bright, . . . making some family decisions.

As the oldest daughters of large families, Anne, Trudy, and Bobbi became "second mothers." According to Anne, "I mean competence was my protection. . . . In taking care of the little kids, in sewing, in school, in whatever. I was the competent child."

Although Amy had an older brother, "I thought I was the oldest, that I was supposed to be the oldest, even though I had an older brother. But it was my responsibility to plan things, to make sure things were okay, to take responsibility, to be the leader of the kids somehow."

Both Jo and Yolanda were raised in rural settings where children often share in work early. From a young age, Jo Martinez's parents and grandparents expected her to help out with the work on their farm. Yolanda Peña irrigated, harvested, and sold an acre of chile to earn money.[7]

Throughout their diverse childhoods and into adolescence, all these women found some niche of competence. Several found prestige as outstanding athletes and several were superior academically. Others were chosen for leadership positions either in classrooms or in extracurricular activities such as drama clubs. For some this sense of capability was more generalized and internalized, coming from writing poetry, building, or being able to defend oneself physically. Lee Powell, who used the word "dork" to describe herself as a child, was recognized and rewarded within her church and Christian youth groups for her speaking abilities. Her oratory skills made her both different and more part of the community.

> It was a gift, but also I worked at it. It was something separate from me. Something I could put on. It got real scary. Up speaking all the time. All these people starting to turn their lives over to Christ. I didn't want all that responsibility. . . . All these people wanted to touch me . . . give me scholarships to the ministry . . . but I fit in more. Not so different. I wasn't crazy about the attention [but] I felt I sort of fit in somewhere.

A lack of adherence to feminine behavior, as it was narrowly defined in this era, and a search for competence appear to be shared among these women. And in their descriptions, these women frequently use boys' and male behaviors as gauges for their differences. It is almost as if competent and active girls could not exist. Their preferences and attributes were not on the continuum of acceptable behaviors, but crossed the line into the masculine. This need to cross a gender boundary to be different or to be competent did not exist for the turn-of-the-century women. Jo Baker could go see the circus being set up with the boys, and Molly Dewson could pitch on the baseball team without questioning their gender identities. They could be exceptional or different but still girls.

Heterosexuality was a virtually inescapable measure of acceptability for young people during this period. Females and males, who were expected to be sex segregated in most other leisure activities, were to come together only on the basis of love, romance, and sexual attractions. Dating was a central activity during adolescence, and the popular media promoted the idea that one's success or failure within this arena determined one's present and future happiness, especially for females (Breines 1992; Douglas 1994).

Not surprisingly, from childhood on, sexual desire was doubly problematic for these lesbians. They did not experience heterosexual attractions and were frequently indifferent to dating. On the other hand, they felt pulled toward women. The heterosexual desire, which they could name and which was considered normal, hardly existed for them, while the attractions they did feel had no name and no acceptable physical expression.

The pressure to date and subsequently "fit in" pushed Jamie to persist in dating. While she felt odd not dating, sometimes dating was even worse. "Yeah, I felt very pressured, but . . . I could never develop a relationship with anybody. I was probably the worst date they'd ever had. I just didn't extend myself. I wasn't rude. I wasn't nasty. I just wasn't myself." Her discomfort echoes Alice Hamilton's seventy years before.

Only one-third of this group participated in dating. Paula

recalled that only her lack of interest in dating kept her from truly feeling good about herself in high school. Gloria dated and went steady, but realized that she was more of a buddy to the boys she dated than other girls were. Anne was relieved that her mother forbade her to date.

Many of these women clearly preferred women, even if this only meant wanting to spend time with them. Particularly the women from small towns had no meaning to give to their interests. When Anne was in high school, she had a strong attraction to one of her friends.

> And I was totally, completely, head over heels in love with this woman. And she loved me. And neither of us had a clue as to what was going on. Not a clue . . . I knew her through the Junior Legion of Mary. . . . But there were these very strange slumber parties. . . . And we would play poker and we would put on Johnny Mathis and dance. And cuddle, never kissing, but a lot of touching. Since neither Frances nor I had a clue that women could be sexual with each other, it never occurred to us. So it was like this extended courtship.

Robin knew she was attracted to women and not men, but she felt like she was "the only one in the world." Jamie knew also, but wondered, "What do you do with it?" [8]

Jean, who was raised in New York City, had heard of lesbians. In her teens, she took herself to a psychologist.

> I guess I felt I wasn't right . . . I didn't name the word lesbian for myself until about nineteen when I was seeing a shrink and told him I thought I was a lesbian because I knew I had desires around women. And this Freudian psychologist told me I wasn't. That was good. I wasn't. That lasted for ten years. Hey, he said I wasn't so I wasn't.

When these women graduated from high school, only Iris and Jo actually had experienced a same-sex relationship, though neither could name what they did as "lesbian." Along with Jean and Anne, Robin, Audrey, Amy, and Lee all had some sense that they were attracted to women more than to men.

Others had more ambiguous senses of their sexuality. A self-recognized attraction to women or even a lesbian sexual experience did not preclude heterosexual activities. Several women became engaged after being attracted to and intimately involved with women.

This concern over sexual desires, regardless of whether they were toward women or men, was not discussed by turn-of-the-century women, while this issue was problematic for the contemporary women. In light of recent studies on the history of sexuality, this change makes sense. In the ideological and social-control contests over gender and sexuality that had taken place throughout the century, women's identities and their sexuality were defined from a foundation of heterosexual desire — desire that was passive and complementary to virility. Desire among women, though rigidly interpreted in this way, was much more integrated into public consciousness by the mid-twentieth century than it had been during the formative years of the earlier group. Not that there was explicit discussion of sexual activities, but an emphasis on having appropriate "sex appeal."

While there were competing definitions of lesbians from those of the sexologists through the self-definitions of the working-class bar communities, most of these women did not have even the word for their desire until later in their lives. Lesbians, women-loving women, had been banished to criminology or sexology texts. Slowly they began to emerge in the pulp fiction of this period.

Just as all women, by midcentury, were assumed to have sexual attractions toward men, they also were expected to desire and plan for marriage. While the Progressive Era women could reject marriage, choose independence, and still retain their womanhood, postwar women faced a different dilemma. Rejecting marriage, like heterosexual desire, put them "beyond the pale."

Among this group, Robin was always clear in her rejection of marriage. She could not say why, beyond that it was "something I was not going to do." Jean came the closest to Robin's rejection.

> When I would see scenes of marriage among cousins I always felt I am never going to do this. . . . Some of it came from feeling different, some of it came from feeling unworthy, not that I chose not to . . . maybe it came from my father saying, "Who's going to marry you?" But I had this feeling, and it's a feeling, it's a long feeling, of long times, that I would never do this. It was like a foreknowledge of my whole life that I would never be in this kind of relationship, seeing scenes of marriage. I thought I would never do this. . . . And I had opportunities in the end and I chose not to. . . . I always felt I would never marry.

When asked if, in their adolescent years, they expected to marry and have children, many of these women paused as if they were searching in all the corners of their memories for some recollection of concern over these issues. When they did respond it was as if that expectation existed vaguely somewhere in their minds. They had not consciously ruled out marriage, but neither had they consciously planned for it. Lee, for example, had a very active imagination and built fantasy futures in her head, but marriage and children were never "up there" in her fantasies. Jamie, when asked about marriage, said, "I just knew I was going to work and didn't think about it seriously." Later she dated a married man, "I thought this was real safe."

Paula, a shy, bright, athletic young woman from a comfortable, Anglo midwestern family, remembers how she tried to reconcile what she wanted with societal expectations.

> And I started thinking about being an anthropologist; that was what I wanted to be. And pretty much stuck with that until I got here [New Mexico]. And at that time, I kinda had thoughts, "Yeah, I'll get married." But you know, I always remember I never wanted to change my name. I was me; I didn't want to change my name. I didn't want Mrs. somebody or other; I always

wanted to be Paula Mitchell . . . so I thought I'd have to meet somebody named Mitchell. And I thought it would be a kick to have enough kids to have a baseball team, but you see, that wasn't really a serious reflection. I mean, obviously I was thinking that because it was the right thing to think, I thought, and no one in her right mind would have nine children.

Carrie, though she later became engaged, never thought about marriage when she was a teenager. When asked if she ever thought about not being married, she said, "No, I didn't ever think of it that way either. I just never visualized myself being a married lady and having kids like some of the other people I knew."

When Amy was asked if she ever thought about whether she would get married, she replied:

I didn't have a consciousness of that, I think, at all until I was in my mid-twenties. . . . Like, this is the sort of thing I'm supposed to be thinking right now, presuming I will have a husband and kids at some point, although the husband was always fairly irrelevant. . . . You know, if I thought of anything in high school, I saw myself as a single P.E. teacher. [After college] I didn't think about it as much as possible. I mean I just kept it out of my mind. I thought about teaching. I sometimes thought about being a parent, having kids, because I've always liked kids. And I think I relate fairly decently to kids, but the idea of relating to men was something I never fantasized about at all . . . at that time. A little bit later I went through a stage where I fantasized a little, but it was all with, you know, you get married to give some legitimacy to what you are doing, which is basically having kids. And the guy is always in the background; you don't really relate to him much.

These women ignored rather than rejected expectations of marriage during this period when there were no positive options for women outside heterosexual marriage. Womanhood was being a wife and mother. If one rejected that, one rejected all that was allowed women within their sex/gender system. Reiterating an earlier point, through the women's activism in the late nineteenth century, that generation's definition of womanhood had been expanded to be able to include never-married women and women who moved into the public sphere. This later cohort's inability to clearly articulate a rejection of marriage reflected to a great extent the narrowness of their era's definition of womanhood and the dearth of alternative "womanhoods."

The earlier group of women also had opportunities to see those alternative models of womanhood in women's organizations, schools, and voluntary organizations. Women coming of age in the mid-twentieth century had no equivalent in their early years to the powerful separatist feminist organizations, institutions, or networks of the Progressive Era. Consequently they saw few models of active public women or female solidarity either in their home communities or in the media. Nor could they participate in such structures as they moved into the public sphere. There were certainly women's organizations that ranged from professional organizations to church auxiliaries, but these groups did not constitute communities nor did they provide autonomous power bases for women. Though Anne, for example, found some opportunities to develop leadership skills within the Junior Legion of Mary, this was no source of feminist thought or support.

Given the number of athletes among this group, some sense of solidarity or community centered on sports teams would have been logical. There is no evidence of such connections from these oral histories. In the pre-Title IX period, at no level from grade school through college did women's sports receive adequate institutional support. Many high schools had only intramural sports for women. Additionally, female athletes generally contradicted the stereotypes of the period, and the benefits women athletes gained through their physical expertise was often offset by a questioning of their femininity (Lenskyj 1986; Twin 1979).

This absence of communities of active women reinforces the argument that these women, when searching for positive models, had to turn toward male examples and male models. Public independent women were rare and considered exceptional.

The women in both generations in this study portrayed themselves as active children who were adventurous both physically and intellectually. The women in these two groups grew up in families that did not have strict gender-based expectations for their daughters during their childhoods and did not strictly enforce stereotypical gender behaviors. Early in their lives, the turn-of-the-century women and the contemporary lesbians sought arenas in which to develop their own competencies.

The meanings of their shared interests, attributes, and activities differed and reflected how gender and sexuality systems changed between the turn of the century and the post-World War II era. While both groups were active individuals and sought areas of competency, among the midcentury women their capabilities, as well as the inclinations they saw in themselves, could not fit within the narrowed gender definition of women of the post-World War II era. They also had few individuals and no communities of women providing alternative models of womanhood. Their only other option lay outside of the feminine, in the masculine sphere.

The later cohort could not escape the issue of sexual desire. The midcentury conceptualization of female sexuality was a double-edged sword. Women could have sexual desires but these needed to be directed toward men and be the passive complement to active virility. For most, there was no name for their attractions for women. Consequently, most of these women held themselves apart from intimate relationships.

A very similar process occurred with this group vis-à-vis marriage. However uncomfortable they felt with the idea of a future marriage, they could not visualize any alternatives. As a result, only Robin clearly rejected marriage, but even she could not say why. As they did with sexual desire, these young women compartmentalized marriage. Unable simply to reject it, they boxed it up and put it on a shelf in their minds to be dealt with at some other point.

For women coming of age during this era, there were no paths to autonomy. Each was on her own.

THREE

"O, the Glorious Privilege of Being Independent"

Defining Independent Womanhood in the Progressive Era

Edith Stedman graduated from Radcliffe College in 1910. Taking a position at the Framingham Reformatory for Women, she appeared to be situating herself for a life and career within the women-centered social welfare networks of the Progressive Era (Gordon 1994). Her plans were disrupted when her brother pressured her to resign from her position to run the family-owned candy store. She hated this job and left after two years, escaping the business in spite of her brother's continuing efforts to control her life and work. At the age of twenty-nine, she joined the World War I effort in Europe with the YMCA. Of her determination she wrote, "The work at the shop seemed useless, and I made up my mind that I wasn't going to miss the greatest cataclysm of my life" (Stedman Papers SL).

As they entered the public world of education and work, none of the turn-of-the-century women claimed full knowledge of or an expectation for independent womanhood. At most they stated this growing notion that they were going to have to be self-supporting, but without a clear vision of how. What their lives suggest is a step-by-step exploration of possibilities and realities. The three most important steps were education, travel and work.

Education

The sense of physical freedom, of not being confined or restricted, in their childhoods is paralleled in the lives of the turn-of-the-century women by an equally important intellectual freedom.[1] In this arena these young women received strong encouragement from their immediate families. Their families fostered in the daughters a sense of intellectual competency, providing forums for discussions and guidance for study. One after the other recalls how her father and/or her mother supported her intellectual growth, read classics aloud to her, and generally stressed the importance of books and knowledge. And when these women did receive formal education, they had already internalized high standards for themselves. The economic and geographical diversity of these families' situations produced an accompanying variability in the basic educations they could provide for their daughters. Nevertheless, each daughter demonstrated a deep and determined commitment to education in the fullest sense of the concept.

Among the working-class women, the need to work precluded regular participation in formal education, but they found other means to continue their intellectual explorations. Mary Anderson left school in her native Sweden after the eighth grade. When she immigrated to the United States and settled in the upper Midwest, she diligently taught herself English, reading newspapers and talking to her employers. This process of self-education became a life-long habit. Frances Kellor completed only two years of high school before joining the work force full time. A pair of wealthy women in her community took an interest in this unusual and talented young woman and tutored her in literature and current societal issues. With the support of these women, Kellor gained the educational background and self-confidence needed to enter Cornell Law School without a high school diploma (Wooley 1903).

After long hours in the garment industry, Pauline Newman still read Jewish newspapers, attended lectures, and tried her hand at poetry. She specifically credits the classes and discussion groups offered through the Socialist Literary Society as a major source of her informal education. Though her brother offered to send her to college if she gave up her radical politics, she refused to compromise her principles (Newman Papers SL). Her additional formal education was limited to the Bryn Mawr Summer School for Working Women.[2]

Among the middle-class daughters, education, though less a struggle, was also a continuing endeavor. Mary Ellicott Arnold attended Drexel Institute's business course at sixteen, a Cornell University agricultural program a few years later, and finally she became a special student at the University of California when she was thirty-nine (Arnold Papers SL).

Jo Baker was raised "in the shadow of Vassar," which her mother had attended. Consequently she was acquainted with women of the stature of astronomer Maria Mitchell. Educated at the Misses Thomas' School, a nontraditional private school in her hometown, Baker notes that within her family "even domestic training was rigorous." In her autobiography, she acknowledges important educational lessons from outside of the classroom. During their summers at her grandmother's in Danville, New York, Jo and her siblings encountered Dr. Jackson's health resort, where, among other challenges to societal norms, women wore bloomers. She also credits her great aunt Abby with providing her with an invaluable lesson. This elderly and outwardly pious Quaker secretly informed the Baker children that there wasn't a word of truth in the Bible. "It would be hard to exaggerate the influence that sort of experience may have on a child, learning so early that it is possible to question the unquestionable" (Baker 1939).

The Dreier girls, after being privately tutored at home, attended George Brackett's School, a private institution for girls in Brooklyn Heights, where the headmaster was assisted by his sisters. His school was dedicated to providing a liberal education for girls that exposed them to the world and did not "shut them in conventional ignorance to preserve their purity" (Payne 1988).

Though the women do not comment on the specific content of these educations, one particular facet was shared. For every one of these women who left comments about their early educations, there were acknowledgments of the importance of female role models. Both Alice and Edith Hamilton were sent to Miss Porter's in Connecticut. While their overall estimation of the school was that what they learned there formally in their classes was of little worth, they found what they learned informally from the women teachers and from other students was very important. Edith Stedman wrote as follows about her love of high school:

> I think I worked harder and got more academic pleasure out of some of my work in high school than I ever did in college. We had a marvelous classics teacher, Carolotta Wiswall, a young Radcliffe grad and keen about teaching. . . . A second cousin, Alice Nichols, several years older than I, and a Radcliffe student, used to spend the night quite often and tell me the most marvelous stories. (Stedman Papers SL)

During the second half of the nineteenth century the cause of women's education received support from various quarters, including those committed to providing women with an education equal to men's, and those committed with equal fervor to a distinctively feminine education.[3] The cohort to which these middle-class women belonged was one that was able to pursue higher education in a diversity of institutions from the elite single-sex colleges that were concentrated in the Northeast to the developing land-grant schools in the Midwest and West. While these women were not pioneers, higher education for women was still a novelty at the time they began to consider their futures. Of the twelve women who received postsecondary education, only Jo Baker clearly states that she expected to go to college.

Seven women in this group graduated from "Seven Sisters" colleges.[4] Scholars have strongly argued the role of these women's colleges as centers for women's education, homosocial culture, and feminist consciousness (Horowitz 1984; Palmieri 1981, 1983). Molly Dewson entered Wellesley College in 1892. As a member of this group, she shares her alma mater with Connie Guion, who graduated in 1906. While Wellesley's all-female faculty was instituted on conservative grounds, many of the young women who attended this school found the female leadership there an inspiration and an argument for women's equality.

Edith Hamilton received her education at Bryn Mawr College, graduating in 1890 from this school which had only been founded in 1885. This college also has a special place in women's education as a result of M. Carey Thomas's leadership.[5] During her years as dean and president she steered the college away from the path set by the founders—conservative Quaker males—and built an institution on the premise that women should have an education equal to the best that men could receive. Lura Beam made her way from Maine to Barnard College in New York City, founded in 1889, and became a member of the class of 1903. The two remaining women who graduated from these women's colleges matriculated at Radcliffe, which evolved from the Harvard Annex. Founded in

1893, it graduated Edith Stedman in 1910 and Martha May Eliot in 1913.

Among the others, Frieda Miller graduated from Milwaukee-Downer College, a women's college in her home state of Wisconsin. Mary Ellicott Arnold, a New Jersey native, attended a coeducational school, Drexel Institute in Philadelphia, where she completed a stenography course.

Jo Baker, who had to give up her dreams of Vassar, graduated from a women's medical school, the New York Infirmary for Women and Children, in 1899. At this female-founded and controlled medical school, Baker was exposed to women whose power as role models equaled that of the leaders of women's colleges.[6] In contrast, Alice Hamilton, who also went directly to medical school, entered the coeducational University of Michigan program and had little exposure there to the strengths of a separatist support system. In her case, a solidarity among the female students as well as a relatively open attitude among the male professors and the Ann Arbor community sustained her. Hamilton's medical school years were among the happiest in her life.

Edith Hamilton alone took a second degree from a female institution, an M.A. from Bryn Mawr College. All the other women who continued in higher education did so at coeducational universities. In this, they had little choice since the women's colleges offered few advanced degree programs (Solomon 1985).

In 1917, Jo Baker was the first woman to earn a doctorate in public health from the New York University-Bellevue Hospital Medical School. She achieved this distinction only after a telling struggle with the school's administration. Though a pioneer in the field, she did not have a formal degree in public health. In 1915, when asked to lecture in this new degree program, Baker offered to lecture in exchange for being able to complete the program herself. They refused her request, choosing instead to stand by their commitment to have an exclusively male school of public health, a field founded by women. After realizing that they could find no comparable lecturer, they finally relented, allowing Baker and other women to attend.[7]

The two other medical doctors, Martha May Eliot and Connie Guion, received their undergraduate degrees at Radcliffe and Wellesley, respectively. Eliot then went on to Johns Hopkins and Guion to Cornell Medical School. Eliot chose Johns Hopkins after her application was rejected by Harvard, with which her family had many ties, as that institution continued to exclude women. Nowhere in Eliot's extensive correspondence with her parents did she complain about poor treatment from males at Johns Hopkins. In defense of coeducation, Eliot wrote to her parents, "If men don't get to work with women they [men] don't get to know their [women's] abilities"(Eliot Papers SL).

How deliberate these women's choices were between single sex and coeducational schools is not clear. Alice Hamilton, as one example, had originally planned to attend the Women's Medical College of Pennsylvania, but finally she attended the University of Michigan, a coeducational institution. The stated reasons were financial. Hamilton, along with Eliot, came to defend these coeducational environments after they had attended such schools. Connie Guion had already completed an M.A. program at Cornell when she entered medical school. She leaves no evidence of any difficulties in her adjustment to the mixed-sex setting.

The fact that the more privileged women of this group could acquire these educations should not be interpreted as meaning there was no struggle involved. These women's stories make it clear that just getting to college or to a professional school was a challenge. These women first had to be aware that such institutions, women's or coeducational, existed. Next they had to determine that they had something to gain from higher education. They needed to convince their families to support them financially and emotionally in their efforts. Finally, in certain cases these women also needed to complete additional preparatory work. Each of these steps was a potential roadblock. Making these decisions and meeting these challenges involved persistence and hard work. Less frequently luck was a factor. For all but Frances Kellor, economic privilege played a major role.

Though Molly Dewson was raised in Massachusetts, home to four of the "Seven Sisters" schools, she maintained, "I had never met, as far as I knew, a woman college graduate, but I had chanced upon a Bryn Mawr catalogue" (Dewson Papers SL). Connie Guion, who did not attend school at all until she was ten, credited her sister with the original suggestion of a college education.

> I continued my education in the public schools of Charlotte until I was fifteen years old, when my sister, Laura, decided that she wanted me to go to college. She had known a man whose sisters went to Wellesley and, apparently impressed, she decided that she wanted me to go to Wellesley as well. (Guion 1958, 1972)

For Jo Baker, Alice and Edith Hamilton, and Frances Kellor, the decision to attain some higher education was based primarily on economic necessity; they decided, since their families would not be able to support them, that they would have to be able to support themselves. Their decisions argue for a consciousness of women's employment options with and without education. It is of note that they never considered marriage as a viable solution to their dilemma. The reason for dismissing this option is not clear, but suggests that these women believed that, married or not, women needed to have their own money. The idea of "marrying up" or "marrying for money" may be developments of the twentieth-century gender system.[8]

Eliot and Guion represent the women who pursued their education already focused on a specific career. They were of the generation who knew women could have careers. Others were more likely to take it one step at a time, unsure when they started in higher education what they would do with their educations. Yet, even for this undecided group, college was not an end in itself but a means to an end. Those who left us their thoughts on what they would do with their educations portray themselves very much as the daughters of the Progressive Era. Eliot, for example, wrote to her parents during her first year of medical school,

> I have had a strong feeling right along that every chance I could get to do any social work would be more than worthwhile in the end. You see even if I am studying here and if I should practise I want to keep attached to the social end of it; in other words be some kind of "social doctor" . . . though just what kind I don't know. (Eliot Papers SL)

This triangle of education, work, and politics was shared and clear among these women.

Even among generally liberal parents, higher education for their daughters was considered a questionable enterprise and the young women had to do some convincing. Lura Beam recalled that "my mother did not believe in [education for women] but was amiable. She said, 'Girls just get married and settle back into Grammar School interests.' My father—then earning for the sake of four females—said dryly, 'She likes books. Let her try to be self-supporting'" (Beam Papers SL).

Molly Dewson remembered, "When I was seventeen, I told my father I ached to know more and I wanted to go to college." (Dewson Papers SL). Jo Baker remarked that her greatest support for completing her preparatory work for her medical school entrance examinations was the unflagging opposition of all her relatives except her mother (Baker 1939). Alice Hamilton spent a year at a local medical school to convince her family that she was serious about her studies.

Several women devoted years to the additional preparatory work that entrance to higher education demanded. Dewson and Guion both found they needed to extend their secondary educations before they could enter Wellesley. Jo Baker disciplined herself through a year of self-guided study to be able to pass the medical school entrance examinations, a trial she shared with Alice Hamilton.

Travel

While these women often described their desire for a college or professional education in terms of personal choice and/or family need, their decisions frequently necessitated that they live away from their families. This physical separation from the parental home was a new development in the lives of middle-class women; before this time daughters generally did not leave their parents' home until they married. Single women of previous generations seldom lived on their own (Chambers-Schiller 1984). Consequently, education also gave these women their first opportunity to break out of the familial sphere and set a precedent in their lives for living and working away from their birth families.

Connie Guion's situation provides an illustration of the complex pushes and pulls involved in these separations. She and her family justified her continued absences on various personal, educational, and kin-related needs. As discussed above, her first separation from her family was conceived and orchestrated by her older sister; but by the time Guion left North Carolina to attend Wellesley, she already knew she wanted to attend medical school. Guion postponed this dream while she fulfilled her sisterly responsibility of educating her younger siblings, earning for their educations by teaching chemistry at Vassar and Sweet Briar Colleges for several years after her graduation from Wellesley. She entered medical school at the age of thirty-one, when her familial responsibilities were completed. Guion's matter-of-fact acceptance of both her sister's direction and the later postponement of her goals for the sake of her younger sisters and brothers attest to the strength of her family ties. As a Southerner, she struggled with the desire to return to the South, twice returning to live and work in her region of origin. However, the South could not compete with the opportunities for growth and autonomy for women that she had found in the urban North. In the end, she lived and worked most of her professional life in New York (Guion 1958, 1972).

Jo Baker, Alice and Edith Hamilton, and Frances Kellor were other examples of women whose movements away from their families were justified on the basis of economics. To support themselves, and sometimes their families, they needed decent educations, but the scarcity of educational institutions for women meant that such schooling seldom could be found close to home. While many women of this generation who graduated from colleges did return to their hometowns, employment possibilities were concentrated in the growing urban centers. The women in this group named their families' needs, the fullest use of their educations, and a sense of mission fostered by both religion and the political/reform movements of their eras as their reasons to work. They continued to live independently, though in several cases they did send money home to mothers or siblings. While many of them did have to return home sporadically to attend to their families, only O'Reilly and Dewson, who grew up in New York City and the Boston area, respectively, had the opportunity to combine work and family in the same location. They lived with their mothers until the death of one of the dyad.

While these women did, to a significant degree, use economic need as their stated justification for educational decisions, it is also clear that among this cohort, the nonthreatening and traditional path to self-support, that is, that of schoolteaching, would not suffice. That they chose less traditional and often less secure fields suggests competing motivations and broader self-expectations. They actively sought employment beyond what might have been required to simply support themselves and their families. Their decisions also speak to a sense of adventure and a need for challenge; few of these women remained in a given position through the majority of their work years. They were, in short, ambitious, though they never used this word to describe themselves.

The opportunities to move beyond the familial sphere, though frequently guised as fulfilling a "family claim," mark an important change and new option in middle-class women's lives.[9] Although much of middle-class America was apprehensive about the shrinking of the nation through the expansion of railroads and the demise of the self-sufficient small town (Wiebe 1967), from the point of view of this small group of women, the new options were not startling or frightening, but welcome. They viewed them as part of a continuing outward spiral, an ongoing expansion of their worlds. These women were eager for new possibilities and they found they could pave them with the support of their families and their culture. For the working-class women, any comparable opportunities were work related, but for the middle-class women the first steps towards autonomy took them into higher education.

During a period when many middle-class and some working-class daughters were viewed as not having essential economic roles within their immediate families, these women's decisions suggest the complex social and psychological consequences of being exceptions to this general rule. The fact that they needed to earn their living and, at times, support their kin, fulfilling a necessary productive role, when paired with the growing though still limited opportunities for women, allowed new life paths and new self-definitions. While women's first moves away from the family were fostered by "family claims," a conservative reason, the result was often progressive for the individuals and for women in general.

As in their childhoods, a silence on sexuality prevailed. While mid-twentieth century middle-class parents would be preoccupied with protecting their daughters' virtue, reputation, and virginity, no such concerns were raised against the plans of the Progressive Era women in spite of their significant freedoms. Though college women were strictly regulated as long as they lived in college dormitories, they had little supervision if they did not. Most of these women traveled to and from their schools alone, and, when they needed to, they negotiated their own housing arrangements. They also made their own decisions about their social lives. While in their twenties, Alice and Edith Hamilton traveled together for a year of study in Europe. Alice, in particular, had to make her own way, confronting extremes of "welcomes," from German professors who refused to allow a woman into their labs, through others who treated her as one of the boys, including inviting her to their drinking parties (Sicherman 1984).[10]

Cultural critics certainly engaged in numerous debates that were sexuality-related, but during this era they were less concerned with college women's virtue than with their reproductive capacities (Clarke 1873). At the time these women were in college and preparing for lives of work, the focus was on their female physiology, with a few scholars concerned that these women were not spending enough time with men.[11] All of this makes sense within the sexuality system of the era where middle-class, Euro-American women supposedly had no pleasure-based sexual desires. Viewed as only having the impulse toward maternity, it was this inclination that social leaders feared would be disturbed by too much education. Nevertheless, none of these women, nor their parents, appear to have been overly concerned about the women's reproductive futures.

Tracing these women's preparations for autonomy suggest that they negotiated paths that accommodated acceptable female goals and behaviors while covertly exploring new opportunities for women. Their particular family situations may have provided the combination of factors that pushed them toward autonomy: the early awareness of the economic vulnerability of women and families; the exposure to independent women as role models; "tender-minded" or absent fathers and competent mothers; and certainly the intellectual and physical freedom they enjoyed. They not only experienced contradictions to the gender ideals of their period, but they were exposed to other possibilities. For each commonality there are certainly clear exceptions, but in each area there are trends that might be considered as significantly preparing these women for their new and nontraditional life decisions.

While these individual and family conditions constituted the pushes, the general environment of the Progressive Era contributed the pulls. For the young elite and middle-class women there was a sense of excitement about education, about doing socially productive work, and about taking advantage of the new opportunities women had in each arena. For the working-class women an equally powerful sense of mission came from their activities in trade unionism and socialist organizations.[12]

Nevertheless, the other side of this argument must include the particular situation of the middle-class women of this second generation of new women. This group did not have to fight for the right to education and the right to work for wages as their symbolic mothers, the first generation of new women, did. They did not have to put their respectability on the line to escape the family claim. Higher education allowed them a genteel means by which to move away from their patriarchal homes. They saw themselves as starting down an acceptable alternative path for women.

Work

This group of autonomous turn-of-the-century women includes four doctors, two directors of the Women's Bureau of the Department of Labor, two educational administrators, two administrators/activists for the Women's Trade Union League, two women who combined social work and writing, the director of the Women's Division of the Democratic National Committee, a union health clinic director, an administrator for the Consumer Corporation of New York City, and an internationally recognized expert on arbitration. These women were more than financially autonomous; they were professional women who were able to find work in which they had real power, including relative freedom from day-to-day male dominance. They were able to build lives in which their primary social, emotional, and political support came from other women. Though they did live within a larger patriarchal society, their own lives were female centered. To understand how they arrived at these positions and sustained themselves as independent working women, we must examine these women's professional paths.

Waged work became the articulated central issue and driving concern in the lives of this group. Although there was an interdependence between the need and the desire to work, the quest for meaningful employment and their status as single women are the shared characteristics that pull these women together as a group.[13] Each woman struggled to determine her own career path among options that were open and acceptable to women during this period, and the type of work they wanted. While each woman decided how hard she wanted to search for her niche, to fight the formal and informal barriers to her participation in a given field, and to adapt creatively to the existing realities for women, this generation did not have unlimited opportunities. In general, a confluence of societal changes that created a need for new professions gave these women a broader range of options than other generations of women had.

The women in this set did not have simple, predictable, or linear career paths. While their decisions to have careers removed them from the traditional female script of completing their education and remaining or returning home to await marriage, the traditional male script of completing an education and entering a career was not fully available to them. Just as acquiring an education was an extended process in their lives, finding satisfying life work also was a struggle. They had irregular work lives, with periods during which they appeared to wander aimlessly or to be "detoured." [14]

The majority of these women were from middle-class backgrounds and they became well educated. Nevertheless, career women were still rare, and there were no set expectations for them when they finished their schooling as there often were for men, who were more likely to have planned for a given career from childhood or had the option of joining their fathers in business or a profession.[15] As a result, these women often took non-career or short-term jobs while they continued the search for meaningful life work, trying various career paths or actually creating their own work. For many this involved physical mobility, often migrating to large cities where they could have the greatest employment opportunities. They actively had to seek work and carve their own paths, a task that takes significant initiative regardless of the social climate. This generation, reflecting the reforming spirit of the Progressive Era, sought work that was both socially responsible and individually satisfying and remunerative. The women express no alienation from their work, more often conveying a sense of vocation, a devotion to their work that had meaning beyond just a way to earn a living.

For working-class women during this period, the possibility of achieving an autonomous existence with a decent income was slight. A class and sex-segregated division of labor preempted opportunities for advancement within factories and trades. Mary Anderson, Leonora O'Reilly, and Pauline Newman all started out as factory workers.[16] Such employment did not provide secure, steady income, especially for women. These three women were able to move out of their trades and expand their employment options through positions in labor and/or feminist organizations, especially with the Women's Trade Union League. The League's commitment to cross-class activism and working-class leadership provided them with an arena in which to develop skills and make personal and political connections that gave them an escape route from factory work.[17]

Mary Anderson's story provides one illustration. When Anderson came to the United States, she anticipated finding greater job opportunities than she had in her native Sweden. Such was not immediately the case; she could only find household service positions during her first years. She states that she knew she wanted more from life than she would get as a private household worker. Anderson taught herself English and searched for better situations. It is interesting that Anderson repeats the "normalizing" theme seen in Jo Baker's autobiography, dismissing her impressive rise from domestic worker and bootmaker to the director of the Women's Bureau.

> My sister Anna did not want me to go, but I wanted to do something different, so we went, Hilda, the baby, and I.... I suppose my experience for the next few years was like that of any other girl who goes from one job to another looking for security and decent wages and living conditions.... I was independent. If I didn't like a job, I quit and got another. (Anderson 1951)

After years of working and organizing in the bootmakers' trade, Anderson's first escape from hourly factory work came when the Women's Trade Union League offered her a position as a general organizer in 1911; she was thirty-eight at this time. Although she was unsure of the stability of such a position, she took the risk and gave up her hourly job. Her skills as an organizer and administrator eventually brought her national recognition and a position in 1918 with Women in Industry Service, a federal agency. Anderson maintained her position with this agency as it evolved into the Women's Bureau within the Department of Labor. It is as director of the Women's

Bureau that Anderson is best known, though she did not achieve this position until 1920, at the age of forty-eight. She held this post until her retirement at age seventy-two. While Anderson's path from bootmaker to the head of the Women's Bureau reflected her personal attributes and ambitions, the existence of grassroots labor and feminist organizations in which white, working-class women could apprentice, as well as the opening of women-focused divisions within the federal government, played important roles in her climb (Anderson 1951). Newman's and O'Reilly's paths to professional positions were eased by similar factors (Shively 1971; James 1981; Newman Papers SL).

At the other end of the economic spectrum are the middle-class and upper-middle-class women who chose to become medical doctors: Alice Hamilton, S. Josephine Baker, Connie Guion, and Martha May Eliot. Although one might expect these four women to have had the least complicated career paths, the turn-of-the-century United States did not provide doctors, especially women and people of color, any guarantees. The medical profession was highly competitive and the regular medical/American Medical Association (AMA) faction had not gained its monopoly on health care. Although women could gain medical educations at single-sex institutions and at increasing numbers of coeducational medical schools, after medical school women faced significant barriers (Morantz-Sanchez 1985; Moldow 1987). Few female doctors could expect hospital appointments or to make a living in private practice. Jo Baker, for example, left her home in Poughkeepsie at twenty-one to begin medical school in New York City. After completing her postgraduate internship in Boston, she returned to New York and opened a private practice. Unable to earn enough money to support herself with this practice alone, she convinced an insurance company that female clients should be examined by female doctors. Still seeking an economically more secure position at thirty-four, she took and passed a civil service test to become an assistant health commissioner for New York City. Demonstrating a sincere commitment to her work, which was lacking among her male colleagues, Jo Baker won recognition reducing infant mortality among the tenement dwellers of New York City. At thirty-six, she became head of the newly created Division of Child Hygiene, and eventually she became a nationally and internationally recognized leader in the emerging field of public health and child welfare (Baker 1939; Baumgartner 1971).

Alice Hamilton stated that she chose to become a doctor

> because as a doctor I could go anywhere I pleased—to far-off lands or to city slums—and be sure I could be of use anywhere. I should meet all sorts and conditions of men, I should not be tied down to a school or a college as a teacher is, or have to work under a superior, as a nurse must do. (Sicherman 1984)

Yet this sense of determined independence was not easily achieved. For three and a half years after graduating from Miss Porter's School, Hamilton remained at home in Fort Wayne, overcoming family resistance, attending to her family's needs, and preparing herself for medical school. She had to change both her plans for medical school and her plans for postgraduate work because of family demands and because the schools she wished to attend did not grant degrees to women. After graduating from medical school and spending a year of study in Europe, her first professional position at the Woman's Medical School of Northwestern University was a disappointment. Over the next several years, Hamilton alternatively held professional positions and did additional postgraduate work while gaining her greatest satisfaction from her work as a resident of Hull House. Not until 1907, when she was thirty-nine, did Alice Hamilton find a focus for her life work—investigating occupational diseases. Like Baker, she was a pioneer in her field, defining the work which needed to be done and developing methods for study and remedial action. And like Baker and Anderson, Hamilton did not present herself as anything but average. These women did not portray themselves as exceptions who were able to overcome what other women could not. Alice Hamilton expressed this view, with perhaps a bit too much modesty, when she wrote, "You see, I simply cannot believe that I am a person of more than ordinary ability, simply I know that chance has given me a more than ordinarily interesting life" (Sicherman 1984).

One factor these women did have on their side was their race. Race privilege interacted with their economic situations to allow them to take advantage of the educational and employment options opening for women. Given the racism and segregation of the era, neither the working-class nor the middle-class women could have followed the paths they did if they had been African American or other women of color. The stories of those African American women who found the means to graduate from medical schools but could not earn livings as doctors illustrate this point (Moldow 1987). Unlike Jo Baker or Alice Hamilton, they could not enter, for the most part, the public sector. The African American women who only had college degrees or less had even fewer options and were often limited to teaching in segregated schools.[18]

With their privilege, these women could play major roles in the development of new professions, new organizations, and new agencies, which, in turn, provided options for pioneering work and entrance into meaningful careers. Much of the earliest social welfare work was defined as women's work, developing rigid sex segregation or hierarchies later. Only during a period of reform would Dr. Jo Baker's ideas on children's health have led to the creation of the New York City Division of Child Hygiene, which she then headed. The same is true for Dr. Alice Hamilton's work with occupational/industrial health. In another example, it was because labor issues were women's issues at this time that Frieda Miller was able to rise within the New York State Department of Labor, from which she then moved on to head the Women's Bureau. The newness of these types of work both allowed and encouraged innovation and creativity, drawing on and rewarding these women's minds and their energy. In these positions, women had real power. They were making the rules. As pioneers in their fields, they not only defined social problems, but also developed and implemented badly needed solutions. The strength of their positions was enhanced by the fact that they were backed by a broad network of like-minded reformers, and, when they moved into nontraditional or male-dominated fields, they were hardly isolated women within a world of men.

While these women insisted that they were ordinary, only doing what any woman in their situations would do, their determination to find work that was meaningful to them often seems extraordinary. The women in this group literally were willing to search the country and, on occasion, the world, in their quest for a satisfying life's work. A few took the option for mobility to an extreme and were veritable nomads, at least during certain periods of their lives. The overall "gypsy award" goes to Mary Ellicott Arnold. Between the ages of eighteen and forty-three, Arnold, with her lifelong companion Mabel Reed, toured Europe, attended Drexel Institute in Philadelphia, worked the Reed family farm in New Jersey, lived in New York City, became an Indian matron on a reservation in northern California, ran cafeterias at Cornell University, and attended the University of California at Berkeley before settling down to work for the Consumer Corporation in New York City for eighteen years. Then, at the age of sixty-one, she was off again with Mabel for ten years working in Nova Scotia, Newfoundland, and Maine. They settled down in Philadelphia when Mary was seventy-one (Arnold Papers SL). Runners-up in this category are Frieda Miller and Martha Eliot who, in their sixties and seventies, were circling the globe, working for United Nations-related agencies. They appeared to have happily accepted assignments that took them to Southeast Asia, Africa, and the Middle East, challenging locations at that time for even the hardiest of U.S. travelers let alone older, middle-class, Euro-American spinsters (Miller Papers SL; Eliot Papers SL).

As seen in the opening of this chapter, Edith Stedman first used travel to escape her brother's domination and seek adventure. At the close of World War I, Edith returned to the United States but was unable to find an equally compelling position. In 1919 she decided to join a close friend who had become a medical worker in China. For seven years, during her thirties, she was a medical social worker there. When she did return to the States, she felt she was starting over again in terms of her career. She finally settled down at Radcliffe as director of their Appointment Bureau for the next twenty-four years. In retirement she spent much of her time in England (Stedman Papers SL).

These women's searches for economically and emotionally satisfying work both necessitated and justified travel. While periods of travel are associated with searching for self-knowledge and the transition to manhood in the traditionally male quest, marriage generally marked the emergence of the adult woman. These women therefore needed an alternative method through which to declare themselves adults and establish independent identities. It appears they utilized these periods of physical separation, of traveling, seeking educations, and finding careers to renegotiate their ties with their families of birth and establish themselves as autonomous wage earners. Edith Stedman succinctly described this process, "I had grown up and wanted my independence, and our wills [hers and her brother's] clashed. . . . I took a room in a lodging house" (Stedman Papers SL).[19]

Through a combination of race/class privilege, personal initiative and determination, and probably some luck, these women sought and found those doors that were just opening for women in the professions. Once they found these possibilities, they pushed them whatever way they could, often with the support of organizations of other Progressive Era reformers. Having these options for autonomy and for challenging work set these women apart from the majority of women workers who faced a racially and sexually segregated labor force in which they were relegated to dead-end, low-paying jobs with little individual power (Kessler-Harris 1982; Matthaei 1982; Jones 1985). As they became policymakers themselves, their own experiences influenced their visions and the solutions they proposed.[20]

While they certainly had greater choices than most women workers, these professional women at the turn of the century were not immune to discrimination or frustration from sexist attitudes. They expressed a consciousness of sexism, especially when they worked with men on a daily basis. Dr. Jo Baker dressed in conservative suits and shirtwaists "because the last thing I wanted was to be conspicuously feminine when working with men" (Baker 1939). Their negative experiences were not so overwhelming as to thwart their ambitions and energies. Consciousness of gender oppression, if anything, fueled their efforts to advance and encouraged their solidarity with other women. There was no denying that women were treated differently during this period of history. Perhaps this cohort was better prepared to handle sexist behavior because they expected it and considered that part of their mission was to challenge treatment based on stereotypes.

Because "mannish" styles of dress and "masculine" appearances came to be used against professional working women, supposedly being a key means by which to identify the "true" lesbian, Jo Baker's commonsense and far less convoluted explanation of her professional style merits note and discussion. In their work, many of these women were involved in activities in which trailing skirts and ruffled sleeves were hazards as well as nuisances. Investigating employment-related health hazards, Alice Hamilton inspected industrial plants and mines, often the only woman who had ever been on such premises.[21] Jo Baker walked miles of New York City pavements and climbed many a tenement stair in sweltering summer heat in her efforts to stem infant mortality among the city's immigrant population. Suggesting that these women's discontent with those aspects of women's clothing that seemed burdensome and frivolous involved a rejection of the female role betrays an ignorance of the basic material conditions of these women's lives. Arguments that "mannish" (rather than perhaps practical or functional) clothes supposedly indicated personal gender maladjustments uncovers the trend among those involved in the emerging fields of psychoanalysis and psychology to develop complex theories of individual neuroses or pathology when simple, materialist explanations would do. That these beliefs were anti-woman and anti-feminist was no coincidence.[22]

Early in their careers, when "respectable" white, middle-class women were assumed to be asexual, these women were able to present themselves as almost ungendered beings in their dealings with men. Only by situating themselves in some in between category could they assume to work with men as equals rather than as "other." Susan Ware, Molly Dewson's biographer, suggests that by middle-age Dewson alternated between a "maiden aunt" and a "one-of-the-boys" image, undoubtably using whatever sources of power she could as our "first female political boss" (1987).

As noted above, Jo Baker adopted a strict conservative dress code. She further elaborates that she dressed as she did so that, "when a masculine colleague of mine looked around the office in a rather critical state of mind, no feminine furbelows would catch his eye and give him an excuse to become irritated by the presence of a woman where, according to him, no woman had the right to be" (1939). Surviving photographs suggest that many of this group dressed conservatively. Even to the late twentieth century eye, their styles seem appropriate to them because they were not, as a group, dainty, delicate, or decorative.

Later this ambiguous positioning was not as possible or as effective because issues of gender and sexual nonconformity were of greater public concern. Both asexuality and homosexuality were outside the category of "healthy" behavior for women. While the emergence of the negative lesbian image has been well documented, the single, asexual female also became suspect.

The single women who headed the Women's Bureau and the Children's Bureau were particularly vulnerable to attacks. Jo Baker, whom Julia Lathrop, director of the Children's Bureau, frequently asked to testify on the Bureau's behalf, wrote of these occasions, "I was called Doctor instead of Miss and so could escape from the eternal remark always coming up among Congressmen about giving money to an old maid to spend" (1939). Politicians argued that the unmarried, non-mother could not possibly provide guidance for and protect the interests of "real" American women. Single women had been eliminated from the definition of "real woman," undermining their effectiveness as leaders and activists (Evans 1989; Ryan 1979).

While these women were conscious of the public-sphere prejudices they faced, there were also certain gender-specific private-sphere issues they had to overcome in their efforts toward independence. Because they were forging a new lifestyle for women, it was harder for these women than for men to make clean and complete breaks from their families. Throughout these women's lives family crises reopened the issue of autonomy; they or their families often expected that they could or should change their lives, rearrange their schedules, and/or put their careers on hold to tend to family concerns. Since nineteenth-century ideals for women so emphasized duty, it is understandable that most women were at least somewhat ambivalent about their nontraditional choices.

The extended Hamilton family provides an illustration of this conflict over family responsibilities. Alice, Edith, and their other two sisters, all of whom left home to build careers and independent lives, had three unmarried female cousins of roughly their same ages who did not leave home. Although Alice and Edith's mother defended her daughters' choices, all the other Hamilton aunts, including one who never married, severely criticized these sisters—Edith, Alice, Margaret, and Norah—as self-centered, especially for not being sufficiently attentive to their father. Consequently, Alice Hamilton, her sisters, and her cousins left behind some of the clearest discussions debating among themselves the issues of leaving home and the proper balance of "advanced individualism" versus self-sacrifice among "new women." In an 1894 letter to her cousin Agnes, Alice expressed her need to be away from the family home.

> My dear, I don't suppose, living as constantly in the home atmosphere as you do, that you realize how different it is from that of the rest of mankind. Whenever I come back home it seems to close around me like a lot of choking, cobweb chains, all this caution and mystery and reserve about nothings. (Hamilton Papers SL)

Two years later, Alice wrote again in a somewhat different vein.

> At any rate if *you* look back and regret, you cannot regret as much, for it can never be as bad to think of neglected opportunities as of neglected duties. Yet I am not sure that I do really regret. Sometimes I do and then individualistic principles reassert

themselves and I think I was right. So perhaps if I had it to live over again I should be where I am now; perhaps at home without any medical training or hospital training or Europe trip. (Hamilton Papers SL)

Regardless of their life decisions, the women in this cohort did not see themselves as abandoning their womanly responsibilities or rejecting their female identity. Instead, they maintained their respectability and avoided regret and guilt by extending their roles, and justifying their efforts for independence as "duty." They saw themselves as needing to support themselves and occasionally their families, use the educations they acquired, and participate in the social reforms that characterized their era. Thanks to the reforming spirit sweeping the country, they were able to find or create social welfare-related professions that provided a compromise between their own ambitions and their fulfillment of these responsibilities. Consequently they were able to seek out relatively adventuresome and comparatively remunerative professional positions without risking their womanliness. Of course, this definition of womanhood had its costs. They had to remain single and presumedly asexual.

While throughout this era, women of color and white working-class women often had to combine marriage, motherhood, and waged work, most of these women came from backgrounds that at least aspired to "separate spheres." As a result, the more privileged among them did not question the need to choose between career and family. Since the previous generations of white women of this class had few choices outside of the family, they saw progress because women now had some other option. Alice Hamilton expressed her strong opinions on this topic when she found out that the woman her cousin was marrying was studying medicine.

And I do think it such nonsense Marian studying medicine. That is the fault of the transition period in which we live. Girls think now that they all must have professions, just because they are free to, not realizing that the proper state of society is one in which a woman is free to choose between an independent life of celibacy or a life given up to childbearing and rearing the coming generation. We will go down the path of degeneration if we lose our mothers and our home-life. . . . I don't mean that she ought not to take up whatever studies she chooses, but she ought not to choose a work which is in its nature absorbing, which cannot be laid down and taken up again. . . . Well, let her do it then, let her study medicine, but if she practices it simply means either avoiding the burden of maternity or fulfilling its duties imperfectly. (Sicherman 1984)

While Alice Hamilton expresses a rather hard line on this issue, others of these women were not so absolutist in their views or their actions. Mary Anderson, having known poverty and living the life of a working-class woman, knew that marriage did not always eliminate the need to work from women's lives (Anderson 1951). And as will be discussed in greater depth in chapter 5, many of these women did establish families, though nontraditional ones, through their partnerships and/or the raising of children.

What is hard to determine is how conscious these women's individual decisions to remain single were. Mary Anderson's analysis of her status suggests a gradual recognition of a preference: "I thought, as a young girl, that I would get married too, but somewhere I lost myself in my work and never felt that marriage would give me the security I wanted" (Anderson 1951).

Anderson's doubts about the security of marriage, which informed both her political analysis (as mentioned above) and personal decisions, reinforce the importance of class differences among these women. While the privileged women did not fully consider the possibility of married women needing to work, throughout her autobiography Anderson consistently defends women's right to work with examples of married women and mothers whose husbands are simply unable to make enough to support their families.

While in medical school Martha Eliot responded to the news of a cousin's engagement by writing, "When I announce my engagement, we can take the paint off the front of the house!! but to tell you the truth if some other opportunity comes for getting it done, don't wait for me" (Eliot Papers SL). Two years later, she casually refers to her future grandchildren.

These ambiguous statements contrast with these women's actions. Any look at these women's life paths, their struggles for education and for meaningful work, strongly suggests that they lived their lives as if early on they intended to be independent. Just as these women were thwarted by societal norms from expressing selfish ambition, they may also have been unable to articulate a rejection of marriage, while behaviorally able to do just that.

While they are not explicit as to their own decisions regarding marriage, some members of this group did critique the institution itself. To marry, to these women, meant limitations, dependence, and a loss of autonomy. With few options for fertility control and severe limits on access to the birth control methods that were available, to marry generally also meant to mother. Many of these women saw this as giving up a tremendous amount of control over their lives. These reservations were, to them, practical and material because to them, more than for the working-class women and women of color, mothering had to be a full-time job.

On the ideological level there were also all the constraints and expectations that came from marriage, as well as the basic role and identity change in which a woman stopped being an individual and became her husband's appendage. Molly Dewson wrote for the 1927 *Wellesley Class Book*:

> Yes, I have no children. And I hope it will not be considered sour grapes as it undoubtably *[sic]* is, for me to plaintively hope that at our reunion all '97's will think of themselves as human individuals rather than as proud progenitors or as part of some human conglomeration. (Dewson Papers SL)

Significantly, four of these women chose to mother. Frieda Miller was the parent of Elisabeth, born in 1917 (Montgomery 1980). Pauline Newman shared parenting responsibilities with Miller (Newman Papers SL). Edith Hamilton helped raise four of her companion's nieces and nephews, and legally adopted one of the boys (Reid 1967). Leonora O'Reilly adopted a daughter, Alice, who died when only four years old (O'Reilly Papers SL). The factors behind these women's decisions to parent were not stated in their writings, but the fact that they did take on this role and the accompanying responsibilities suggests that motherhood, in and of itself, was not the reason they didn't marry. Importantly, each of these women continued her career and each mothered with another woman.[23] While these mothers account for a quarter of this group, there is no research on the number of professional, single, turn-of-the-century women who were biological, adoptive, or foster parents with which to compare this group.[24]

Other women in this study expressed regret that they never had children. Molly Dewson again: "All '97 children are so simple, sensible, sturdy, and attractive, I almost wish I had married myself" (Dewson Papers SL). This finding is consistent with Katherine Bement Davis's finding that among the 1,200 single women in her survey who wished they had married, "227 women regret the lack of children, while only 102 specify a husband."[25]

Like other active women of their generation, they expressed the belief that, through a particular combination of privilege, personal choice, and economic necessity, they were able to lead lives that were acceptable alternatives to the few options open to previous generations of women. They did not see themselves as rebels, but instead felt that the fight for the expansion of the definition of womanhood had already taken place, and they were matter-of-factly taking advantage of that change.[26]

It is important that these single women left few statements

defending their choice not to marry. This void contrasts with the numerous statements justifying their moves away from their birth families. Historian Smith-Rosenberg (1985) wrote that this generation's struggle was to "remain single *and* separate from their families." It seems that not marrying did not challenge gender norms as these women saw them, while leaving their families for reasons other than marriage did. What set these women apart from earlier generations of single women was that they were seeking full, independent lives of work, communities, and companions. Such autonomous lives were possible only because of the new economic opportunities for professional women.

But work and independence do not alone make a life. While these women and their culture constructed the choice for professional women of this era as marriage and family or career, these women challenged this dichotomy in their actions more than in their words. As will be discussed further in chapter 5, they created alternative families and communities that were women centered. A number formed lifelong partnerships with other women. Four of them raised children in female-headed families. Though not theoretically separatists, they found their greatest freedom within women-centered worlds of their own creation.

FOUR

"I Was Going to Have to Do It All on My Own"

Toward Independent Womanhood after World War II

After five years away, completing her education as a health care provider, Bobbi Denova moved home to her parents' house. One night, viewing the movie *The Sound of Music,* she fell in love with the mountains of Austria. A short time later she happened to meet an Austrian ski instructor who encouraged her to go to Europe. She decided that she would, and "the minute I got home [from the ski trip] I wrote to every Embassy." She received information about an overseas program through the American Council of Nurses. "I got myself a passport. And I went." She had no money saved, knew no one there, and spoke no German. "I had a sense I belonged there and needed to be there." She stayed there working and exploring Europe from 1965 to 1967. When she came home she lived with her parents, but was unhappy and looking for other options.

> And I remember my dad coming out on the back steps with me, and says . . . I was looking for an apartment, and my dad says, "I know you're really unhappy, but I'd like you to stay home and live with us." He says, "We could work things out." And my unhappiness was because I had been to Europe and I had been around and I knew somehow I could not stay at home. I'd vegetate. So I decided to go to [New Zealand].

She moved to New Zealand, again alone, without a job and knowing no one. While there she met Jamie Henson. Together they moved from New Zealand to New England so that Bobbi could acquire additional professional training. They finally settled in Albuquerque in 1974.

The fifteen women raised in the post-World War II era moved into adulthood unsure of what direction their lives would take. Their clearest shared commitment was to education, and, through education, they hoped to find professional positions. They also had begun to separate from their families and move away from their hometowns. Less certain were their expectations about marriage and independence. Throughout their early adult years, which spanned the mid-1950s through the mid-1970s, the opposite sex and plans for marriage were not priorities in their lives, but they had not dismissed the possibility of matrimony totally. They knew they were different and were grappling with conflicts between what they thought they should be doing and thinking, and their yearnings for something else. This "something else" was generally vague. They knew they were not in step with their cohort, yet the individuals in this group seldom could define the bases of their dissatisfactions. Most had some orientation toward independence, and they felt competent enough to begin to explore the world beyond their families and hometowns. Some had a sense of their attraction toward women, but, as they were entering adulthood, they had no meanings to put on these desires.

The themes which evolved out of the years that took these lesbians through early adulthood to maturity were education, travel, work, and sexuality. Woven through the first three of these are issues of separation and autonomy. While the contemporary women shared these concerns—education, travel, work, separation, and autonomy—with the Progressive Era women, the societal and personal support they received in their quests was very different. All of the earlier group's efforts were framed within larger cultural changes that both allowed and justified their choices. Although not all the turn-of-the-century women were actively involved in the Women's Movement, many were. Together they benefited from the new educational, employment, and social opportunities that opened to women. They could have a shared consciousness that what they were doing in the public sphere was important and necessary for women and for the whole society. They knew they were probably in the vanguard, but they expressed a sense of being with, not apart from, other women.

This contemporary group came to maturity during an apolitical period. The gender and sexuality systems they confronted were static, at least through the mid-1960s. Women's options were more ideologically than materially constricted. Challenges to the *de juris* sexism were thwarted by a gender "Catch-22." The myth of equal opportunity promoted the idea that women could do whatever they wanted, but no "real" or "healthy" female wanted any more than a home, a husband, and a family. Consequently, the postwar never-married lesbians found their possibilities on their own. This group took advantage of what educational paths were open to them. They searched for meaningful work. They traveled using both education and work as justifications. They did not marry, sometimes consciously rejecting marriage, sometimes not. They enjoyed intimate, sexually active lives with other women, and came, in most cases with great caution and deliberateness, to claim lesbian identities.

They built these lives on personal foundations of competence, having accepted in childhood that they were different from other women.

Until the women's, gay, and other political movements erupted in the 1960s, these women constructed their private lives quietly. They felt they could not proclaim that they were lesbians without jeopardizing the economic base of their independence. They also could not take a public stand as independent women. So deeply heterosexual was this culture (and still is in many ways) that women as solitary human beings did not exist. Unattached to a male, a woman was incomplete. Even further outside of the boundaries of the sex/gender system were women who sexually and/or emotionally made other women primary.

This chapter traces their paths to autonomy through education, travel, and work.

Education

Although these women pursued their educations with serious commitments, with several earning advanced degrees, unlike their turn-of-the-century counterparts, most had negative memories from their earliest formal schooling. Their identification with education evolved. Retrospectively, they could name the overt sexism of the educational system plus that of individual teachers and counselors. At the time, they were only confused. "Sexism" was not part of the postwar vocabulary.

Gloria Whelan had one teacher who told her she "walked like a farmer," and kept her in during recess, making her practice "walking like a girl." This same teacher also tried to convince her parents to keep her back a year, not because of her school work, but because she was not "mature." Bobbi Denova stated that "my father was very, very adamant about education." While she did well and has mostly happy memories, she remembers going with her father to get the results of an assessment test. The examiner told her,

> "They indicate you could be an architect. But obviously you are a woman so you can't do that. . . . Maybe you could be a nurse." Then he says, "No, you don't want to go away from your mother. . . . Why don't you have your mother teach you how to sew?" I went from elation to the dumps so quick. And I was angry. I didn't know why I was angry at the time. I was thinking I don't want to stay home and sew.[1]

Anne found school pretty "stupid . . . school itself didn't mean much." Even among the six women who did not have seriously negative memories of school, the joy of learning academic material was not what they recalled from their early years. These women remembered liking to play with other children, recess, sports, and music.

Racism in the public schools was an issue for all the women of color. Both Yolanda Peña and Jo Martinez spoke Spanish as their first language. In New Mexico and San Francisco, respectively, Yolanda and Jo were put in special education classes because they lacked fluency in English. According to Yolanda,

> All of a sudden I was yanked from the English class, the normal class, and put into the special class. And I don't know why, except they were giving me these devious little tests that I had to do, and I guess I flunked them. I couldn't speak right or do what I was supposed to do, and so I had to learn, go back and learn English from the very beginning. It was an emotional thing. I knew I didn't belong there and it was so shocking, it was terrible. I thought I was retarded.

Jo's parents had migrated to California in the 1940s to work in the war industries. Because Spanish was Jo's first language, she, along with all other students who did not speak English, were placed in special education classes.

Throughout this period, *de facto* and *de juris* racial segregation produced numerous barriers for the women of color. In

New York City, Trudy Hardin's entry into first grade was complicated by race. Her teacher there was the first white woman she had ever seen. A few years later her family moved to a neighborhood where she was the only black girl in her public school class. Everyday she was chased by the white children when she got off the school bus.

In the South, Lee Powell went to segregated schools until junior high. She found that even black teachers based their expectations of students on their class backgrounds and skin color. She described these teachers as "nasty" and "cruel." She had no positive memories of school until junior high.

There was, however a shared aspect of these women's educations which Trudy summarizes succinctly: "I liked reading, but I didn't like school." Many of these women identified reading as one of their favorite activities, one that broadened their views of the world. Jo, whose small Hispanic village had no library, had a teacher who would bring her copies of the *New Yorker*, *Newsweek*, and *Life*. She also befriended a man who settled on the edge of their village. He was the first person she knew who received newspapers and publications in the mail. He would pass these on to her, and "I thought that was the greatest thing there ever was." Anne McConnell remembers how important it was for her to receive a gift of secondhand books from the local doctor's wife.

> They were mine. I had never been into heavily reading until this point. But, because they were mine, I read them. And there were tons of them. There must have been three boxes of books, so some of them were way over my level. I read those books. I loved those books. And that hooked me on reading.

Although these women ranged from outstanding to indifferent students, with many negative experiences in school, by the end of high school almost all these women had begun to view additional education as a necessity. They had connected acquiring an education with work, career concerns, and separating from their families. Not all of these women clearly articulated these issues, but a number did.

All but Iris went immediately from high school to some post-secondary education. For most this meant college. It is at this life junction that class differences are most clear. Only five of these women had always expected to go to college. Three of these five, Audrey, Carrie, and Amy, were the most economically privileged of the group. Going to college and going *away* to college were basic expectations for young women of their class backgrounds. Their mothers had gone to college, and all had lived away, boarding at school. Carrie went 1500 miles away to school. Although Amy went to college quite near her parents' home, she made a deal with them that they were to treat her as if she were hundreds of miles away.

For the other women, additional education was unexpected. The processes by which these women came to the decision that they had to have more education again display significant diversity, but for most it was a gradual evolution of an idea. If they got additional external support or encouragement, it was greatly appreciated, but many of these women persevered with little emotional or financial backing.

In several families the gender-based bias against higher education for females was strong. When Jo raised the possibility of college with her father, he said, "No, you're not going. Don't even think about college. It's not for girls." This was from a father who had himself set an example of using education for upward mobility. He had completed college via night school, while working full time. Neither was her mother supportive.

My mother thought I was crazy that I wanted to . . . I couldn't quite define it and say, "I want to be . . ." I knew I wanted to go to college, but I wasn't quite sure what I wanted to be, but I assumed I was going into P.E. 'cause I was good at it. No other reason. I think my mother expected me to get married and have children and that was that. I'm not sure she . . . she couldn't understand all these other things I wanted to do, or thought I wanted to do, or got involved in. Does that make sense to you? She went to eighth grade and then she got married. So I went beyond that so why shouldn't I get married and settle down.

Jo managed to get to college through the support of her grandparents and the physical education teacher at her high school.

Yolanda didn't even have the small encouragements Jo received in school and from her grandparents. Her only alternative was a technical-vocational school. She felt she needed that schooling because "I couldn't just get a job; I needed a skill."

Among the women from stable working-class families, finishing high school was assumed, but it was considered sufficient education for girls. Gloria Whelan's father refused to allow her even to take college prep courses in her high school until her mother intervened.

I remember I was so disturbed by the strong message from my father that I couldn't go to college . . . that at night, I would just cry myself to sleep in frustration. . . . My friends were going to college, and I was going to have to be a secretary. And one time my mother heard me sobbing, and she came downstairs to find out what was wrong. And I just burst out and told her everything. So she really went to him and talked with him. And it took her a couple of days to convince him, but then he finally broke down and said okay. We'll let you do it.

These daughterly ambitions were clearly problematic for certain fathers. In Gloria's case at least part of the issue was finances. If money was going into higher education, it would be for the sons of the families. Women were not expected to be independent, but these young women had such expectations.

This connection between higher education and future employment possibilities came up among other working-class women. Jamie connected her decision to go to nursing school with a conversation she overheard. "Well, I knew by this time that I had a choice—secretary, teacher, or nurse, and, at some point in my life, I had heard my mother talking to a neighbor who was a nurse, and she said, 'When you're a nurse, you can always find a job.' And that stuck in my head."

And getting to school was only part of the process. Juggling jobs and finding the time and energy to complete their school work continued to stress these women. For several, serious deprivations were involved. Jo remembers that all she could afford to rent when she started college was a place which was little better than a chicken coop. When Gloria entered graduate school, she

> was hurting. I didn't have any extra money for anything. Basically my house was pretty empty in terms of food. I had maybe bread, tuna, and eggs. And that's about it. And coffee. I pretty well sustained myself on those. And then my friend, she knew I was hurting so she had me over for dinner once a week, so I had one good meal a week.

If the quest for higher education is one theme consistently found among these women, the other commonality is a determination to separate from their families and hometowns. Only Robin has never moved away from her hometown. While as children these women had expressed their love of physical freedom, as young adults they began physically moving away on a larger scale. Most of them left home via schooling, and the means and motivations between getting an education and leaving home are intertwined. Anne remembers the night the recruiter told her she would have a full tuition scholarship to go away to college: "It was like getting your dream. It's sort of like kids who have always wanted a horse and then Christmas morning they wake up and there's the horse. It was like I can really do it. It's okay. I don't have to go to PA (the local junior college). I can really do it. I can get away from home."

Jo remembers, "I had to pick the cheapest school in the state. And I couldn't go to. . . . See the cheapest one would have been going to [New Mexico Tech] because I would have been at home. But it had to be the cheapest one away from home for me. I mean, that was my goal."

Although both Trudy and Anne realized that as the "second moms" their leavings would be hard on their younger siblings, they did not hesitate to leave. The two hesitators were Robin, whose father had been sick, and Jean, whose father had died. Yolanda did not leave immediately either, but after completing her course at Albuquerque Technical-Vocational Institute and working for a short period of time, she enlisted in the military. Though Iris did not go directly to college after high school, she did leave her hometown, coming to New Mexico to be a "rich hippie."

It is in this pursuit of education, as well as the use of schooling as a reason to leave their families and hometowns, that this contemporary group most closely parallels the turn-of-the-century women. Getting to college was a struggle for all the Progressive Era women as well as for most of the contemporary women. Among the lower middle-class and working-class women, even when their parents were supportive, most were unfamiliar with colleges and universities. What guidance these women received in school was based on the recognition of their potential by individual teachers rather than systematic educational or career counseling. Given these odds, it is clear that the women in this group, with the exception of the three most privileged ones, actively sought higher education, and did so with a strong sense of needing to be self-supporting. They are not clear about the source of this motivation. They know they did not receive messages from their families nor from their schools.

Breines (1992), in her study of the 1950s, characterizes most young, middle-class, white women as non-planners. Because the functioning gender system for white youth constructed females as satellites to men, young women could not plan their own futures. A woman had to wait until a man chose her as his wife, and then she followed whatever future he had planned. Families, educational systems, and the popular media all contributed to this myth, and few discordant messages existed that would have encouraged young women to behave differently.

That so many of this group went away to college or for professional training should be analyzed as an even more deliberate decision to leave home when compared to the earlier generation. The earlier group had fewer choices in pursuing a college education; they had to leave home to go to school, while the contemporary women did not. Except for a few, most could have lived at home and attended college. Clearly, this group also wanted to be on their own. While not all of the women could articulate this intention, more could among this generation than among the earlier one. There is a sense from their stories that they knew they needed more social space than their families and hometowns could grant them.

These women, who entered college between 1954 and 1971, were part of the generation of women who reestablished a female presence on campuses after the great postwar influx of male veterans ended.[2] In 1950, only 24 percent of the bachelor's degrees granted in the United States were earned by women. Not since 1910 had this figure been so low (Kaledin 1984; Solomon 1985). By 1960, the proportion had grown to 35 percent; by 1970, to 42 percent; and by 1980, 47 percent. Absolute numbers of women in higher education were rising significantly as well.[3] Mabel Newcomer (1959), in *A Century of Higher Education for American Women,* presents data on the economic backgrounds of women college students in 1958. While private women's colleges continued to educate the daughters of business people and professionals primarily, at state teachers' colleges, 30 percent of fathers were manual workers, 24 percent were white collar workers; 22 percent were businessmen, and only 21 percent were professionals.

Unlike the turn-of-the-century women, the contemporary women included in this study were not exceptional within their generations on the basis of attending college. Both the numbers and percentages of women participating in postsecondary education had risen significantly. By the time these women graduated from high school, even the daughters of the working class were graduating college in large numbers.[4]

Although college educations were an option for increasing numbers of women, sexism in higher education continued.[5] Many of the issues feminists have since identified as formal and informal barriers to equality in education are obvious in these women's stories. Some of these include a lack of female role models; independent women seeing themselves as the exceptions, rather than models; women defined as sex objects; little information about nontraditional fields or financial aid possibilities; and the idea that parents might sacrifice for a son's education but not a daughter's. The lack of athletic scholarships for women before the passage of Title IX in 1972 was a clear factor for several women who were excellent athletes and would, if graduating from high school today, be almost guaranteed such assistance.[6]

The education this group sought was practical and traditional. As undergraduates, four majored in education, three in English, two in religion, and one each in psychology, sociology, and drama. Nine of this group taught or planned to teach. Audrey and Yolanda chose social work and human services respectively. Bobbi and Jamie both went into traditionally female medical fields. In their choice of fields this group replicates the pre-Women's Movement distribution of career goals among college women. In 1965, for example, even at elite Stanford University, 36 percent of the senior women planned to be elementary or secondary school teachers.[7] In this distribution of majors, these women show no deviation from the averages of their generation. In 1970, 36 percent of the bachelor's and first professional degrees granted to women were in education; 26 percent in the arts and humanities; and 17 percent in social sciences. However, the percentage of women college students who planned to teach was only 36 percent, a lower proportion than among this group (Carnegie Commission 1973).

There were no significant class differences among the original career aspirations of this group, but economics did keep Yolanda, Bobbi, and Jamie from entering four-year colleges immediately after high school. While it is not surprising that the three women from the most privileged backgrounds—Audrey, Amy, and Carrie—all attended private schools, it is interesting that both African American women also did. Anne, an Anglo from a poor family, also graduated from a private college. All three of these women received scholarships.

None of these women remembered receiving any significant formal career counseling, though many were informally mentored. They certainly did not receive any counseling that recognized that they might be self-supporting. Overall they were on their own to figure out what to do with their education and their lives. This was an exceptionally daunting task for students who were first-generation college. While still in high school, Gloria remembered planning to work.

> Well, I figured I would go to college and get my degree. Then I would teach in order to pay my loans. . . . So I had always planned to be a professional. I think I always planned to be able to take care of myself financially. . . . I knew that I was not going to be able to take the easy street and have somebody support me. I was going to have to do it all on my own.

In the process of deciding what they would prepare themselves to do, these women balanced their own preferences with a consciousness of what was open to them and possible based on class, race, and gender. Jo wanted to be a veterinarian, but found out quickly that women were discouraged from this field. When several schools ignored her requests for applications, she also suspected that her Hispanic surname elicited a racist reaction. Jamie Henson thought it would be great to be a gym teacher, but knew her folks couldn't afford to send her to college. Lee Powell felt that teaching was simply all that was open to college-educated Black women.

Class influences worked the other way as well. With her family's resources, Audrey could aim a bit higher and plan on going to graduate school to get a Master of Social Work (M.S.W.) degree. After graduating from college Phi Beta Kappa, Amy decided she needed a teaching credential to have a steady job. Because she didn't want to ask her parents to support her any longer, she found out about an internship-type program.

> And you taught two classes and you continued to take classes at [the university] and at the end of that twelve month period, you had a master's degree and a teaching credential, and supposedly a foot in the door because you actually had been working in some school. So I applied to that and got admitted to that program and . . . how deliberate? I think most of my decisions at that point were not discussed with anybody, not thought out that carefully, just, this seems the best route without that much analysis. . . . One of the attractive things about the program . . . is that it would involve some pay, and one of the things that had happened through my college career is that I had been incapable of asking my parents for more money . . . so I tried to get a job . . . supporting myself.

Not depending upon her family for money was another way Amy declared her independence.

These career plans might also be viewed as reflecting the fact that these women had few role models of independent women except their high school teachers. Paula, who originally aimed higher and wanted to be an archaeologist, was actively discouraged from her ambition by a leading woman in the field.

> You know, it's funny, I had Florence Ellis as my advisor, and although she's a brilliant . . . anthropologist, she was rather negative about women being in the field . . . at that time I wanted to

be a field archeologist . . . and she really discouraged me from that because they didn't pick women to do that kind of thing very much in those days. And they didn't want women to distract them, you know, in these digs, although I never really noticed myself distracting too many men. . . . She probably really discouraged me. . . . And I had gotten involved with sports again . . . and I decided I didn't want to live without that the rest of my life . . . so I decided to become a P.E. major, plus the fact I'd realized . . . I'd have to have a Ph.D. before I got a darn job anywhere. . . . And I didn't see my parents affording to send me through my doctorate . . . I didn't feel I should be that burden . . . I should get myself a job and support myself.[8]

In spite of the constraints of gender, class, and race that these women faced, as a group, they had higher than average educational achievements for women of their generation. Of this group of fifteen women, one has a Ph.D., seven have M.A.s, twelve have B.A.s, two have advanced professional training in the medical field, and one has received significant computer programming skills from her job. While the women from working-class and poor backgrounds confronted greater difficulties in earning their education than the middle-class women, the educational levels they achieved are slightly higher than the level of the more privileged members.

As did their Progressive Era counterparts, these women continued their formal education throughhought their adult lives. For most of them, their reentry into education was related to their careers and reflected a growing awareness of new job opportunities. When Gloria entered college as a young, working-class, first-generation college student, she was in awe of her professors. As her comfort and success in this academic setting grew, she decided that she could aim higher. Though not without self-doubt, she pursued her master's and doctorate degrees. Jo Martinez returned to school for her master's in 1968 when she was thirty-three, and for her administrative certification when she was thirty-nine.

At the time of these interviews, 1986–87, seven of the fifteen women were in school full or part time. Only two of these women were taking classes for personal growth. The other five were preparing for career changes. Their career goals included medical doctor, psychologist, human-services consultant, hospice counselor, and accountant.

These women used education to gain entry into traditional and secure female professions, especially teaching, along with nursing and social work/human services. The high proportion who have additional degrees suggests that they continued to move to better jobs through education. These opportunities did not become apparent to them until after they had entered higher education or the professional ranks.

Travel and Separation

In some ways these women's struggles with individualism and the "family claim" echoed those of the turn-of-the-century women. While the power of the "family claim" had diminished by the mid-twentieth century, establishing autonomy was not necessarily easier for the contemporary women. With few models of independent womanhood, there was still no female rite of passage to adulthood except for marriage. Women were generally expected to remain part of the family's household until they married, though working away from home for a few years was acceptable. For example, in May 1948, *Life* magazine had as its cover story, "Career Girl: Her Life and *Problems*" (my emphasis). The subtitle read, "The Hopes and Fears of Countless Young Career Girls Are Summed Up in Her Struggle to Succeed in New York City." After profiling a remarkably incompetent and unhappy young woman, we are told at the end of this article that Gwyned Filling plans to work for only five years. It is also noted that she worries that she is jeopardizing her chances to marry by working that long.[9]

The majority of women in both generations first left home to attend postsecondary school. Past that period in their lives, there is an important difference between the Progressive Era women and the contemporary lesbians. The former group traveled in search of work, while the latter group settled into a job or a profession much earlier, and then traveled. Possible reasons for this variation will be discussed in the following section.

The women in this cohort did not follow any one pattern of travel and separation to establish themselves as autonomous individuals. Eight simply did not move back to their families or hometowns after graduating from school. Both Jean and Jamie became the "man of the family" after their fathers died, helping their mothers financially and emotionally while still young. Only when their families appeared to be on solid footing did these two women move away, and then both went overseas. Four women—Iris, Lee, Bobbi, and Yolanda—repeated the pattern of returning home, then moving away several times.

Eventually most of these women could articulate the connection between leaving home, traveling, and searching for autonomy. For Audrey, who came from a wealthy Anglo family, the connection was clear. For her, personal autonomy was in direct opposition to her mother's expectations, which were partially based on the fact that Audrey had a physical disability: "Mother never thought I would be able to take care of myself. She never thought I would get married and never thought I would work. She thought I would stay home with her . . . I thought I would leave and be a cowboy [sic] or a detective."

Audrey eventually did become a "cowboy," owning a ranch in central New Mexico. But this settling down followed many moves. She left home earlier than any of the other women, to attend a Catholic girls' boarding school. This community sustained her through some difficult years as she underwent a serious operation to alleviate some of the pain from her disability. She moved to another state for undergraduate college, and then to yet another state to earn her master's degree. While she moved back to her home state for her first professional job, she left after two years. After that time, she moved progressively east, through three states, working and building an autonomous life.[10] By 1966, at the age of thirty, she was in a relationship. Between 1972 and 1974, she and her lover adopted three mixed race, special-needs children, and then this family moved to New Mexico to the ranch. Finally, in 1986, when their children were on their own, Audrey and her partner moved up to Albuquerque.

Amy agreed that geographical distance was a factor in her graduate school decision. "It was. Putting a little more distance. I was really not comfortable with life in general at that point in my life, and adding more distance between me and my family was something that seemed important. Getting further away."

Yolanda's escape route was the military, one of the few options at the time for young people without resources for college. It was not without complications, though, for young lesbians: "I was still unclear as to what to do. I just knew I had to get out, out of town. Still unclear as to my goals and what I wanted to do. So I hit upon an idea, join the Air Force. . . . It was just a way to get out. And I wanted a big adventure, which I got."

Iris is the only informant in this group who did not go directly into some postsecondary education. She was also the only one who described herself as a hippie. After high school, she became "tired" of her hometown. With money from her savings account she and a friend caught a bus for Albuquerque. They ended up on a commune in Taos, where they stayed until the weather got too cold. They went to Los Angeles, staying there for about a year before they decided to head home to the South. Iris tried college, but also began to work for a national corporation. After several years, in 1977, she transferred to Albuquerque.

Jo described her decision to move out of state as something

she knew she should do, almost deliberately as a rite of passage into full adulthood.

> Well, Alice [her lover] and I talked about it. And essentially I had moved away from home to her, and then to Mt. Gold [New Mexico], and was still pretty much cared for in a sense by Alice. Not in the traditional sense, [but] she was always there for me. And so she really felt I needed to be absolutely by myself, where I didn't know anyone. So I said "shit" and went. I interviewed in San Diego and I interviewed in two other places. And I liked Santa Barbara . . . so off I went.

These decisions to just pick up and move on their own may not appear unusual today, but these travels took place from the late 1950s on and were exceptional choices for young, unmarried women to make. Such mobility was still an adventure for young men as seen by the popularity of Jack Kerouac's *On the Road*. Moving from one town to another may have been the closest that young women could get to this experience.

Six women were quite nomadic. In addition to living in Europe for several years, Jean, a New York native, also lived in California before moving to New Mexico. Both Yolanda and Carrie explored the country before returning to their home states. Eight other women moved a moderate amount. For example, Anne lived in three different locations in Texas, and went back and forth between New Mexico and Texas twice before settling there. Some moved often while others moved far.

Robin Edwards was the major exception; she never moved away from New Mexico. Her dream of attending an out-of-state university was not possible given her family's financial situation. She did move out into her own apartment in her early twenties, even though she had been allowed a great deal of freedom at home. Perhaps she felt less compelled to move far because her life plan—not to marry and to have a career—was accepted throughout her life by her family and social circle. She received this affirmation and did not have to move away to establish an independent identity and escape family and community pressures to conform to gender and sexuality norms. She was also her mother's only child and they had no extended family in the area.

Just as the Progressive Era women's lives challenge the explanations sexologists and psychologists developed concerning unmarried women and lesbians, the paths these women found to separate and achieve autonomy pose an interesting contradiction to contemporary psychology such as feminist object relations theory (Chodorow 1978). In spite of a diversity of mother/daughter and father/daughter relationships, these women put themselves first and chose paths in early adulthood that led toward economic and social self-sufficiency. Their struggles for independence are especially noteworthy given the hegemonic nature of the gender and the sexual messages given their generation, as well as the relative lack of autonomous female role models.

Just as their earlier counterparts had seen the hardships when the heterosexual, male-centered nuclear family failed, most of the women in this group had seen the weaknesses of these familial and gender systems in their childhoods. This knowledge, and their early sensitivity to being different and not conforming, may have made this group especially sensitive to the rigidity of the post–World War II gender images. Without finding some flexibility in the female role, these women may have felt they had no options between total conformity and "dropping out" and getting away. Even if object relations theory is correct in giving infancy and childhood experiences significant formative power for adult autonomy, the early adult years of these women's lives appear to have been another critical period for choosing between relational dependency with family responsibilities and personal independence.

Work

Neither travel nor autonomy would have been possible for these women without a base of financial self-support. With the exception of Iris, these women focused on acquiring the necessary education and training for entrance into safe and secure jobs, generally at the professional level. While the choices made reflected the options easily open to women during the late fifties and sixties, their career paths were quite different from those of the turn-of-the-century women. The earlier autonomous women took longer to find their careers, and, as mentioned above, their adult travels were often predicated on this search for meaningful work. The later group also traveled, yet eight of the women who moved stayed in the same type of job. An example of this different life pattern is Audrey. From the time she received her master's degree in 1960 to the time she moved to New Mexico in 1974, she was always employed as a social worker. She then changed professions, becoming a rancher, but this was after she had settled down geographically. Jamie Henson and Bobbi Denova traveled because they were certain they could always find positions in their health-care field.

Several factors may have influenced the different patterns between these generations. First, the sex segregation and regularization of the professions may have made it clearer to the contemporary women that they had only a few viable options for self-support. Unlike Alice Hamilton and Jo Baker, who created their own fields, women at midcentury were not developing new vocational fields. Although working-class women had greater opportunities for higher education and to become professionals during the postwar period than earlier, this meant that few of the professional women in this contemporary group had family resources to depend on outside of their own earnings. The turn-of-the-century women had earned their living at a time when new opportunities were emerging. The content of their work, the experience of working, and the context in which they worked were new and exciting. Mary Anderson and Edith Stedman, for example, focused much of their autobiographies on their work, conveying a sense of its importance and excitement (Anderson 1951; Stedman Papers SL). Their work was not compartmentalized. While it was not their whole lives, it was intertwined with their social communities and their political activities. Among the contemporary group it was the exception rather than the rule for a woman to describe her work in any detail. Jo, for example, felt she did innovative work in her position in California, but she did not present the actual tasks involved in any of her other jobs. Overall, like many other twentieth-century Americans, they typically portrayed their work as routine, as a means to make a living.

Although these women originally entered traditional female professions, many did not stay in one position or location. While Robin has held the same position since she graduated from college in 1969, the other women have had more complex career paths. Yolanda, as an example, worked for one year as a drafter after completing her Technical and Vocational Institute course. She then enlisted in the military for several years. After she was discharged, she used her G.I. benefits to attend college and earned a B.A. in psychology. She then worked as a social worker for several years before receiving a commission in a different branch of the armed services. Today she is still in the Reserves, working in a nontraditional job in private industry, and taking courses toward her M.A. "Well, I want to be a professional. I want to be . . . a training development consultant so I could have more freedom. And I want to make the money I'm making now and not work so hard. And write."

When she was in her early thirties and after working as a teacher, Trudy felt the pressure to get into a field that offered a stable, decent income.

And I thought maybe I'll try law and so I signed up to take the LSAT. And while I was doing that I was thinking, do you really want to sit behind a desk with a long yellow pad, wearing stockings and . . . pumps? You know, you have to play the part. Even my friends who are lesbians who are lawyers play the part. They dress the part. And I thought no, I don't really want to be a lawyer. If you wanted to be a lawyer, you'd be a criminal lawyer, and there's no money in criminal law. The reality is you're getting up there and you need to make some money. So I thought I'm just not going back to school until I decide what I want.

Most of these women have expanded their employment expectations in the direction of desiring more interesting and challenging positions, and more autonomy in their work situations. Only after they entered higher education or the world of work did they find other career possibilities or consider them achievable. Of the nine women originally involved in teaching and education, only Gloria, Robin, and Trudy are still in the classroom. Lee has joined Jo in higher education administration. Jamie and Bobbi are part of a private medical group that contracts their services to local hospitals. Paula left teaching after twenty years and now works for a woman-owned wholesale business.

Class and race issues do appear to have played some role in these women's career changes, their abilities to make these shifts, and the direction of their career choices. As mentioned above, Trudy Hardin, Jo Martinez, and Lee Powell, three women of color, as well as Gloria Whelan and Robin Edwards, two Euro-American women from working-class backgrounds, have made the decision to stay in secure public educational systems. Yolanda Peña and Iris Miller both work for large private corporations. It seems the women of color and, to a lesser extent, the working-class women prefer positions with guaranteed salaries and benefits.

The three women whose parents were in private-sector businesses eventually started their own companies. Amy Adams's and Carrie Stern's parents both provided the capital they needed to set up their businesses. Audrey gradually moved away from institution-based social work into freelance work and finally started her own company. She inherited the money she needed to start her enterprise.

In Carrie's case, her parents originally hesitated to provide the money she needed, and she felt their reluctance was related to her gender. Her story provides an interesting example of how class and access to material resources can interact with the gender ideology in constructing women's work options. Carrie had begun showing and breeding border collies when she was eleven. This interest grew to be the main focus in her life, an avocation that was much more than a hobby. As a teenager, her parents got involved in this business, investing as part owners in a kennel. Although Carrie was also involved in this aspect of her interest, her parents never thought to bring her fully into making financial decisions nor did they think she might want a career in this area. In fact, Carrie believes they never considered that she might have a career at all. "They never even knew what I took in school," and she compared this with the time, energy, and care they took to make sure her brother had a professional situation. Only after Carrie had been out of college a while did her parents realize that she was struggling to find some meaningful work. They urged her to go to school to get a teaching certification. She did so and taught grade school for two years, but found that she missed working with dogs. She decided she wanted to start her own kennel and train dogs to be used by sheep ranchers. She lived and worked in Pennsylvania at the time but went to New Mexico to present her parents with a business plan. In the belief that they had agreed to back her with the necessary capital, she went back East, packed, and moved, arriving in Albuquerque only to find that her parents hadn't taken her proposal seriously. She was now on her own.

For the next five years, Carrie built her reputation working for a leading local dog trainer and running his business. After that time, her parents "were ready to help and ready to take me seriously."

There are, in these examples, indications that parental career patterns as well as class background influenced these women's directions once they moved out of traditional fields. Anne, for example, is co-owner, with her lover, of a feminist bookstore. Her father was not a success in his businesses and was frequently out of work, but when he did work he was self-employed.

Four of the women from working-class backgrounds have found the means to balance the demands of economics and quality of life. Jean, Bobbi, and Jamie all work less than full time as semi-independent contractors. All three expressed the wish to have more time to pursue their other interests as the reason behind their work-related decisions. Robin, who has a full-time position, cut back on her work hours by resigning from after-hours, work-related commitments.

The Heterosexual Imperative

As discussed in chapter 2, most of this midcentury group distanced themselves from actual heterosexual involvements and kept thoughts of marriage vague or, at least, on the back burner. Others participated in heterosexual dating and a few became engaged. That they came so close to marriage while also having deep, intimate, and, for some, sexual, relationships with women, captures the confusing sexual landscape that women of this era experienced before they knew and claimed their lesbian identities.

Jo Martinez, who had been involved with Alice Henry since high school, became engaged while in college. She thought, "Sure, I'll get married. I didn't really know what that meant 'til he really started getting serious . . . I'm not saying I'm naive. I'm saying I never put myself, marriage and sex, and all that, and children together." What brought Jo to a reality check was having to select silver and crystal patterns. At that point the meaning of what she was doing hit her and she ended the engagement.

Jean, though she never thought she would get married, had several relationships with men and even set marriage dates. But, she remembers, "I always felt this sense of doom about these marriage dates." They never happened. After the last involvement she left for Europe.

Carrie told about the "cowboy" to whom she became engaged just before she left on a postcollege trip to Europe. This man followed her and her female friends when they left for a long planned overseas trip. The more time she spent with this man, the clearer she was that she couldn't live within his world. "He liked to dominate." Finally, one day Carrie, her friends, and the cowboy were all drinking at a bar in Spain. Carrie remembers that she was drunkenly daydreaming about kissing the woman she had loved in college. At that exact moment her fiance kissed her, and Carrie responded with a passion she had never expressed with him. He was thrilled. Only the next morning when she was sober did she realize what had happened. While this incident only confused the cowboy, through it Carrie reached the decision that she couldn't marry this man.

These examples suggest that heterosexuality was so normative in the gender and sexuality systems of the post-World War II era that even loving and being sexually involved with another woman could not displace those expectations. Most of these women had only seen or heard of a future at home with husband and children. Though they felt they wanted to be independent, have adventures, and love women, neither their home communities nor the larger culture provided words or positive images of women doing what they themselves wanted to do.

While many of them did find the category "lesbian," as will be discussed in chapter 6, the lesbians they found had been constructed by sexologists and psychoanalysts—pathetic, abnormal, and mannish, quasiwomen at best. They had enough sense to reject these models, as best they could, until they found a more positive option. Consequently their same-sex desires generally remained unnamed and their life plans were unarticulated.

In general, the women in this group do not appear to have found their careers as fulfilling or as central to their lives as the turn-of-the-century women did. This is not surprising. In part this reflects changes in the work place, with more modern fields' developing rigid sex and race hierarchies and the traditional professions' reinforcing their gateways. It may also have involved the culture's new emphasis on recreation and leisure activities. Furthermore, these women were restless within their positions, frustrated with the traditionally female fields they first entered. Coming to maturity before the feminist movement, their first career decisions were made from a narrow range of options. They have had to be creative and ambitious not only in their search for satisfying and remunerative work, but also in their efforts to balance earning a living with making a life.

But earning a living did come first, as Audrey's story illustrates. In a culture that clearly restricted women's work options, these women appeared to have shared a knowledge that their abilities to be self-supporting would be even more seriously jeopardized if they claimed a lesbian identity. The work of lesbian historians finds clear class divisions among the lesbian communities of the postwar period. In Buffalo, the working-class lesbians who publicly proclaimed their sexuality and fought for lesbian bar space—the street dykes—had a hard time finding and keeping jobs. Their middle-class counterparts may have occasioned some of the safer bars, but they were not going to take any risks that might endanger their positions in education, clerical, or medical fields (Kennedy and Davis 1993).

Like Kennedy and Davis's cautious lesbians, this group put self-support and economic issues first, perhaps only because they were forced to do so in their quest for another type of female identity. They had found ways to get an education and separate from their families. They had extended their areas of competence.

But these women also were cautious in their career choices. It is possible that they knew as gender nonconformists and sexual "outlaws" that they needed all the camouflage and security they could get. They may have hesitated to be pioneers or enter nontraditional fields where they would have stood out and had their lives more closely scrutinized. Because these women did not consciously and permanently claim lesbian identities early in their lives, it is not certain if their sexual identities influenced their education and career choices.

Questions of sexuality and gender cannot be separated from economics. The lives and choices of both the turn-of-the-century women and the postwar lesbians demonstrate also how, for women, the gender and sexuality systems functioned differently than they did for men, straight or gay. While most men were expected and primed to earn their own living, neither generation of women was. The gender system each generation faced, both of which marginalized self-supporting women, were experienced as a separate and significant layer of struggle within a sex- and race-segregated labor force, a layer that continues to be problematic for most women regardless of their sexuality. And sexuality functioned as an additional constraint, though one whose parameters we are still struggling to define.

FIVE

"Such Beautiful Lives Together"

Community and Companions among Progressive Era Women

Mary Elisabeth Dreier and Frances Kellor met in 1904 when Kellor became general director of the Inter-Municipal Committee on Household Research and Dreier headed its legislative group. By Christmas of that year the notes between them were affectionate and loving. In August 1905, Dreier wrote, "But you know I do love you and how beautiful and pure and true you are, I shall be glad to see my darling. Surely next week." That year Kellor and Dreier began to live together. Twenty years later, in 1925, the shyer and publicly reserved Kellor writes, "We have had such beautiful lives together and seem to have grown closer—if that is possible . . . I know I have never loved you more tenderly." When Kellor died in 1952, among the sympathy notes to Mary Elisabeth was one from Frieda Miller and Pauline Newman. Yet, in 1960, when Dreier wrote of her long relationship with Kellor, she stated simply, "Meanwhile, Miss Kellor and I had become close friends and she moved into my home with the consent of the other members of the family and became one of our family" (Dreier Papers SL).

Although Progressive Era women such as Dreier and Kellor rejected the traditional female "script" of marriage and motherhood, they did not become or see themselves as rugged individualists, setting out to conquer frontiers on their own. Nor were they "unloved, uncompanioned, uncared for, homeless, childless, with her work in the world for sole consolation," as feminist theorist Charlotte Perkins Gilman, in 1906, characterized the unmarried woman.[1] Through women-centered institutions and organizations, these single women formed female communities that provided unity and continuity between their public lives of waged work and politics, and their private lives of friends and companions. These communities not only provided power bases for political work, they were also sites where women were mentored and promoted into social welfare and other reform-related employment and where they found the lifelong friends and companions who constituted their emotional support systems and served as surrogate families.[2] Through them, this era's autonomous women became more than individuals resisting gender norms and heterosexual pressures; it was the collective nature of their resistance which gave this generation's challenge its substance.

Communities

This group of women built their public and private lives with women they met through education, politics, or work. Alice Hamilton, Mary Anderson, and Frances Kellor were linked through Hull House in Chicago (Sicherman 1984; Anderson 1951; O'Connell 1980). Through Hull House they knew and were influenced by this organization's important leaders: Jane Addams, Florence Kelley, and Julia Lathrop. Florence Kelley became Molly Dewson's boss within the National Consumer's

League after she moved to New York City (Ware 1987). While Mary Elisabeth Dreier, Frances Kellor, and Leonora O'Reilly had all been involved in settlement-house work in New York City, their most important links were through the Women's Trade Union League (Moore 1980; Shively 1971; Montgomery 1980; Newman Papers SL). Mary Anderson, Frances Kellor, Frieda Miller, and Pauline Newman were also part of this organization nationally, which was under the leadership of Margaret Dreier Robins, Mary Elisabeth's older sister, during its most active and influential years.

While Hull House and the Women's Trade Union League connected the most women, other significant formal and informal memberships extended out from these hubs. Among them were Jo Baker's memberships in Heterodoxy and the College Women's Equal Suffrage Association (Schwarz 1986; Baker 1939); Lura Beam's employment with the American Association of University Women (Beam Papers SL); Frances Kellor's involvement with the Chicago Women's Club (O'Connell 1980); Leonora O'Reilly's founding of the Working Women's Society and the NAACP (Shively 1971); and Edith Stedman's affiliation with the YWCA during World War I (Stedman Papers SL). Connie Guion held a position at the New York Infirmary for Women and Children beginning in 1925 and had numerous connections with other women physicians (Guion 1958, 1972). Edith Hamilton was part of the Bryn Mawr College network. Although Mary Ellicott Arnold left no evidence of formal homosocial connections from her early years, in retirement she worked for the Women's International League for Peace and Freedom (Arnold Papers SL).

The ties and claims these women had broken with their families of birth were replaced by their work-related communities. Where family connections may have eased young men's entries into professions, women-centered organizations served similar functions for these new women. Such organizations not only provided links among women doing similar work, they also helped locate and create employment or opportunities for advancement for many of the women in this group. These functions were limited to Euro-American women (Gordon 1994).

Mary Anderson's rise within the federal government was discussed in chapter 3. Anderson chose Frieda Miller, who had long been active in the WTUL, to succeed her as head of the Women's Bureau, just as Frances Perkins had suggested Miller follow her as head of the Division of Women in Industry of the New York State Department of Labor earlier. Molly Dewson's training, gained through the Women's Educational and Industrial Union, the National Consumer's League, and the Red Cross, prepared her to move into Democratic party politics with invaluable experience and contacts. After Franklin Delano Roosevelt's election to the presidency in 1932, she headed the Women's Division of the Democratic National Committee and became the most powerful woman in mainstream politics in her day. Recognized for her health-related work at Hull House, Alice Hamilton was appointed to the Illinois Commission on Occupational Diseases. Later, the U.S. Bureau of Labor hired her as an industrial investigator. Frances Kellor's social welfare work led to her employment as director of the New York State Commission on Immigration and the New York State Bureau of Industries and Immigration. No doubt Jo Baker's medical training at the New York Infirmary for Women and Children and the New England Hospital for Women and Children prepared her well for work with maternal and child health, and provided her with an introduction into the larger child welfare network.

Charismatic and powerful women leaders stabilized these organizations, provided role models for the next generation, and fostered a personal loyalty that cannot be divorced from these women's commitments to institutions and their principles. Mary Anderson wrote of her relationship with Margaret Dreier Robins:

There was one friend who stood out above all—Mrs. Raymond Robins. From the time I first knew her until the day of her death in 1945, she was our inspiration and support. . . . Almost everything we undertook was at her inspiration. She was always seeing far ahead what could be done. Sometimes we were aghast at what she thought we could do, but finally it was unfolded before our eyes and it was done. (Anderson 1951)

This sentiment is echoed in other women's writings. When Edith Stedman was offered a position at Radcliffe, she wrote:

However I came away with very mixed feelings; another situation for which I had no training! I didn't know what went on in the place or what my particular duties would be. I wondered if I hadn't been hedgehopping too long and at the age of forty ought not to become a stable character, but when I thought of Miss Comstock all the hesitations dropped away. The job and she too, might give me bad moments, but I knew that I wanted to work under her more than anything and that I had come home. (Stedman Papers, SL)

Jane Addams's importance to Alice Hamilton can be seen in the fact that Hamilton, a twenty-two-year resident at Hull House, established a separate home only after Addams's death. At that time, many Hull House associates had felt only Alice could replace Addams as head resident. Hamilton's subsequent refusal to take that position speaks to how closely her friendship with Addams and her dedication to Hull House were intertwined (Sicherman 1984).

In a world that generally provided only male models of power and achievement it is not surprising that these older women were important figures to individual women and to the building of women's communities. It is also not surprising that white, middle-class, native-born women felt at home in all-female communities. Because many of these women gained their educations at women's colleges or professional schools, their first steps outside their familial circles took them into a woman-centered world. Many, when they entered the paid labor force, worked among women. Even for those who did enter male-dominated fields, communities based on gender solidarity often provided their social and emotional support. They had been "inside" such communities all their adult lives, and they also found out quickly that the world outside was still misogynist, often in very rude ways.

It is no mystery, then, why these women "chose" to be part of same-sex communities. While some women, including some leaders, may have justified and defended their separatist activities on the basis of inherent gender differences, in truth, the white, professional women of this generation had few choices. Not only were women's organizations the most promising options open to them, but these were the only spaces in which they were received with both respect and affection. The atmosphere of the Heterodoxy Club allowed radical women to relax from the rigors of their struggles, have fun, and even cry at Amy Lowell's poems. The importance of women-only spaces such as the Heterodoxy Club was demonstrated by its longevity and the loyalty of its members (Schwarz 1986).

Rigid segregation along gender lines had not been a shared feature of these women's childhoods. There is no indication that they would not have gladly continued in a fair, mixed-gender environment if such opportunities had been available. The new women of this generation appear to have attributed "difference" to women's and men's culturally enforced roles. Their personal experiences of gender-segregation and sexism came from their educational experiences and work, not from their families and childhood restrictions. Gender segregation was externally imposed rather than something they had known since infancy. Consequently, the argument that they were primarily replicating in these communities the female-centered worlds of their youths is not convincing. It seems more likely that these political and socially active women made pragmatic rather than psychologically based choices, recognizing the sound strategy of strength in numbers as well as finding that only in autonomous women's organizations could they, as women, have independence and assume leadership.

The choices of working-class women were different, and their decisions to work with women's groups, more complex. The separatist or female-dominated organizations and homosocial communities of this generation of women were predominantly a middle-class phenomenon. When middle-class women did attempt to initiate cross-class organizations, they were competing with the commercial and increasingly heterosocial activities emerging in working-class urban communities (Meyerowitz 1988; Peiss 1986). The working-class women who did join cross-class women's organizations gained significant benefits through their contacts with wealthier women. Anderson, of all these women, probably gained the most from her associations with both Hull House and the Women's Trade Union League, as well as the individuals she met within these groups. Leonora O'Reilly, as another example, was able to extend her education and achieve a middle-class position as a teacher through the support of individual middle-class women and their organizations. For example, in 1907 Mary Dreier provided O'Reilly with a lifetime salary (James 1980). Pauline Newman's skills as an organizer were first recognized by the Women's Trade Union League. Through that organization she was able to leave her factory job, becoming a full-time organizer.

These benefits, to O'Reilly's and Newman's credit, did not buy their unquestioning loyalty. Class differences did threaten these institutions, and both of these working-class women were torn between gender and class loyalties. O'Reilly consistently questioned the validity of middle-class women's involvement in labor issues. Pauline Newman shared many of O'Reilly's perspectives. Her views concerning Margaret Dreier Robins were somewhat different from those expressed by Mary Anderson above. To O'Reilly she wrote, "Now you know I think an awful lot of Mrs. Robins—but the only fault I find with her is that she has made all the girls of the League think her way, and as a consequence they do not *use* their own minds and they do not act the way they feel but the way Mrs. R wants them to" (Dye 1980).

In fact, Pauline Newman and her fellow organizer, Rose Schneiderman, resigned from their work with the League to become full-time organizers with the International Ladies Garment Workers' Union (ILGWU). But, it seemed, the sexism of the male-dominated unions was worse than the classism and ethnocentrism of the WTUL. Both returned to the WTUL (Dye 1980; James 1980).[3]

In her study of the New York chapter of the WTUL, Nancy Schrom Dye argues that an acceptance of basic gender differences underlay these women's commitments to this cross-class women's organization. A more political and less ideological alternative analysis is also possible, suggesting that the working women realized that as individual women within male-dominated organizations, they had little power politically and even less support personally. Within the ILGWU and other unions, women rarely became national leaders, and their personal autonomy was limited because their immediate supervisors were men. Within the Women's Trade Union League, they were recognized and valued as leaders with the power of an organization behind them. The long struggle of women to gain respect and recognition from male-dominated unions is well documented (Foner 1979, 1980; Henry 1915).

Although class differences surfaced within women's organizations, both working-class and middle-class women needed these collective female power bases as private individuals and as public political women. Men and their institutions would not give the formal recognition of equality and were generally assessed, as individuals, as not being able to give the emotional sustenance women needed. Alice Hamilton was politically mentored at Hull House especially by Florence Kelley. Hull House was her base for her reform work, and it was through this settlement house that she found her life's work and came to meet many of the individuals who remained important political connections (Sklar 1985). She also developed close friendships with Jane Addams and Julia Lathrop. Then, in 1919, she became the first woman faculty member at Harvard University. She broke an important barrier, but it is clear that Hamilton's time at Harvard was generally miserable, just as Newman and Schneiderman's lives were as organizers for the ILGWU. Neither formally nor informally could Harvard provide what Hamilton needed for a full life (Sicherman 1984). It is significant that Alice Hamilton, who more than the others identified with a male life pattern and resisted identification with women-only organizations, suffered the isolation of the token.[4]

As the new century progressed, professional women increasingly worked among men. All of the women doctors and all of the women in city, state, or federal positions, in spite of the composition of their most immediate work circles, did not have the luxury of a single-sex employment environment. As competent as these women were in their positions, they generally neither acquired nor exercised great personal power, nor could they develop the friendships with these male bosses, co-workers, or employees that they could with women. Women's organizations and individual Republican women had to mount a major campaign to pressure President Coolidge into reappointing Mary Anderson as director of the Women's Bureau (Anderson 1951). Molly Dewson wrote her political autobiography, *An Aid to the End,* in part as a retort to Jim Farley's book on the New Deal. She long felt that he lacked appreciation of the Women's Division of the Democratic National Committee and of her personally (Dewson Papers SL; Ware 1987). Other evidence is seen in the fact that when these women retired or left the male-dominated work situations, they do not appear to have maintained many friendships with their male co-workers. In contrast, the multitude of benefits they gained from their connections with female bases of power kept them involved with such communities even when they moved on to other types of work.

An analysis of these communities clearly shows that women found both the emotional intimacies associated with women's culture and the personal and collective power and support needed for gender-based political work. It was precisely because such a diversity of their needs could be met by women as individuals, as leaders and role models, and as peers and friends, within these organizations that these homosocial worlds had such influence and elicited such loyalty during the first few decades of the twentieth century.

Nevertheless, the women's continued reliance on homosocial worlds, like their "choices" in the work world, contains many contradictions. Their decisions to base themselves in women's institutions were both a conservative adjustment to their exclusion from male-dominated power centers and a progressive choice to build alternatives to life under patriarchal power. Though they saw their political activism as advocacy for women generally, this group led lives very different from those of most women, especially in that they did not marry and most did not raise children. Their consciousness of women's issues must have differed from that of women who had to contend with patriarchal pressures daily in their private as well as their public lives.[5] That they were single women promoting reforms for women was used against them. Jo Baker made an important point, though, when she noted how, in the 1930s, the now questionable never-married women were being replaced in women's and children's welfare agencies not by married women and mothers, but by men (Fitzpatrick 1990).

At a time when the functions of the family were declining, these women, who chose to live outside the patriarchal family structure of their era, constructed communities that fulfilled many of the roles that families supplied during the nineteenth century. The emotional work of the family—women's work in the overwhelming percentage of cases—is only now beginning to be fully discussed and integrated into political and economic analyses. Such "work," which is hard to quantify and fully describe—the nurturing, support and intimacy, as well as all that goes into making and maintaining a home—were frequently shared in these women's circles. And these circles fulfilled many of the functions associated with men in the patriarchal family, as discussed above, as well as those believed to be women's domain.

Companions

Within every strong female network, in educational institutions, political groups, and social organizations of this period, were female couples who formed lifelong partnerships and who might, if they were of the current generation, call themselves lesbians. Although friends were important for all of these women, there is strong evidence that at least nine of them had women companions around whom they built their private lives. Martha May Eliot met Ethel Durham in medical school and they lived together, except for one year, until Ethel's death in 1969—fifty-plus years (Eliot Papers SL). Pauline Newman and Frieda Miller were companions from about 1917 until Frieda's death in 1973 (Newman Papers SL). The cross-class nature of the WTUL produced this unlikely coupling of Miller, a monied Midwesterner, and Newman, a working-class Lithuanian-Jewish immigrant. From 1905 until 1952, Mary Elisabeth Dreier shared her home with Frances Kellor (Dreier Papers SL). Molly Dewson's original introduction to social reform work came from her college professors at Wellesley and, through this work, she met Polly Porter (Ware 1987; Dewson Papers SL). This couple lived together from 1913 until Dewson's death in 1962. Mary Arnold made her commitment to Mabel Reed at the age of sixteen (Arnold Papers SL). Edith Hamilton's most documented relationship was with Doris Reid, who had been one of her students at the Bryn Mawr School of Baltimore (Reid 1967; Sicherman 1984). Jo Baker had several relationships, the longest with Dr. Florence Laighton (Schwarz 1986).

These relationships have yet to be fully explored even by feminist historians. Rather than analyze their significance and impact on women's work and politics, historians continue to either treat them as an embarrassment, worth a brief mention at most, or as a marginal factor, interesting to lesbian history but not a major influence in women's history. Susan Ware (1987), in *Partner and I,* initiated a discussion of these relationships in her study of Molly Dewson and Polly Porter, but the full challenge these women's lives posed is still underexplored.[6]

Their relationships did influence these women's public lives. Unlike marriages, even the alleged companionate marriages of like-minded activists of their era, these relationships allowed women to enjoy the benefits of companionship and intimacy without a conflicted separation from their female communities of support.[7] Their loyalties were not divided between women and an individual man.

Although the phrase "Boston Marriage," a nineteenth-century term for the relationship of two unmarried women, suggests that these partnerships were substitutes for or somehow parallel to traditional matrimony, these women's own writings suggest that among these female couples visions of their relationships placed them at a critical tension with heterosexual marriages. This is not to deny the characteristics these relationships shared with marriages, and marriage was the only model of societally validated relationships available for comparisons. But the differences are also important. These relationships need to be analyzed not as deficient or quasimarriages, but unique and creative couplings.

In attempting an analysis or even a description of these women's lifelong relationships, it is important to find the reasons they came together. If there is one cause, a common thread, among this diverse group it is the waged and political work which was shared between the two. This is unlike either the traditional or companionate marriage ideal. This conclusion is based more on these women's actions than their words, since scant are their reflections on their decisions. For example, the first evidence of Jo Baker's partnership comes when she decides to set up residence and practice with another woman doctor. This occurred after she had completed her medical schooling and postgraduate internships and residencies and was ready to settle down (Baumgartner 1971). The other medical women, Martha May Eliot and Ethel Durham, roomed together during medical school. They reluctantly separated for a short time during their internships, but came together when they had completed their training and had some control over the location of their work (Eliot Papers SL). A similar pattern is evident for the other women. Most met in the course of their work and, through this shared concern, came to share their lives.

The partnered women of this generation generally built their relationships only when they had already declared their independence from their families and each member of the dyad was already financially and socially independent. Their partnerships most often complemented and aided their professional activities, in contrast to the energy-draining conflicts recorded when their married counterparts tried to combine marriage and career (Payne 1988; Antler 1987). These single women were mature individuals when they chose their companions, at ages significantly later than the average marriage age of women for this period. While Mary Ellicott Arnold tells us that she made her commitment to Mabel Reed while they were both teenagers, the rest of this group postponed their decisions until they were at least in their late twenties (Arnold Papers SL).

Many of these women would never have met each other if they had not pursued educational and employment opportunities that took them away from their families and hometowns and exposed them to a broader spectrum of people. They also had that period on their own to grow as individuals, build their own networks of friends, and prove to themselves that they could function competently and autonomously in the world.

In most cases, one member of a couple became much more active or prominent. Molly Dewson was by far more public and active than Polly Porter, as was Edith Hamilton compared to Doris Reid. Mary Arnold appeared to have been the initiator and vocal member of that couple, as Martha Eliot was in hers. Importantly neither greater age nor greater economic resources appears to have determined which of a couple would lead a more public life. There is no evidence of one sacrificing herself and her independent life, work, interests, or friends to support the other either economically or emotionally. As close as these women were, as much as they shared friends and work, one's life did not subsume the other's, nor did they become two completely overlapping spheres. In many ways, the compromises they worked out most closely resemble the ideal of the contemporary dual career couples if any model, and, if for this reason alone, are worthy of analysis.[8]

Each couple evolved its own solution to the inevitable difficulties of two careers. Doris Reid's career as a stockbroker developed only after Edith Hamilton had retired from work that took her outside their home.[9] Consequently, when they became guardians of Reid's nieces and nephews, it was Edith who ran the household. Polly Porter was also more the homebody than Molly Dewson. Dewson took on her greatest work and responsibilities long after Porter had retired from regular employment

(Ware 1987). While Newman remained in New York City and seems to have assumed more of the familial responsibilities than Miller, Pauline continued to work well into her seventies (Newman Papers SL). Overall, their arrangements appear to have been flexible and developed to meet their particular needs. These arrangements did not mimic either the marital ideals or realities of this period. Perhaps because these couples did not receive public recognition, they had greater freedom from scrutiny and judgments to explore alternatives to marital norms.

Also unique were the agreements these women worked out vis-à-vis joint finances and shared homes. Arnold wrote of her relationship with Reid, that, from age sixteen, "We have lived together ever since and continued, without a ripple, to hold all things in common" (Arnold Papers SL). Susan Ware, Molly Dewson's biographer, argues that Polly Porter's inheritance provided the means by which these women could build a comfortable and secure life together (Ware 1987). Although Dreier does not state that she supported Kellor, she does remark that Kellor worked all her life without a salary. Given the poverty of Kellor's childhood, it does not seem logical that Kellor had an independent source of income. Within these couples the sharing of monies appears to have been an agreeable arrangement.

While Jo Baker, Martha Eliot, and Edith Hamilton all shared homes with their partners, it is not clear if they shared money. Although Pauline Newman and Frieda Miller were together for fifty-plus years and raised a daughter together, they did not share money. The great difference in their class backgrounds may account for their being the only couple who left evidence of conflicts over finances. How money issues contributed to a late crisis for this couple is discussed below. Pauline also resented Frieda's assumption that Pauline would take care of various family responsibilities and traditional wifely duties, such as remembering birthdays and helping with their grandchildren (Newman Papers SL; Miller Papers SL).

All of these factors—when they met, where they lived together, money concerns and decisions about moving and though they are extremely important for understanding what these relationships looked like, still do not tell us how these women saw their partnerships. These women's public and private writings are remarkably public-sphere focused.[10] The nature of their attractions is difficult to categorize. They left few passionate words from the early years of their involvements. Although the women do not actually say that their relationships were sexual, we cannot assume that all of them were either asexual or sexually naive.

Letters exchanged between couples show them to be affectionate and playful with each other. For example, Mary Elisabeth Dreier wrote to Frances Kellor:

> Sweetheart, It is one am [1:00 A.M.] and I just came in from our meeting, very tired. Your beautiful dear note was such a sweet surprise. Somehow dear, there is such a sweet consciousness of the beauty of our love. I want you to feel so strongly its beauty and strength and my soul gives out to you in a way the body can not limit." (Dreier Papers SL)

They did profess their love, but the meanings of these expressions do not easily translate from their nineteenth century understandings of intimacy and sexuality to the homophobic, heterosexist world of today. Even the closest reading between the lines and the piecing together of their lives still make it very difficult to get a strong sense of how these women and their partners saw their lives and the challenges they faced in starting and maintaining their relationships.

Unfortunately, toward the later years of their lives, when the labeling of same-sex relationships as abnormal became more widely accepted, some of the women were faced with pain and confusion about the choices that had given them full emotional lives. While many of the single women of this generation were forced to reconsider the decisions they made, those women who had been intimately involved with other women had their respectability and mental health most deeply questioned.

While we do not know the attitudes of the specific women in this study, we can again use Katherine Bement Davis's sample of unmarried women for comparison. In *Factors in the Sex Life of Twenty-Two Hundred Women,* Davis found that 50 percent of these women had experienced "intense emotional relationships with other women," including 234 women who had had sexual activities with other women. Approximately 47 percent responded that they felt "shame and disgust" for homosexual relations, while 27 percent felt "approval" for these relationships, or that homosexual relationships were "natural" and/or "legitimate" (Davis 1929).

These actions and attitudes provide critical background for an analysis of how these women responded to the changing sexual and gender systems of the early twentieth-century United States. This group left evidence, both public and personal, that they felt under siege, judged and labeled both as single women and as women who loved women. For several, the growing questions about their choices hit them at vulnerable times in their lives, at the end of their work lives, with their health failing, and when they were losing their friends and lovers to illness and death.

Edith Hamilton's relationship with Doris Reid, for example, was discussed both by Reid in her published memoir of Edith and by Barbara Sicherman in her book on Edith's sister, Alice. The contrast between the two stories is striking. Doris Reid's account of how she and Edith Hamilton came to live together betrays neither great emotional involvement nor strong familial opposition. After presenting Edith as a friend of the family, with whom she and her parents bought a house in Maine, she states, "My mother took a very dim view of my living alone in New York, and suggested that Edith spend the winter with me" (Reid, 1967). Edith Hamilton was in her fifties at this time,

Doris in her thirties. She then says nothing about why they continued to live together, except that Edith did not want to live in Baltimore anymore and that she disliked the summer weather in Connecticut where her sisters had bought a summer home.

Several pages later is Reid's first reference to "our children." A bit later she writes,

> Owing to certain family developments, the Reid children came to live permanently with Edith and me in New York. She did not think of herself as "deciding" to take them on. In the circumstances it seemed best for them to leave Baltimore and come to us. Here they were. In her mind that was all there was to it. (Reid 1967)

The Reid children included Dorian, two younger sisters, Betsy and Mary, and a younger brother. Reid also fails to discuss the fact that Edith officially adopted only Dorian. Nevertheless, Reid goes on to describe how Edith combined the new family and her new work, both of which entered her life comparatively late. She paints a picture of Edith, sitting in her chair, in their New York apartment, writing about ancient Greece, able to concentrate though the children were around because she would turn off her hearing aid. Later Reid describes their home, busy with Dorian's college friends. These young people found Dorian's "parents" to be unusually open and accepting of their nonconformist political views and personal appearances.

Reid's final contribution to this puzzle is in an ambiguous statement about one of Edith's translations. Reid explains why Edith translated a Greek word in First Corinthians as "love" rather than "charity." "These two quotes throw a light on Edith herself. They explain, at least in part, the devotion she gave and inspired. She did not 'refuse the great initiation.' To her, St. Paul was clearly writing about 'love on earth' " (Reid 1967).

What Reid means by "the great initiation" and its connection with "love on earth" remains an open question. However, it is tempting to read this inclusion as Doris Reid's response to the theories Jo Baker assailed and even the attitudes of feminists such as Charlotte Perkins Gilman. It may also have been directed closer to home—at Alice Hamilton and her judgments about Edith and her relationship with Doris.

Barbara Sicherman, in her collection of Alice Hamilton's letters, found a different view of Edith and Doris, one that sheds light on the complex ways the shifting views were dividing independent women at this time. Sicherman includes a letter written by Alice to the third Hamilton sister, Margaret. Margaret, also an unmarried woman, was a teacher at the Bryn Mawr School in Baltimore, a position clearly linked to Edith's position as headmistress there. In this letter Alice discussed what she saw as the connection between Edith's relationship with Doris and Edith's resignation from the Bryn Mawr School. Alice felt that Doris had pressured Edith into an awkward and contentious resignation without considering the impact of such a battle on Margaret's situation.

> Of course I will never say such a thing to anybody but you but I can't help seeing that because of this affair with Doris Edith first destroyed your home and now may destroy your work. It all comes back to the Doris affair in the end. Doris and she have talked it over and over. Doris is young and her judgment poor, she wants Edith back in England where she was better and where she was free from worries . . . and all the serious business side of which a man would think first, and which you and I would consider most important, all that is lost in a sea of personal relations. . . . Oh I do so wish Edith's temperament were a little stiller, a little less tempestuous and extreme. My heart sinks when I look ahead for her. (Sicherman 1984)

Alice's views of herself and Edith are rather clear. Alice chose between career and marriage, as did Edith, at least on a formal legal level, but what this choice meant for Alice is different from what it meant for Edith. From this letter, her other writings, and what we know of her life, Alice had many friends but no intimate, passionate relationships that might have involved sexual activities or which could be seen as an equivalent of marriage. Her home was at Hull House for much of her adult life and, after that, with her sister Margaret. In her own words here, she dichotomizes male and female approaches to business and relationships. She similarly compartmentalized women's choices earlier when discussing her future sister-in-law's intention of studying medicine. All emotional involvements, intimate partnerships, children, and sexuality appear to be what Alice Hamilton believed she, and other career women, had to sacrifice. She judges Edith harshly for not doing the same, and also, perhaps, for making Doris a more important person in her life than her sister Margaret.

That her judgment of Edith's life was also influenced by the sexologists' "morbidifications of same-sex love," to use Faderman's phrase, is suggested in the ongoing struggle between Alice and Edith. Sicherman comments that Edith resented what she saw as a lack of support from her sisters, and relationships among them were strained for several years. In February 1923 Alice wrote to Margaret that Edith had stated, "that until I can assure her [Edith] that I do not and never did consider her [Edith] in any way abnormal mentally, there can be no coming together again, and as she can not see how that can happen she thinks we never can." Sicherman explores this issue no further except to state that by 1925 the sisters "were again on good terms," though never again as intimate as before.

Was Alice's view that same-sex relationships were "sick" behind this entire conflict? It remains unclear. Alice's concerns for Edith's mental health may have been related to their family's mental health history. Not only had their father, Montgomery Hamilton, become depressed and reclusive late in life, but the fourth Hamilton sister, Norah, had suffered mental breakdowns throughout her adult years. Nevertheless, these two accounts strongly suggest that the relationship between Doris and Edith was seen as problematic by Alice and Margaret Hamilton, if not by Edith herself.

As a result of a very different type of crisis, Pauline Newman left an equally challenging picture of the last years of her relationship with Frieda Miller. Early in the 1950s Newman and Miller bought a summer/retirement home together in Coffeetown, Pennsylvania. When this house was damaged in 1955 by Hurricane Diane, Pauline had to deal with the damage since Frieda was out of the country at the time, still working for a United Nations agency. Pauline's letters before this time were already fussing over the amount of time Frieda was away and how lonely she was. Yet for a while things were calm. In December of that year, Pauline wrote to Frieda, "Always remember that in spirit I am walking beside you" (Miller Papers SL).

By 1958 something more drastic had happened, though it is never clear what the exact problem was. Pauline wrote in her datebook on April 27, 1958, "At E's [Frieda's daughter, Elisabeth] talked with her and David re FSM [Frieda Segelke Miller]." In December she wrote, "Skirmish w/FSM."

With the beginning of the new year another issue was introduced: it seems that Frieda was having some sort of relationship with a man. She was close to seventy at this time. By the end of March, Pauline states, "I think the 'break-up' has come." In spite of this break, Newman was in constant contact with Elisabeth and her family. And they were truly a family, for Pauline seemed more involved in the day-to-day lives of Elisabeth, her husband David, and their two sons than Frieda (Newman Papers SL).

For the next several years Pauline continued to comment in her date book on two sources of pain that appeared to have been directly related to this "break-up." The first source was the house in Coffeetown; apparently she sold her interest in it though she continued to go there. The second was the man in Frieda's life (Newman Papers SL).

Pauline's pain from this break is seen starkly in the journal she kept during a solo trip to Europe. She wrote of her loneliness. "There are very few women traveling alone—as far as I have observed there are always two—old they may look and be—but they are together still—more than I can say for myself." Sadly, there is no evidence left by either of these two women to indicate if their split was resolved before Frieda had her stroke in 1969. Pauline and Elisabeth took care of her from that time on until her death. The sympathy notes sent to Pauline at that time acknowledged their relationship and compared it to a marriage (Newman Papers SL).

Whatever was behind this crisis, there is enough to suggest that questions of sexuality, "normalcy," and life-choices were troubling individuals and dividing never-married women.[11] Additional evidence of the struggle over the redefinition of women's sexuality is seen in two major studies that focused on sexuality and the single woman: Davis' 1929 study and the 1934 volume co-authored by Lura Beam, *The Single Woman: A Medical Study in Sex Education*. Both books were sponsored by mainstream sources: Davis's through the Bureau of Social Hygiene with Rockefeller money and Beam's from the Committee on Maternal Health. The effect of both books was to expose a far greater diversity of sexual activities among women than was commonly accepted. Both also sought to open up sex education.

Though she took as "objective" and scientific a tone possible, Davis's findings, especially on masturbation and homosexuality, were controversial and an embarrassment to the Bureau of Social Hygiene. They decided that her "female" interests were not those of the bureau, and she was let go at the age of sixty-eight. This dismissal was personally and professionally devastating to her (Fitzpatrick 1990). She was effectively silenced as a proponent of an alternative definition of women's sexuality.

This series of events may have been why Beam's volume was co-authored by a male medical doctor. She did note that even though *The Single Woman* was published by a medical publisher and advertised only in medical journals, the writers were concerned that John Sumner, of the Society for the Prevention of Vice, might raise objections to the explicitness of this book. Beam explained why she declined to take on another such project:

> As I neared the end of these studies, someone asked me if I would be willing to work on a new study of homosexuality. No, because sex has peculiar laws of development. I have seen "sexologists" in which it appeared to be going backwards. Sex has so much mystery that workers think they can never find anything else so near the secret of life. Homosexuals are, if possible, even queerer than heterosexuals. . . . It was in the reading background of books on sexuality that I discovered that the reader should have prior knowledge of the writer's occupation. Gynecologists and urologists are never factual in the same way. (Beam Papers SL)

Beam makes it clear that further studies involved going into treacherous territory.

Both of these volumes are long out of print. These works suggest that there was an active struggle over the emerging definitions of women's sexuality, especially woman-to-woman intimacy. At least some women social scientists and their allies resisted the acceptance of a male-defined female sexuality and the collapsing of gender and sexuality definitions, including the condemnation of a "mythic mannish lesbian." These researchers and writers used the weapons they knew best—social science research—but their dry, quantitative approach did not capture the public imagination.[12] Furthermore, men still held the purse strings within private foundations and educational institutions, and this reality, along with other societal forces, stunted the impact of these progressive works.

The stories of these women's lives, especially the aspects that contained evidence of women-centered alternative families and their full emotional and sexual lives, have been lost to several generations of historians, feminists, and lesbians. Also missing are the discussions of the private and public ways this generation of women resisted the demonizing of singleness and same-sex love.

Taken as a whole, these partnerships were creative, egalitarian partnerships. They were recognized as being of equal importance and commitment as marriage by the couples' close friends. While there is no evidence that these women ever identified as lesbians or were labeled as such by their associates or by the larger public, neither is there proof that they were not stigmatized on this basis. Although sexual mores had begun changing in the 1910s and knowledge of homosexuals and lesbians had become commonplace by the 1930s, these women may have been protected from condemnation on the basis of their professional status and their discreet behavior (McGovern 1968; Katz 1983).[13]

But overt public acceptance or rejection is only one level at which the sexual system functions. The other level, and the one that seems to have gained power in this century, is the packaging of sexual and gender norms as homogenized standards of individual mental/psychic health. Evidence suggests that these women saw this change coming and viewed it critically. For example, Edith Abbott, another never-married woman in this network, negatively evaluated Wellesley College's School of Social Work in part because of its emphasis on psychiatry and treating the individual. She wanted social work to continue to do "scientific" research from which to develop new social policy (Fitzpatrick 1990). These women's personal choices were similarly reevaluated. No longer were they resisting a system based on the collective legal and economic oppression of women. They had become individual "freaks."

The single and woman-partnered leaders of this generation could not control how women's sexuality became a sociopolitical issue. When those who were brave among them tried, they did not have the unified force of women's organizations behind them. This splintering allowed a harsh reaction against those women, such as Katherine Bemet Davis and others, who did speak out about sexual realities.[14] Silenced, this generation could not contribute to the development of a woman-defined public discourse on sexuality that might have drawn from analyses of their public and private lives and choices.

The "morbidification" of these same-sex relationships links changes in the sexual system with changes in the economic system and with women's position within each. As Joanne Meyerowitz (1988) argues, single working women were objects of societal pity and worthy of concern and charity as long as they were viewed as impoverished, marginal victims, but once women were recognized as financially able to choose to live without men, the ideology changed. The acknowledgment of women's sexuality produced a parallel shift from a sympathetic view of single women as sexually vulnerable or sexually neutral to a negative evaluation of them as sexually active and dangerous.

The turn-of-the-century independent women used their social and financial independence to reject the limitations of the patriarchal private sphere and marriage, and to build alternative communities and families for themselves. In their optimism they did not realize how their collective power and the examples of their lives would be undermined by the emergence of new gender and sexuality systems. First, during the prosperity of the 1920s, the younger generation accepted a new emphasis on consumption, leisure, and pleasure. The homosocial world of the female reformers was portrayed as antiquated and prudish to a generation of women raised with new opportunities for heterosocial leisure and mixed-sex education and employment. Young women were encouraged to be less concerned about having economic, legal, and political equality with men than they were in having equality in manners and morals. The flapper played while she was single, and when she did marry, she presumably continued to be more her husband's buddy than a submissive wife and dutiful mother. This mythic new heterosexuality came to be perceived as truly reformed sexuality and gender orders. Consequently when the Depression hit, analyses of the resultant family crises were devoid of any gender consideration. The gold diggers and working women of the previous decade were scapegoated. Discrimination against women was justified as being good for the country.

The vision of emancipation shared by turn-of-the-century women was undermined by these material and ideological developments. The new gender and sexuality norms that emerged split their generation, while a reliance on separatism and homosocial communities had no "modern" appeal to young people schooled in heterosexuality. These women did construct alternative work and political opportunities, from which developed surrogate families and marriages that were women centered; but these new models did not survive for future generations.

"We're Not the Only Ones"

Lesbian Identities and Communities after World War II

Jo Martinez had been involved in a relationship with Alice Henry for more than four years when she discovered a larger lesbian community.

> When I met all these lesbian women it finally occurred to me that there was a community like this. Not just me and her. In Mt. Gold, I'm sure there were other gay women, but even when they came over, to be with Alice, to visit or whatever, they were so hidden, that I never saw it. . . . But when I found gay bars, I loved them. . . . And it was, "This isn't so bad. We're not the only ones."

If finding meaningful work and achieving financial independence was difficult for the women of this group, their paths to a positive lesbian identity were treacherous. Many of these women knew early of their attractions to women, and they describe their first sexual relationships with women as thrilling. However, the struggle to give meaning to these experiences was

133

complicated by their ignorance of gay life and the various dangers lesbian oppression presented.

While World War II had fostered a brief improvement in the lives of lesbians and single women, public and psychiatric attitudes regarding these two groups hardened, if anything, in the 1950s. In research from the 1940s, Kinsey and associates reported that one in four women reported sexual attractions to another woman; between 3 percent and 12 percent of the single women were lesbians; and those lesbians with the most extensive same-sex experience reported high levels of comfort with their sexual orientation. However, in 1943, only 9 percent of the young women polled believed that a single person could be happy and they viewed nonmarriage among women as a "quasiperversion." Among the fifty never-married women interviewed between 1982 and 1984 by Barbara Levy Simon (1987), all of whom had come to maturity by World War II, a full 82 percent (41) refused to discuss issues of sexuality. Thirty-five of these women had primary relationships with another single woman. Simon concluded that "Freudianism has cast lasting shadows over the social respectability of single women carving out lives together," and that their silences "may also indicate their *resistance* to collaborating with investigatory processes that Michel Foucault has characterized as part of the 'policing of sex,' a process of 'regulating sex through useful and public discourse.' " These women knew that among the general public, close relationships among women continued to be suspect (May 1988).

The end of World War II saw a backlash against whatever freedoms the war had allowed lesbians and gay men. In the 1950s all homosexuals were labeled as security risks in the military and government service. An April 1953 executive order barred gay man and lesbians from federal jobs. Witch hunts and purges became the reality for lesbians and gay men in the military from the 1950s through the 1960s. For every individual actually fired or given a dishonorable discharge, an equal number resigned rather than face the consequences of a public inquiry. The loss of these government jobs may have been particularly hard on lesbians since the federal government had provided one of the few employment areas in which women received decent pay, job security, and chances for advancement, a tempting situation for many self-supporting lesbians. The Cold War era was indeed a very chilly one for lesbians in the United States (D'Emilio 1989; Berube 1990; Penn 1994).

Lesbian Identities

Not surprisingly, as young women the lesbians in this study faced a major challenge in their search for a sexual identity. Several of these women, when they first suspected they were gay, followed the classic pattern of going to the library and looking up what was written on homosexuality. What they found was what the male sexologists and their followers had left—uniformly negative images of twisted and pathetic lives. Finding such "deviant" images of lesbians caused several of these women to reject the only definition of their sexuality available to them. They could not claim such identities for themselves or find common ground with such creatures. Not surprisingly, delayed "coming out," defined as acknowledging themselves as homosexual, was often a consequence of sexual literacy. Yet such knowledge was not sufficient to destroy their desires, keep them from sexual involvements with women, or push them into an acceptance of heterosexuality.

Libraries and the tomes of sexologists were not the only sources of "danger." Fear of lesbians pervaded the culture. Young women of this generation had internalized the warnings against loving women, with and without knowing the lesbian label, although several of the women did not know *how* they knew they had to hide such attractions. While a few of the to-be-lesbians could see the problems clearly, for others multiple levels of denial and silence were functioning.

Audrey was in college in the late fifties when a classmate, not suspecting that Audrey was lesbian, brought news back from San Francisco about the gay community there. Several years later, in 1961, Audrey went to San Francisco to visit a friend whose partner was running "The Front," a lesbian bar. Audrey found women at the bar "wild, tough, very butch-fem." Although she knew by then she was "probably a lesbian" and was intrigued by the lesbian subculture she saw, "I knew there was no way I could come out. I was just out of graduate school. I was a professional social worker. I was making good money. There was no way I could jeopardize my career or my chance for a livelihood." Nevertheless, within two years, Audrey was involved in a closeted lesbian relationship, a relationship that lasted twenty-one years, the adoptions of three children, and several career changes. She came out in a much more public way during the 1970s and has been active within the lesbian-feminist community.

Iris, an Anglo raised in the deep South, had a never-married aunt who owned a movie theater that featured "arts" films. Too young to remember the names of the films, she recalled,

> Occasionally they would get in these gay flicks, and I honestly never really went and watched them because I tried watching a couple of them and they were really bad. But I don't know the name of the movie . . . all these gay women came, and it was butch-fem, butch-fem, butch-fem! I thought what's going on here? I was like really excited and really scared and like . . . I don't know what to do . . . and I think that was the point that I knew that I was probably a lesbian, but I really didn't know a lot of good things about it. I just knew the butch-fem stuff and some of the stuff I read.

For both Paula and Gloria, the professors in their physical education (P.E.) classes unwittingly introduced them to the idea of lesbianism. Paula recalled,

I had never even heard the word until I think I was in a sopho-
more class in dance. It was the funniest thing, you know, all
these stupid dance classes we had. It was nothing but women
P.E. majors and we had to dance together. I never heard the
word lesbian until Dr. Small mentioned it. I had never even heard
the word; I didn't even know what it was. And didn't, even when
she said it . . . [but] I didn't want to appear that I didn't know
things. You have to be cool.

All of the women who were in P.E. in college talked about
the rampant homophobia they found in their departments, each
of which housed several closeted and/or suspected lesbian professors. Though these women went to schools in different re-
gions of the country, all received warnings about "special
friendships," and talked about the particular rules that P.E.
majors had. They remember still how irked they were at having
to wear skirts even when the dress codes were relaxed for
women generally, allowing others to wear slacks on campus.
Robin feels she is still trying "to unhitch all that negative crap
. . . I still have flashbacks. It made me paranoid . . . I wish I were
born now. I assume it's a little bit easier now. I'm not saying
'poor me, poor me.' Each generation's getting a little better.
Maybe I'm jealous. I wish I could have done what they do
[today]."

But these anti-lesbian rules and lectures gave name and meaning to what had been unstated and ambiguous in these young
women's lives. By making their desires concrete, such prohibi-
tions became subverting. Women who never knew other lesbians found they were not alone. Finding communities and a
shared history became possible.[1]

But such additional steps were not easy or automatic. Amy
actively resisted recognizing the lesbianism of some of her
friends and role models.

There was some consciousness on my part, that I always tried to
keep blinders up in front of [the lesbian issue]. You know, it's
like I could think it if I let myself, but it wasn't . . . there wasn't

that much pressure early in college. There was some later on and I at one point did try to talk to the woman who was . . . the Dean of Women . . . I tried to talk to her, but it was a taboo subject with her, because of her own situation I know at this time. So it's like she wouldn't help at all, and I needed somebody to draw me out and she wouldn't. So I just stuffed it—again.

"Stuffing it" was very much part of the culture of the 1950s; if "it" didn't fit in the perfect family portrait, it didn't exist. But this denial, for the women in this group, appears to have served another purpose. The complications claiming a taboo sexuality would bring into their lives were not what they wanted at this point. While Audrey was conscious that she had to stabilize her economic autonomy first, Amy Adams followed the same process, yet without the words and consciousness Audrey had. The result of this difference was that Audrey could feel in control, making informed choices, while Amy remained confused.

These women's desires, however, did not need names to be real. Perhaps these young women already knew to trust their bodies more than they trusted this culture's counsel. Without knowing why or what their feelings meant, they acted on their attractions. The average age at which these women had their first lesbian relationships or affairs was twenty-one, with the range being from sixteen to twenty-nine.

When they did become sexually active with women, the dangers they had heard about became real and the consequences came in many forms. For Bobbi Denova the pressure was self-generated. She broke off her first relationship because she feared she could be jeopardizing her education and her career.

And then all of the sudden it dawned on me what it was . . . that this wasn't right. I severed the relationship. Not that I said to myself in so many words what wasn't right. But I thought I can't see her anymore because all the nuns are around and all my classmates are around. I really developed a relationship with my classmates. And I knew this wouldn't go somehow. Inside I knew more than thinking it out with my thoughts. So I severed that.

Bobbi's statement that "inside I knew more" captures the essence of this other "problem which has no name." How did these women receive the message that same-sex relationships were not for public notice? And additional questions involve the locus of disapproval. To what extent did these women believe what they were doing was "wrong," according to their own moral codes? Or did they just know on some level that this culture did not accept such relationships?

Postsecondary education, especially when residential, stands out as a mechanism for social control against both homosocial and homosexual bonding among women. Deans of women and female residence directors, along with faculty members, felt justified in intruding into women students' intimate lives to regulate their affectional and sexual behavior.

Carrie Stern was prepared when she was called into the dean's office and confronted about her affair. As a result, she was able to bluff her way out without any penalty. Paula Mitchell was not so fortunate. She was suspended from college, ostensibly for cheating, but she is convinced she was targeted because of her sexuality. Although these women and others in this group survived and completed their educations, these scares undoubtedly had an influence on their later degrees of "outness" and closetedness.

One of Anne McConnell's professors introduced her and her lover to the local lesbian subculture of bars and parties. This professor was fired shortly afterward when, according to Anne, one of the priests at this small southern Catholic women's college breached the confidentiality of confession, using information from one woman's confession against this professor. Later, after another anti-lesbian purge during Anne's senior year, Anne made a decision:

> I had figured out . . . that being a lesbian was not a piece of cake. One of the women in the group [she was part of] found Christ and blew the whistle. Nine women lost their jobs and it really

put the fear of god in me. . . . Being a lesbian is not an easy
choice . . . so graduate school was my year to really try the
straight life.

At the end of that year, Anne fell in love with a woman who
became her partner for ten years. "We were married." She
became part of a closeted social circle where her friends seldom
spoke of being lesbians. Anne claimed a lesbian identity but
never ventured to the bars. This still was not enough to protect
her from homophobia. Several years later she lost her job in
higher education because of her sexuality.

Several of these stories highlight the treachery involved in
closeted lives. These women have themselves debated how issues
of solidarity and support were problematic when no one named
their shared situation. Robin Edwards's supervisor, who later
became her friend, came down very severely on her when she
was a student teacher. According to this supervisor, Robin was
forbidden to see a certain student on campus or she would fail
her teaching semester. Robin didn't test the threat, but to this
day she wonders if this woman was trying to teach her how to
survive in the school system or if this teacher's self-hate, as a
closeted lesbian, caused her to be especially hard on suspected
dykes. Were these closeted women also resisting a label they
knew to be wrong and unfair, or had they accepted that they
were "perverts?"

What was clear was that closeted lesbians of this era could
not fight back against unfair, sexuality-based discrimination
without opening not only their own closets but the closets of
coworkers and friends. The military utilized this system during
this era, when the comparatively flexible rules of World War II
became rigidified in the McCarthy/Cold War era (Berube 1990).
Yolanda Peña described a system where, if an individual was
caught in any indiscreet act or situation, the military authority
would promise leniency if s/he cooperated and named all the
other "homosexuals" s/he knew. Yolanda survived several of
these witch hunts and argues that it was a crap shoot for those

caught, with one never knowing if one would be treated with leniency even if you named names, and never knowing what information they really had against you to start with.

Gloria Whelan had internalized all the anti-lesbian lectures and rules that appear to have been standard for women entering physical education classes during this time. In spite of these warnings, she found herself attracted to an upperclasswoman.

> We had so much fun that sophomore year. But there was a lot of heartache too because I loved her so much and I didn't get enough in return. But I didn't know that . . . I knew I had these strong feelings for this woman, but I didn't know I was gay at that point because I had never acted on it, being gay. I had never come to grips with it.

Several years later, peer pressure led her to break off her first real lesbian relationship, and she, like Anne, tried dating men. There were dangers there, too, for the woman who wanted a career. After a pregnancy scare, she went back to graduate school and gave up on heterosexual relationships. Yet her lesbian desire was still problematic. Gloria became very depressed after her next serious relationship ended, one which was complicated by professional ties. She connects this crisis more with an overall lack of self-confidence than with struggles about her sexual identity specifically. She was lucky enough to find an enlightened psychiatrist who helped on both issues. While she had accepted her gay identity by the time she finished her advanced degree, she did not become part of a community of lesbians until several years later, when she was somewhat more settled and secure in her work.

As mentioned above, Amy Adams kept her blinders on through college. She had finished her M.A. degree and was teaching when she had an affair with a woman who had been her friend since they were teenagers.

> We had gotten closer and closer and what she had, it seemed, kind of been aiming towards since we were very young, hap-

pened. Like, around Christmas time, that we became lovers. And she couldn't handle it. It's like she had been engineering this for eight or nine years . . . and within a couple of months she had broken things off. And I felt at that time very clearly that if I let myself, let myself any slack in being depressed over this, that I would never recover.

Amy eventually had a serious relationship with one of her students. When it seemed that this relationship might become public, she made several self-protective moves. She left the relationship, her job, and the area. Although at this time she was living in a metropolitan area with a large and politically active lesbian and gay community, she never sought out this community. She never "met" another lesbian until she was about to leave the region.

While neither the turn-of-the-century women nor the postwar lesbians had control over the discourse available to them with which to name and claim their desires, the earlier women did have communities of women and models of successful, independent womanhood whose presence in their public and private lives contradicted new and old stereotypes. The young lesbians of the 1950s had only negatives from their culture, especially negative images of lesbians and negative experiences if their attractions became public. If they did find any communities, the positive aspects of which will be discussed below, these communities had little power to protect them or provide them anything comparable to what the Progressive Era women gained from their networks. Even their individual mentors or friends were, at best, ambivalent in their support and instruction.[2]

In spite of all these problems, these women persisted as lovers of women, claiming their desires even if they could not name them, enjoying the pleasures these relationships and affairs brought. What came too was the confusion between the external dangers and the emotional and physical joys. Iris Miller re-created the entire evening of her first lesbian experience:

Three friends and I went to a concert and did some drugs. One of them was a boarder, so we all went back to Mrs. Howards' [the boarding school they attended]. We had to devise this little way to get in because we were out late, late. She didn't want, Miss Bonnie didn't want to let anyone in after midnight because they had a curfew, so we had to devise a way to get in. And me and Cindy were the only two that got in. . . . We had to climb in the French Room, climb in the window there, go around two or three classrooms, and then sneak up the stairs, which was real easy because Miss Bonnie and Miss Pearl, who were the two Mrs. Howards, were like eighty and ninety years old. This was like pretty easy to do. So we got up there and one thing led to another and we just kinda started touching and feeling, and then the . . . drug just kind of took over. And it was really great! It was really great. It was nice. . . . But then like we didn't do it again. I think it scared both of us, so we didn't do it again and we really didn't talk about it.

Robin Edwards, who had long desired a physical relationship with a woman, remembers it "sure was nice." She didn't feel guilty, but felt bad that she didn't know what she was doing.[3] Anne McConnell became totally wrapped up in her first affair in college.

It was . . . I don't know. It was young love. I couldn't breathe when she walked into the room. It was just amazing. She seduced me though. I didn't seduce her. . . . But we weren't really conscious except, being raised Catholic, we knew that anything that felt that good had to be sinful. This we were sure of. So we knew we were in trouble. We weren't quite sure what it was because we didn't know what was possible. And then after a couple of months of this, we discovered what was possible. . . . But neither of us knew it was possible for this to be a life commitment. . . . We knew we loved each other. There was a lot of very positive stuff about the loving. . . . It did not seem appropriate that something which harmed no one, and was a very loving thing, was grounds for sending someone to hell. It wasn't logical.

Anne's questioning of the morality behind the prohibition against homosexuality fit with the other questions of her generation—the morality of war, of racism, of materialism, and their actions of resistance. Before the women's and lesbian/gay movements, Lee Powell, Trudy Hardin, and Jo Martinez were activists, especially in civil rights; Amy was active in anti-war work. The atmosphere of questioning and resistance provided for these women a space to reconsider the rules, restrictions and definitions they had inherited, as well as a more personal sense that they were entitled to the freedom to be whoever they were and love whomever they wished.

This "right to love" and of feeling right with their desires were both powerful components in these women's struggles toward lesbian identities. Paula was very clear when she described the meaning of her first lesbian experience. She felt as if she had discovered herself.

> My junior year, . . . we were on a sports day trip. Another woman, actually, we got physically involved and it just seemed so right. I mean it was the rightest thing that I had ever done, and I didn't realize 'til then, I mean, actually named myself a lesbian 'til then, and even though I'm sure other people thought I was. . . . Well, then I realized that that's what I had been all my life and just hadn't known it. And it just seemed as if everything fell into place for me. I didn't have to be worried about getting married, or changing my name, or ever having a [hetero]sexual involvement. Not that I was ever terribly worried about it. . . . I knew I didn't want the whole world to know. . . . I didn't feel guilty about it, or bad, or awful; it seemed just right.

While these early relationships felt wonderful, their meaning could not easily be articulated. According to Jo, what started out as casual sex quickly became complicated.

> I don't know. I was just very arrogant, and I asked her if she'd go to bed with me, and she said, "Yeah." So we went to her apartment, which wasn't too far from there, and made love. What can I say. I'm not sure I knew what that all meant. It's interesting to say the least. It certainly created some problems for both of us.

Jamie, who had been the "worst date," felt as Paula did, that she had found her place.

> Yeah, we were all in nursing school . . . everybody slept with everybody, and it was really very innocent. . . . And somehow we wangled it so that we were sleeping together. It started in innocent back rubs. . . . I don't think it took very long at all . . . I was in hog heaven. I was really happy. I can say that that was probably the first time that I felt comfortable with any relationship. . . . It was good, I was happy, and basically didn't have any guilt feelings. . . . Still, I didn't put a name to it . . . again I didn't know where the hell to go with it.

While cautious, these women positively embraced their homoerotic experiences in spite of the "outlaw" or "outcast" status such sexuality conferred on them. They all ultimately chose to continue to explore this sexual option, though, as discussed, several tried to be straight for short periods in their lives. And with or without claiming a lesbian identity, these women translated this sexual alternative into a lifestyle. The average age for entering a serious relationship was twenty-six, with six women over thirty before they settled into a long-term commitment. Overwhelmingly, these women have chosen an adult pattern of serial monogamy. On average, their longest relationships lasted ten years. Eleven of the fifteen women were buying or had bought homes together with lovers. While these relationships share many qualities with heterosexual marriages, with the exception of Amy whose partner was supporting her while she was in school, these women have all maintained economic autonomy.

Communities

The process by which these women reconciled their choice to build lives with other women with the available sexual identities revolves around their introductions into self-identified lesbian communities. Claiming a lesbian identity, for these women, was not based on an individual love affair, or even on an acknowledged sexual preference; claiming a lesbian identity most often occurred when a woman came into contact with and became part of a lesbian community, and through that community became aware of a lesbian subculture.

While earlier in this century, middle-class women may have acknowledged their variant sexual identities among small intimate groups, as seen in the Salt Lake City study, or among progressive feminists such as the Heterodoxy community, publicly "out" middle-class, white lesbians were generally unknown in the United States (Bullough and Bullough 1977; Schwarz 1986). Lesbians born in the United States, such as Natalie Clifford Barney and Gertrude Stein, chose to live in the presumably more tolerant atmosphere of Europe (Benstock 1989; Wickes 1976).

Researchers are beginning to uncover the histories of pre-World War II working-class lesbian communities that were starting to assert a lesbian presence in certain urban centers. Such visibility had increased during World War II as growing economic opportunities and a relaxed social atmosphere made the war years positive for many single women and lesbians. These women were able to support themselves better than they ever had before, and, as stated above, working women were viewed in a positive light. Women left the domestic sphere to meet the demands of paid work and voluntary patriotic activities and enjoyed a new freedom in public (D'Emilio 1983; Berube 1990; Kennedy and Davis 1993).

Kennedy and Davis's (1993) informants in Buffalo identified the war as the "turning point in lesbian life." Women had more money and more access to public space. For those individuals who migrated to war industry centers or joined the military, it created a new "erotic situation." According to John D'Emilio (1983),

> The war plucked millions of young men and women, whose sexual identities were just forming, out of their homes, out of towns and small cities, and away from the heterosexual environment of the family, and dropped them into essentially sex-segregated situations—as GIs, as WACs and WAVES, in same-sex rooming houses for women workers who had relocated to find employment.

Combined with the above-discussed factors, the result was a significant growth of lesbian and gay communities. Harassment of lesbians and gays, in the military and in defense centers, was relatively minimal; the state and private industry needed workers too much to risk publicity that might scare off potential employees. Even wartime fashions—tailored clothing generally and slacks for women—eased many lesbians' lives. They could find and wear the clothes they liked and blend in with other women.

The gay communities that had grown and flourished during the war did not disappear when it ended. Women and men realized that small-town U.S.A. had no place for them, and many chose to stay in urban centers such as San Francisco, Los Angeles, and New York City. In Buffalo, this decade brought greater confidence to that working-class lesbian community. More so than in the forties, these lesbians were willing to reach out to newcomers, fight for public lesbian space, and build an integrated community. The emergence of the butch-fem dyad who announced their sexuality by appearing in public together was key to this change (Kennedy and Davis 1993).

At the same time, many lesbian and gay communities faced increased local harassment and bar raids as part of a trickle-down effect from federal anti-gay persecution. Concurrent with this repression, middle-class lesbians and gay men began to organize themselves, founding "homophile" groups that aimed to educate the general public about homosexuality and press for legal protections. Gay historians argue that the collision between the permissive wartime climate and the postwar backlash forced lesbians and gay men into a greater self-consciousness as victims of a common oppression and fostered an increased community solidarity. For example, Kennedy and Davis (1993) conclude that the lesbian bar culture was "a pre-political form of resistance in an extremely hostile heterosexual world." Although class stratification existed within the gay and lesbian communities and class-based tensions separated the homophile organizations from the public subculture, both developments produced increased general awareness of and self-awareness within this sexual minority.

Lesbian communities were key to the women in this study. Among them, only Paula named herself a lesbian in conjunction with her first sexual involvement with a woman. Seven others did so through frequenting the gay bars. Another seven claimed lesbian identities after becoming involved in lesbian-feminist groups. For some, this process occurred before any sexual involvements, while for others there were years between their forming a relationship and claiming a lesbian identity.

Lee Powell is the only one in this group who grew up aware of lesbians and gay men and their communities. In the urban, African American culture of her youth, gay men were visible in important community roles, especially as musical directors for the churches. They were also moral arbiters because, as Lee described it, gay men had the dirt on everyone and were very skillful with the "dozens," an African American art of verbal confrontation. People could not gossip in a negative way about them, the gay men, unless they were willing to risk retaliation. Lesbians, "bull daggers," played more marginal roles in Lee's home community, but they were there, often working in nontraditional jobs, living as couples, and raising families.[4]

As work in the arts became more central to Lee's life, she became friends with some gay male co-workers. At twenty, Lee had been going to the bars with a gay male friend for months.

She knew she was a lesbian but had not had a woman lover. On her twenty-first birthday she decided to act and spent the night with a woman she had gotten to know at the bar. Even though this one-night stand was not a particularly good introduction to lesbian sex, Lee persevered in exploring this community.

Robin Edwards describes how she came to an awareness of the lesbian community.

> We would all go to the Caravan [a straight bar] for happy hour. But we [Robin and her girlfriend] kept being left behind. They'd say, "Well, we're going home now," or make up something. We'd sit there and like it's eight o'clock, thinking, what's wrong with these people. So one time I got pissed at Sue in the parking lot. I said, "Goddamn it, what's going on here? You ride with me and we're supposed to spend the evening doing something and then you take off with those folks." She got out of the car, went over to those others, talked to them and came back. And she just said, I'll never forget it, "Get in." On the way, driving down Central, she said, "Remember when I told you there was a place I'd never take you?" I said, "Yeah?" She said, "We're going there now." And I said, "Damn. Alright. It's about time."

Before connecting this group of friends with the clearly lesbian bar culture, Robin could maintain her "innocence." To be part of the bar culture was to accept oneself as a lesbian.

Amy first identified as bisexual, and appears to have quite deliberately arranged her coming out. She agrees with this analysis but claims she was not conscious that this was what she was doing at the time. As described above, she had been teaching in the same high school for five years when she had her first sexual relationship with a woman. She was in her mid-twenties. In 1976, when she ended that relationship, she quit teaching, moved to Albuquerque, and sought out and became part of a feminist C-R (consciousness-raising) group. Within a few months, she came out as a lesbian: "I think that it really . . . I mean, one of the first things that I did when I came to Albuquerque was go to the women's bookstore, and start moving in that direction. But it's like I couldn't do that while I was in this other situation; I had to change my situation."

On the other hand, Bobbi Denova holds the record among this group for delay in claiming this identity. Settled in Albuquerque with her lover of eight years, best friends with another female couple, she still managed to avoid entertaining the possibility that she was a lesbian. In her mind she simply fell in love with another woman. Though she knew this was an intimate relationship which she could not publicly celebrate, it was clear that she did not think this was a "lesbian" relationship. Her commitment to Jamie had a private meaning for which there was no special term in her mind. The concept of a sexual identity did not exist for Bobbi for years.

This situation changed when a younger acquaintance, very much involved in the emerging lesbian-feminist movement in Albuquerque, came out to her and questioned her about her identity. Only then did she make the connection. What makes her process worth quoting at length is the contrast between her consciousness and that of her long time lover, Jamie Henson. According to Bobbi,

> It was years and years. We never talked about it. I don't know if it was the youth part of it, or if it was denial. I don't know what it was, but we were in a relationship and it didn't matter. We didn't have any commitment and things were loose and we didn't think about how we fit anywhere. And [the island] was a paradise . . . I don't know how to explain it. There were no negative things, no negative thoughts or feelings about it at all. . . . It was something we just kinda skirted around and never talked about. Maybe we thought that it might destroy our relationship, or traumatize us somehow. But having Connie say that so easy to us, it was kinda like oo-wee, I know who I am. Now I have a name. Now I can fit in a slot. And it wasn't unpleasant at all. And it kinda opened a door for Jamie and I to start communicating on a different level. From that point on, we would start talking about a relationship and, as we did, we committed and became more firm with each other. Why didn't we talk about

being gay or having a commitment, talking about other women, or being with other women for all those years? I don't know. I don't remember being unhappy or missing anything.

Jamie, on the other hand, was aware that she was "queer." She was also aware of the power of that label. Out of fear of losing Bobbi, she kept silent all the years it took for Bobbi to come to a consciousness of lesbianism. Certainly for Jamie the taboo against lesbianism was contained within the label, the named sexual identity, not the sexual behavior. On the other hand, it also demonstrates how, without a named sexual identity, there can be no discourse.

> Again, I felt very at home and no guilt. [But] we never acknowledged ourselves, and . . . I was always afraid to say anything. If I had come out and said how do you feel about being queer, boom, she'd have been gone, that's the way I felt. . . . Many times I wanted to say something to her about being a lesbian, and I just knew that if I brought that word out, made us face it, that again I'd be left, she'd be gone. Took 'til here . . . and there was a support group.

By the time Bobbi did accept her lesbian identity, their relationship had a very firm base and they had several communities of support. This new awareness allowed them to explore the larger lesbian community. Bobbi described the change:

> And I don't remember having a negative feeling about it [the word "lesbian"]. It's strange, what I often think about, it's real strange what a mind will sometimes do. It will just shut doors on things you don't want to deal with. And you need someone to come along and kick these doors open. And you need to have them kicked open at good intervals. So that you start seeing and exploring. There was a whole new different world out there. And it's interesting because there are so many different circles of women, and they are all very different, and yet they all kind of touch each other. And I think about how we've come through different circles, not that one is better or one is lesser than the other, but you go through these different circles that meet your needs as you start your growth. And it's kinda nice.

Each woman's path toward and reaction to claiming a lesbian identity was unique. Some lived carefully but also enjoyed being part of the public lesbian community. All became involved in some part of the lesbian-feminist/activist community in Albuquerque during the late 1970s and early 1980s. But within this diversity of reaction was a shared sense of relief, a sense of peace, or a sense of being home. Regardless of the consequences and the oppression, these women were glad to know there was a name for what they were, that there were others like themselves and a place to be among other lesbians.

Five of these fifteen lesbians—Jo, Carrie, Paula, Robin, and Lee—found communities when the only overtly lesbian communities centered on bars.[5] Jamie, Bobbi, Gloria, and Anne had circles of friends, most of whom were closeted lesbians. While several of these women were involved with lesbian-dominated softball teams, it was not until the emergence of feminism that they had the opportunity to be part of communities that fulfilled the types of functions seen among the Progressive Era reformers.[6]

Most of these women have earned the title "community builder" from their contributions to women's or lesbian organizations and institutions. Anne McConnell, Amy Adams, and Lee Powell have owned "women's" businesses or run centers for women. But these were not just opportunities for them to work in women-friendly environments, or in the case of businesses, make money—small businesses such as theirs don't make much money. These establishments became employers of other lesbians and feminists, provided lesbian-friendly environments, and most importantly have served as community centers. They were alternatives to the bars as gathering places, sites for forums and debates, and places from which to organize political and social activities. Among the other lesbians, most have been involved with at least one of these institutions, as employee or participant in some service or group.

Political, social, and cultural efforts have benefited from the energies of these women and have been the basis on which they have been integrated in the large and dynamic Albuquerque feminist/women's/lesbian community.[7] Two women's production companies, SIREN and WIMIN, the Albuquerque Women's Community Association, the National Lesbian Feminist Organization, the Gay/Lesbian Hotline, the National Lesbian Conference, the National Organization for Women, and the National Women's Political Caucus—New Mexico Chapter, and the University of New Mexico's Women's Studies Programs and Women's Center have all been the most formal vehicles through which lesbian and women's causes have been advanced, networks have been formed, and social circles established.

While none of these local organizations have the power or national presence of either Hull House or the Women's Trade Union League, neither does this latter group include women with the wealth needed to individually sustain an organization. Nevertheless, some of the leaders have contributed significantly from their much more modest resources. These women's and lesbian institutions and organizations are part of new national and international networks that are again promoting women on the basis of their being women and even promoting lesbians on the basis of their being lesbians.

These communities play different roles in different women's lives. Both Lee and Jo bridge the women's and racial/cultural communities of Albuquerque, while many of the Euro-American lesbians who were not born in New Mexico have few ties to communities outside of lesbian and/or feminist circles. But, perhaps more importantly for the lesbians in this research, lesbian communities exist. Most certainly they are not without their problems and differences; nevertheless, there are places to be lesbians.

It is a complex task to assess the extent to which these women challenged their era's gender and sexuality norms. The core issue differentiating this generation of women from the turn-of-the-century women is that the contemporary women came to maturity during a period when there was no organized women's movement. Aside from Audrey, who was involved in an international women's religious organization, none of them participated in or found support from a women's network. Their struggles for autonomy and sexual identity were individual processes. Though most of these women identify themselves as feminists, and many have been involved in feminist, lesbian, and other types of activism, these movements did not exist in any accessible form early in the women's lives.[8]

The lives and struggles of these never-married lesbians provide insights into the changing gender and sexuality systems of the twentieth century. During the postwar period, the ideology of heterosexuality was perhaps at its strongest; the ideal gender role of the adult woman was narrowly defined as the economically dependent wife and mother, and the endorsed female sexuality was limited to a passive role in marital intercourse. Yet women were continuing to claim educations and to enter the work force, and lesbian communities were growing and beginning to organize themselves. It could be argued that these women sought out the cracks in the gender and sexuality systems. For example, they could become educated because earning a college degree was acceptable for women. They could be self-supporting, though this was less respectable. By identifying themselves as autonomous females, as economically, socially, and sexually independent, they rejected the ideals and were willing to risk whatever stigma was involved in being independent.

However, the consciousness with which they ignored, rejected, or resisted the norms is harder to identify. Most of these women did have a sense that they wanted to be independent, even when they were not sure if they were eliminating the heterosexual model and/or marriage from their lives. It appears that either an endorsement of this independence or, at least, an absence of heterosexual pressures from their families laid the foundation for this decision. As a result of this familial environment and their own varied achievements, these women's sense of self-worth was never dependent upon heterosexual success. It appears therefore that they were able to put the problematic issues of sexuality and relationships aside while they pursued the difficult but acceptable goal of economic autonomy. These women were then able to discuss the importance of getting additional education, which they connected with financial self-sufficiency.

At a time when women were defined by their relationships, defined as daughters, wives, or mothers, this group of women also used education as a vehicle for separating both from their birth families and whatever residual expectations were connected with the environments of their hometowns. This particular type of separation appears to have been essential for social autonomy. Through their years of education and travel, these women learned that they could not only support themselves, but could build full lives in new places. It is not that they abandoned their families or other loved ones. In several cases there was a years-long process of going away and moving back until some resolution of ties and responsibilities emerged. Furthermore, in a good number of the cases initial separation was painful, but the women endured the loneliness, homesickness, and material deprivation that accompanied these breaks. Yet, while these women easily verbalized their desire for education and economic independence, they are far less likely to have articulated this need to physically break away from the domestic sphere. In retrospect they can; but it appears that, without a feminist movement and public discussion of these issues, these women would have stated only what was ideologically sanctioned in our culture during this time period.

These women's lives suggest that a similar process may also

have been taking place vis-à-vis issues of sexual identity and adult relationships. They could decide they didn't want to be married, but they were less likely to clearly state a rejection of matrimony. They could also enter into sexual relationships with other women without major moral qualms, but they could not clearly articulate the meaning of these intimate relationships. Yet, they acted as if they were fully aware of the implications of such choices, both before and after actually becoming sexually active with another woman. The negative connotations of the "queer" and "lesbian" label seem to have caused these women to reject or hold such an identity in abeyance until they could come to some internal resolution of its meaning. The choice to claim a lesbian identity appears to have been very deliberate, something these women closed their eyes to until they were ready emotionally, financially, or socially. This process was aided by coming into contact with other individuals or a community of support. Bobbi's process, though the extreme, provides a good example. For Bobbi there was a clear compartmentalization between her relationship with Jamie and the externally imposed label "lesbian." Nevertheless, she acted as if she well knew what lesbian oppression was all about, while, in a sense, waiting for someone to come along and tell her being a lesbian was "okay."

A self-definition as "different," which appeared in most of these women's childhood memories, appears to be central to understanding how these individuals came to live outside our culture's gender and sexuality norms. Though not always comfortable or thrilled with this status, these women accepted themselves and expressed no desire to be average, to follow the norms. They had, through this self-conception, set up a different set of life rules for themselves. Having already rejected the basic female roles and expectations, claiming an education, and setting a course toward independence, accepting a lesbian identity was less traumatic, less threatening to their senses of self, than it might have been for women who had not already gone against the grain.

Another significant pattern in these women's lives was gaining a means to economic and social independence, before dealing with issues of sexuality and relationships. Class factors have been found to be important in studies of lesbian history, often being lines between publicly "out" working-class lesbians and closeted professional lesbians. Such findings provide a clue to understanding this group of lesbians who generally remained closeted until they had achieved their professional positions and, for some of them, until the women's and gay liberation movement had begun to change public attitudes. They knew or acted as if they knew they would be risking their chances for a good job if they came out earlier. Audrey certainly articulated this understanding, but few of the other women did so clearly. The interconnectedness of the economic and sexuality factors in these women's lives suggests how the two issues might constrain each other. Although these women were compelled toward financial independence, one might wonder why they first chose such traditional fields. In addition to the issues already discussed, this might have been because those fields were safe, secure, and good cover for the woman who knows or suspects she's a lesbian. These women may not have been willing to be in the limelight the way a woman in a nontraditional field would have been at that point in history.

On the other hand, the ways that jobs limit the extent to which lesbians can be out is a well-known and well-discussed consequence of homophobia and the lack of legal protection for lesbian workers. The restlessness of these women within the work force, while reflecting their efforts to take advantage of new and better work opportunities, might also indicate a search for a safer and freer job environment. Jo and Anne were both fired from jobs because of their sexuality. Amy left one of her jobs voluntarily. Gloria never ventured into a gay bar until her job was secure.

The creativity with which these women negotiated their way through the 1950s and 1960s is impressive. Because the gender and sexuality systems of midcentury labeled both economically independent women and never-married women and lesbians as abnormal, these women had to struggle for their autonomy on several fronts. They also had to make priorities and choices among those struggles. The consciousness with which they made decisions varied, limited by the lack of any organized women's movement or an accessible theory of their oppression. Nevertheless, these women did reject the gender and sexuality norms of their era and eventually came to a point of conscious resistance through participating in lesbian, gay, and/or feminist communities.

SEVEN

Spinsters and Lesbians

Resisting and Surviving as Independent Women

Jo Baker tells us very little in her autobiography about her private life past her childhood. She doesn't speak about the women with whom she lived and whom she loved. But Jo Baker and the women in her social and political circles were not isolated women, ignorant of the battles that were taking place over gender and sexuality during their adult years. We know, for example, that Jo Baker traveled in 1934 to Great Britain with her partner at the time, Ida Wylie. There they met with Radclyffe Hall and Lady Una Troubridge, women who had long been friends of Ida's (Schwarz, 1986). This trip and meeting took place six years after the publication of Hall's *The Well of Loneliness* and the ensuing controversy. Baker wrote her autobiography eleven years after Hall's novel appeared and ten years after Katherine Bement Davis's study on women's sexuality. Baker was sixty-six when it was published.

Recovering Women-Centered Lives

While Baker's autobiography certainly can be read as a subversive text, neither Baker nor any comparable woman of her generation in the United States ever came out and said that they—respectable, white, professional women leaders—were lesbians or claimed their intimate relationships with other women.[1] What does this tell us about her and the other women of her generation? Not only did many of these turn-of-the-century women, who had enjoyed such womanly solidarity throughout their lives, face their last years intimidated by the labels society now placed on them and questioning themselves about their identities and their lives, but subsequent generations lost these women's stories and their voices. Their full and creative lives, with their varied lessons, contradictions, and conflicts, were hidden, and these women as individuals and as a diverse movement were marginalized.

This erasure was due in part to their own successes, but the gender system, which they had critiqued and helped to dismantle, reformulated itself under very different economic and social conditions. The new and revised heterosexuality did not seem burdensome in the prosperous 1920s. Meanwhile, a powerful political backlash, a coalition of many forces, denigrated the women activists, especially those who lived women-centered lives. Scrambling to redefine their work and stem the political/legislative reversals in this new era, women did not or could not fight the personal as well as public attacks. In these struggles they were seriously hampered by their inability directly to confront the issues that were ideologically most undermining: new sexuality ideals and new definitions of womanhood.

All the women of the post-World War II group came to claim their lesbian identities. Some claimed them within the early bar-centered communities while others waited for lesbian-feminist organizations. They have all contributed to women's and/or lesbian activism, as well as to many other political and cultural struggles. It is at least a bit ironic that these lesbians, who grew up in an era that so stigmatized or so ignored them and all never-married women and lesbians, are among the best-placed survivors of the 1950s. Their early efforts for economic self-sufficiency and self-defined sexuality have allowed them to take advantage of recent societal changes, especially those fostered by feminism and gay liberation. The communities, culture, and activism they know in middle adulthood are similar to those the Progressive Era women knew from early in life. These cohorts faced their times of ideological marginality and personal questioning, as well as their times of validation and women-centered solidarity, at opposite life stages.

While the issues of independence and sexuality are at the core of the comparison between these generations (and both represent a very particular and limited subgroup of each), their lives argue for an integrated analysis. Economics and family structures, gender, class, and race systems, as well as political movements for change constrained and promoted these women's differing struggles for social, sexual, and material autonomy and self-definition.

The Progressive Era women, daughters of the nineteenth century, saw their generation's struggle as one against a gender system that was based in economics and the law. For them personally, economic independence and social autonomy allowed them the freedom to contribute to the numerous reform activities of their lives. And while this group, the second generation of new women, came from somewhat varied class backgrounds, they generally shared having supportive families, intimate and national female role models, rigorous educations and educators who took them seriously, powerful women's institutions and communities, and the Progressive Era's spirit of change and innovation. They used these benefits to create new lives as women.

As Jo Baker suggests, their childhoods were important, but not for the reasons Freud and sexologists expressed. These women did not experience harshly patriarchal families. Their childhood freedoms prepared them for independence at a time when there were sufficient contradictions in women's traditional roles to endorse their choices as liberal challenges.

As discussed in chapter 1, a number of these women lost their fathers at early ages. Most of the remaining fathers' businesses suffered during the economic uncertainties and crises of the late nineteenth century. As young women, they saw their fathers, generally gentle, decent, and supportive men, have their traditional roles undermined by forces beyond their control. Could these parents then argue against their daughters' determination for education and financial independence? At a time when middle-class masculinity was differently defined, perhaps these fathers, and mothers, could accept that they could not provide for their daughters, subsequently supporting them in their efforts to be part of a reformed economic and gender system.

If these were the beliefs with which these young women left home, those who entered the middle-class "new woman" track and attended college found enough continuing agreement on these issues among those sharing and providing their educations, while the working-class women found social critiques in the radical political movements. "Enough" does not mean unanimous, but enough was sufficient for these women who were determinedly seeking opportunities and for whom pushing limits was already second nature. This was true in terms of society's views of them as well. They had adequate acknowledgment from those closest to them, so that they were in the vanguard, going in the "right" direction, and able to escape serious and debilitating self-doubts when those who opposed them condemned their decisions. They were and continued to be part of a large movement of women.

Having seen an unstable patriarchal and capitalist economic

system in their childhoods, the Progressive Era women became self-supporting. Many of them set out to reform the system they critiqued. While they researched, educated, and developed public policies, they also constructed relationships, communities, and families. Their private lives were perhaps more innovative than their public writings portray. While adventurous and ambitious, and while they may have envisioned themselves as individualists, they were part of kinlike networks. It is easiest to see how these circles of friends and colleagues provided mentors, promoted these women into Progressive Era employment, and introduced them into larger national and international networks of reformers. It is harder to see how they replaced female kin in each others' lives. Nevertheless, in a diversity of ways, with blood family at times overlapping with constructed relationships, they cared for each others' emotional needs and built homes to replace what they sacrificed to become independent. They formed friendship networks, developed egalitarian intimate relationships, raised children in female-headed households, and maintained homes for themselves and the families they founded. Neither these women nor their historians have preserved and analyzed all the lessons from their lives.

After World War I, new anti-woman sex and gender norms took root as women's power declined. Conservative times and Republican administrations thwarted postsuffrage political efforts such as the Sheppard-Towner Act while most women's lives improved somewhat during the prosperous 1920s. Privileged women did have greater freedoms and choices in leisure and education, a right to work and the means to plan their childbearing. Experiences which, for the Progressive Era women, had been significant departures from the worlds of their mothers became commonplace for middle-class women born after the turn of the century. College attendance, travel, and working for wages were no longer pioneering endeavors. For working-class women, repressive measures limited radical and labor activism while the opening of sales and clerical positions produced fewer women radicalized by labor union activities. In general, women had less time to be on their own as their age at marriage dropped.

A political and social generation gap was exacerbated by hostile antifeminist media portrayals where the homosocial activism of their mothers' generation was portrayed as the ludicrous rantings of maladjusted matrons.[2] On the other hand, the heterosexual and heterosocial opportunities available to young women of both middle-class and working-class families were sold to them devoid of sexual dangers.

The Great Depression fostered a restructured sexual division of labor within the waged labor force, which halted the inroads women had made and redirected them toward the developing clerical and service fields. The increase of women in the work force had not really touched the centers of male power as defined by the traditional male professions and the increasingly important world of business. As the professions women had founded and led matured, such work allowed fewer opportunities for individual innovation and initiative. This standardization coincided with a diminishing of the reform spirit of the Progressive Era and its sense of communal duty. An individualist ethic was emerging.

By the time the country was thrown into crisis by the Great Depression, very few people still held a political analysis of women as oppressed by a system of male dominance. A mature woman had only one place, firmly reembedded in the family.[3] The decade of the Depression set the tone that lasted until the reemergence of the Women's Movement. Men were the center of societal concerns, while women's primary role was to bolster the fragile and threatened male ego. In her book on the 1950s, Breines (1992) argues that by the time the nation returned to "normalcy," sociologists such as Harvard's Talcott Parsons could safely state that a healthy, stable family needed to be built on dichotomized gender roles. He and his generation of social scientists noted that while this necessitated the subordination of women, this was not a problem, for the mature woman would be fulfilled through her domestic responsibilities.

This study found that this construction of the family with its supporting definition of womanhood *was* a problem for the female children of this era. On the most basic level, their families did not replicate the perfect suburban families portrayed in sociological theory and on television as typically American. Certain of their "deviations" were indications of national trends, such as married women entering the waged labor force, while others—poverty, racism, incest, and other forms of child abuse—remained hidden realities that this culture is still struggling to confront. These women remember their childhoods as contradictions of freedom and censure, competence and denial.

While social scientists dreamed of happiness in strictly dichotomized gender roles, producers of consumer goods for baby boomer families discovered how to double the market by defining everything from infant receiving blankets through furniture, from bicycles through sneakers, as gendered.[4] Gender transgressors were easily marked as outside the system's boundaries by these products. While these women's families often seemed caught between enforcing compliance and allowing freedom, both generations knew the "pinks" from the "blues."[5] And the message was not just one of difference: both boys and girls knew that boys had it better.

For several of these young women, crossing the gender boundary into a strong identification with boys and male privilege was a tortured but necessary decision for psychic survival. For others confronting other challenges—poverty, racism, and abuse—assuming early economic or familial responsibilities seemed to have produced the self-esteem needed to move beyond the narrow female role. Their decisions might not have been ideologically endorsed, but, from their view, they had no choice but to transgress.

While television and the marketplace were new mechanisms

for gender role enforcement for the post-World War II generation, by midcentury the educational system, which had so supported the Progressive Era women in their quest for new options, was in the business of reproducing sexism, racism, and
class hierarchies. Education still being very much the gateway
for upward class mobility and economic self-sufficiency, especially for women, schools and teachers gave conflicting messages
of equal opportunity and gender-based restrictions.

When these women entered schools of higher education, their
experiences diverged even more from those of the turn-of-the-
century women. Higher educational institutions emerge in their
stories as sites of invasive enforcement of gender and sexual
norms, with women faculty and administrators often acting as
agents of compliance. All homosocial bonding and solidarity
were suspect, for special friendships and attachments might indicate "latent homosexuality." But just as these women gleaned
and hoarded all the information they could use to further their
education, separate from their families and hometowns, and
became independent, they took these mostly negative messages
about "homosexuality" and put them to their own use. These
women were survivors as well as resisters. Just as they survived
the sexism, racism, and other challenges in their childhood while
resisting the female role they were urged to play, they later
survived the homophobia while resisting the overwhelming heterosexuality of the era. And like the Progressive Era women,
they needed physical distance from their families and hometowns to define their independent identities.

Perhaps even more clearly than among the earlier women,
sexuality and economics constrained each other in these
women's lives. Audrey most clearly articulated the decision
these women appear to have shared when she described how
she could not risk her livelihood by coming out as a lesbian.
Each woman negotiated this balance between her competing
desires for social autonomy and sexual intimacy. Just as they

postponed claiming lesbian identities until they found one that did not undermine their social position and sense of themselves, so too they moved into lesbian relationships, communities, and activism only as their economic stability could be maintained.

Perhaps nowhere is the feminist truism that the personal is political more applicable than in lesbian history. Not only are the private lives of both of these generations important for an understanding of changing gender and sexuality norms, but there are political reasons that these stories, particularly the Progressive Era women's, have been hard to find and analyze. We have not valued the "female" sphere with the same level of inquiry as we have the male sphere. These lives urge that we refocus on the connection between the personal and public in our lives.

It is also easy to give lip service to our diversity. While all women's lives in the United States involve racism, economic/ class issues, sexuality, and other power systems, it is easier to ignore the influences of these systems in the lives of women closest to this culture's hegemonic centers. Varying combinations of privilege and oppression from their societal positions influenced the ability of turn-of-the-century women and contemporary lesbians to support themselves financially and determine their own sexual/affectional lives. They also informed the degree of investment the different women had in maintaining their respectability and their social position. Class and race arrogance often cannot be separated from a vulnerable economic toehold based on those same privileges.

Families: Permission and Constraints

Before we venture into that analysis, we must address the role of birth families in these women's quests. While most of the women in both groups felt a clear need to separate from their families, it was often not because their families were not supportive of their efforts for independence. This suggests that they were leaving more than their families. Just as they built new communities, families, and relationships, they had also left their home communities in addition to their families. While individual families may or may not be strongly patriarchal, much of our culture remains centered in a nuclear family structure. It makes sense that women, who saw themselves building lives in which they were not primarily wives and mothers, needed space away from communities where those roles were the overwhelming norms, if not the only options, for women. Alice Hamilton's letters to her cousin, Agnes Hamilton, demonstrate this point. While Agnes did not marry or mother, she was still caught up in familial and community caretaking. It is also interesting that in the Hamilton family, the women who remained behind did not get angry with Alice and her sister for abandoning them, the women, but for abandoning their father.

The importance of building alternatives to patriarchal families and communities highlights the significance of alternative communities in both generations' lives. Just as the earlier cohort did not see themselves abandoning womanly qualities, they also were not really abandoning womanly needs or roles. They wanted to reestablish and redefine those needs and roles outside of a patriarchal situation. These women also needed to separate from their families if they were to form nonfamilial ties, especially since these new bonds could not be legally recognized in most cases.

Class and race do not function in any simple way on this issue. Among the turn-of-the-century women, women from different class backgrounds—Leonora O'Reilly, Mary Elisabeth Dreier, Molly Dewson, and Mary Anderson—all continued to reside with members of their birth families well into their adult years. Geography appears to have interacted with their particular family's characteristics. If they could work close to home and have considerable freedom, they did live with their families.

Among the contemporary women, the women of color separated from their families just as much as the white women, but they also reestablished ties, to differing degrees, with African American and Hispanic communities. Again, the degree to which women could have social freedom and find work determined their need to separate. Robin Edwards, whose family and community accepted her early declaration to be single, has not needed to move, while Audrey Streig, whose mother did not expect her to be able to be independent, had an early and strong determination to separate.

It is also important not to underestimate the difficulties these women had in accomplishing these separations, and much of that involves money and work. This is especially true for the contemporary lesbians. The older generation had many more familial and community supports. Not only did the postwar women come from poorer families overall, but they were facing an educational system and work force with rigid gender (and racial) segregation, built on the assumption that women were not independent wage earners. Many of these women were the first in their families to pursue higher education. No one told them the options open to them about the different types of schools, financial aid, and scholarships. And their original traditional educational and career decisions strengthen this point.

While it is somewhat clear, given our current state of feminist research and theory, how issues of gender, class, and race structured these women's educational and economic options, there is almost no mention about what it means for women to establish themselves as independent apart from their birth families and family-centered communities.[6] Because women have been defined, and often confined, by their familial connections, but have also found important material support and emotional fulfillment there, this conundrum must be analyzed as a major barrier to independence. The addition of demands and restrictions of our changing sexuality systems to these women's lives deserve an even more complex evaluation. Their lives argue that sexuality and economics, as well as family, class, and race, have functioned separately at times, and in varying combinations at others, influencing their paths to autonomy.

Sexuality, Racism, and Economics

The silence of the turn-of-the-century "new women" on sexuality and their private lives, a legacy left for the post-World War II women, was not simple Victorian reticence. Their gender and sexuality analyses were very much limited by their class and race positions. With further research we may also identify generational, regional, and life-choice differences among single women and between them and many of the women active during this first wave of the women's movement.

During the Progressive Era, race was intertwined with class, while racism was on the rise.[7] Many reformers of this era, including these women, shared their culture's prevailing xenophobic view of eastern and southern European immigrants as a different and inferior race.[8] Most African Americans still lived in the rural South, and other people of color resided in areas removed in many ways from northern urban centers in which these women lived and worked.[9] While these women were occasionally aware of racial issues and occasionally addressed them, their lives and their analyses were often no less racist and white-centered than those of most other women and labor activists of their time (Giddings 1984; Gordon 1991).

The sexual issues that were of concern to feminists and activists in the late nineteenth and early twentieth centuries centered on women's right to say "no" within marriage and to control her fertility. It is ironic that all sexual dangers for women were originally linked to heterosexuality or marriage, for by the end of these women's lives, ideologically the reverse would be true.

Heterosexuality had become the only safe haven for "real" women.

The nineteenth-century sex radicals' demand that women have the power to decide how many children they would bear was consistent with that era's sexual ideals of controlled sexuality in marriage and women's primary maternal drive. This definition of sexuality, including the single standard of moderation in marriage urged by the Moral Purity crusades, was one of the means by which the white middle classes built their claim of race and class superiority. They defined their morality and controlled passions in stern opposition to the "uncontrolled" and "immoral" behavior of other classes and races.

New linkages were also being assumed between nonmarital sex and violence and disorder. During this period, the traditional friends of African Americans were abandoning them, convinced by the white supremacists' creation of the myth of the black rapist (Giddings 1984). Sensational stories about "white slavery" sold newspapers but also resulted in the passage of the Mann Act (D'Emilio and Freedman 1988). Female homosexuality among prison inmates became a concern for criminologists and prison administrators (Freedman 1981; Fitzpatrick 1990). Social scientists sought the origins of disruptive sexual behaviors, including prostitution. The attribution of uncontrolled sexuality to non-whites and the poor, and the association of nonmarital sexuality with violence and disorder, cast extramarital sex as sinister, and this view continued as a base even as some parts of the older sexuality system were challenged.

Sexual definitions had never been simply split along gender lines, but were cut across also by other societal tensions and power systems. Nevertheless, the never-married women of the Progressive Era, some of whom studied sexuality, were unprepared to deal with sexuality when those issues touched their lives. The changes taking place in the sexual arena would eventually force this issue on them. The beginning of this move included the separation of sexuality from procreation, the acceptance of female sexual pleasure, and the promotion of sexual expression as necessary for health and happiness.

At the same time that women's—even middle-class women's—sexuality was being redefined, sexual behaviors were increasingly named and categorized. For example, while Freud contributed to the acknowledgment of women's sexual needs, his theory of sexual development also designated only certain sexual behaviors as mature and healthy. For women, these were limited to sexual activities that were passive, vaginally centered, and heterosexual. Other desires or activities were immature, cases of arrested development. This narrow and rigid definition left women little room to protest its boundaries, for discontent was itself a sign of maladjustment.

Psychologists and psychiatrists were joining criminologists and other social scientists on the sexual battleground. Over the next half century, these professions struggled over the right to define normal and abnormal sexual behavior, the right to determine the best response to sexual deviance, and the right to design programs for the prevention of sexual variance. While women reformers had an early and leading presence among the criminologists and social scientists, the psychiatric community did not welcome them, and their voices were not heard among the leaders of this specialty (Morantz-Sanchez 1985). Eventually even women medical doctors and social scientists were squeezed out of the debate, and men alone became the major contributors to the revised gender and sexuality norms. What they developed certainly reflects their power, for sexuality for women and men was defined around male sexual needs. Sexuality, especially women's sexuality, was contained within a revised but still male-centered and male-dominated nuclear family.

Women who desired options outside of these definitions were stigmatized. The collapsing of nonconforming gender behavior

and nonconforming sexual behavior into the person of the female homosexual was the creation of European and U.S. male
psychiatrists and sexologists. This menace, whose sexual deviance could be identified by her masculine dress and behavior,
became an important villain against whom normal women
would be measured in the public consciousness. The extension
of their definition of this deviance to include specifically the
unmarried, independent "new woman" was deliberate. Various
feminist historians have argued that this designation was part of
the reaction against women's growing opportunities for social
and economic autonomy.[10]

While the Women's Movement had had its opponents
throughout its history, accusing these women of deviant sexuality produced a weapon against which neither they nor their
feminist and radical allies were able to mount an adequate
defense.[11] The women who voiced opposition to these definitions did so either indirectly, as Baker did in her autobiography,
or from a professional distance, as Katherine Davis and Lura
Beam did in their studies. While there is no one reason ex-
plaining the remaining silence, several factors seem to have
played a role.

From their critique of the gender system as they knew it,
these women defined womanhood to be large enough to accommodate their differences and choices. They had justified their
nonconforming gender behavior because they were resisting a
system that was unfair. But their discussions of sexuality were
limited, focused on the sexuality of others—either men or
women different from themselves—and grounded in the nineteenth-century understanding of sex. Women as sexual victims
came within their definition of womanhood, but women who
acted with sexual agency posed a problem.

To have claimed a lesbian identity would have meant claiming sexual agency and a nonheterosexual female sexual identity.
These women were unprepared. Until now it had been unneces-

sary to define their attractions and lifestyles. Even the truly single and celibate women among them were suspect. To have admitted to lesbianism as it had been defined by the sexologists would have made them immoral and negated their positions as respectable females. This, in turn, would have eliminated their economic options as independent women, public employees, and educators, as well as their moral power as reformers. They were still dependent upon the male-controlled marketplace for their income.

Next, since behavior that was labeled "female homosexuality" first came to the attention of middle-class women via some of their own work in female reformatories, accepting that identity would have linked them to poor and working-class women, women of color, and "criminals." Claiming common ground with these "homosexuals" across class and race and social position may have been far more than they could do.

They may well have been aware of repercussions for the Women's Movement. It could have split them from many of their primary allies—the safely married women of similar class and racial backgrounds. These issues also divided the never-married women, as discussed in chapter 5. Finally, while they knew such a sexual identity would have threatened their ability to continue the work they were doing, it may well have threatened their sense of themselves as well, or pushed them to deny the linkage.[12]

Could these women have constructed their own definition of lesbianism or women-centered intimacy and sexuality at this time? Carroll Smith-Rosenberg (1985) finds among modern women writers a countering definition of same-sex female sexuality. Though she includes Radclyffe Hall in her discussion, she focuses more on Virginia Woolf and her book *Orlando*. She contrasts the joyful, playful androgyny of this work with the dark, sinister, sexual transgressors found in the works of modern male writers, James Joyce in particular. While this reasoning is interesting particularly in light of the post-World War II lesbians' identity struggles, it is not clear how relevant these European voices are to the gender and sexuality struggles in the United States and its particular class system and racial tensions. Were we too bound, as a nation, to a history that feared sexuality and linked sexuality outside of marriage to violence and societal disorder to allow a competing definition to emerge?

The bottom line was that these women could not have been the leaders they were, and could not have achieved the positions they did, if they had claimed a deviant sexuality. And the gaps between their realities, the sexual understandings of their day, and the limited names and definitions available to them produced their vulnerability and their silence. They divorced themselves from sexual identities and labels, be they "lesbian" or "invert." While it is certainly not only the responsibility of the targeted population to confront and contradict stereotypes and discrimination, no powerful counterforce could develop without someone from within these women's networks providing leadership by naming the issue and providing a political analysis.

As women's political organizations declined in number after suffrage was achieved and as progressive political forces were repressed after World War I, sexuality was among the many issues stripped of political content.[13] What were once causes based on justice and equality, especially gender and sexuality concerns, became neuroses among the middle classes and delinquencies among the poor.[14]

The legacy of silence of this generation of feminists was a relatively unchallenged redefinition of womanhood that became entrenched during the national crises of the Depression and world war. While that definition in and of itself was problematic, how it was used as a mechanism of social control sheds light on the sexual and gender systems the second cohort faced. Though not every step from theory to hegemony is covered, an expanded connection between nonconforming gender behavior and "deviant" sexuality emerges in the stories of the midcentury cohort.

Economics and sexuality are linked, and our racial history contributes an additional basis for divisions among us. While the limited ideological definitions of women gave psychological pressure to keep them in heterosexual relationships and marginalize resisters in their own minds as well as that of the public, it also was a useful tool to justify labor force segregation and stratification on the basis of gender and the low wages of women's work. As long as women do not develop an analysis that links sexuality with economics, class, and race, we will remain divided in other areas where these forces intersect as well—issues involving prostitution and other sex works, state-funded abortions, welfare, and other programs for poor single mothers.

These stories begin to fill the gaps in and between lesbian and women's history. "Romantic friendship" emerges as an inadequate phrase for describing the worlds and lives built by turn-of-the-century women. Within this small study I have found a diversity of families, some with children and many extended through kin and social networks. As their historians, we need to resist reducing their lives to find commonalities, or relying on simple oppositions based on class or race.

This group of contemporary lesbians inhabits some of the historical space between the stereotypes developed by sexologists and social control agents and the bolder lesbians who fought for lesbian love and space at the cost of social respectability, economic stability, and upward mobility. These cautious lesbians, whose lives were at odds with the choices presented to them as women and lesbians, still shared with their generation a sense of rights and entitlement to personal happiness. They didn't buy the self-denial and dependency which was being sold to the women of their era, nor the deviance-based lesbian identity that had become part of the popular culture.

Communities of women and social movements were essential supports and vehicles for each group's challenges. With a political analysis, though severely limited at times, of their situations and the social and cultural space in which to live either women-centered or lesbians lives, both generations constructed innovative partnerships and families. With many others of their eras, they struggled to create alternatives out of the contradictions this culture presented to women.

These women's lives are two more pieces of women's history, lesbian history, and the history of sexuality. Together they argue that the complexities of women's lives cannot be separated out and filed in discreet folders marked sexuality or economics, private or public, race or gender. Together they argue that our struggles for economic independence and sexual self-definition are intertwined, treacherous, and joyful; that they are not linear progressions; and that we need individual and community efforts to deal with our differences. In our postmodern, capitalist, male-dominated culture, we must fight for and control our own words and desires, our own bodies, and our money.

On Methodology

In this book I analyze the lives, from childhood through adulthood, of two particular groups of "independent" women: Progressive Era spinsters and contemporary never-married lesbians. For this study, I define "independent" as without economic, legal, or sexual/affectional ties to an individual male. While controlling for the economic and legal ties is a rather straightforward process, determining the sexual/affectional ties is more difficult. While women of both generations had some affectional ties to some men, and at least some of the contemporary women had been involved with men sexually, no women of either group constructed significant portions of her adult life around a male partner. With this working definition of independent women, I sought out my subjects.

Subjects

Spinsters

The fifteen women in the Progressive Era group are never-married women who led women-centered lives. They were not randomly chosen. In any historical research, you are led by your sources. In this case these women were chosen because they left accessible diaries, private papers, or other first-person material that contained some level of self-reflection.[1]

All fifteen of these women are Euro-Americans, eleven from the middle or elite classes and four from the working class.[2] Among the latter are two women who emigrated to the United States early in their lives, including one who was Jewish.

These are not "typical" women; generally they were economically privileged and highly educated. They shared the privilege of race. Most were leaders and prominent women of their generation. The working-class women were from more typical economic situations, therefore their achievements must be seen as even more noteworthy. That a number of these women had female partners is not surprising, but the number who raised children is.

Though these women did not claim lesbian identities, some historians have placed them in lesbian history (Cook 1979; Rich 1980; Smith-Rosenberg 1985). While this is certainly not an uncontested placement, these intimate and affectionate partnerships among middle-class women, termed "romantic friendships" or "Boston Marriages," are frequently juxtaposed with "passing women," the mostly working-class women who assumed male identities for economic reasons and/or to marry other women (Katz 1976). More recent research identifies early working-class communities and African American performers, who, along with the other groups, formed the basis of modern lesbian identities in the United States (Faderman 1991; Vicinus 1992; Nestle 1993; Kennedy and Davis 1993).

A number of these Progressive Era women have already become visible to us through U.S. women's history's focus on this time period, a focus certainly justified by women's prominent and changing roles at the turn of the century. However, they have not been viewed through the particular lens of a shared single state.[3] They also did not leave us clear specifics of their sexual/affectional lives. While a few, such as Alice Hamilton, claimed the societally endorsed option of celibacy, most were silent on sexuality. It is primarily through contemporaneous social science research that we have any sense of what their sexual lives might have been (Davis 1929).

Lesbians

The contemporary group consists of fifteen women who never married, identify themselves as lesbians, and grew up in the post-World War II era. At the time of the interview (1987–88), all lived in central New Mexico. Women were recruited for this part of the study through personal networks and lesbian community events.

In contrast to the earlier group, these women are from a greater diversity of class, race, and regional backgrounds. My original intent was to reflect, in this sample, the local population according to race, class, and region of origin, but this was not possible. Only two Chicanas and two African American women were willing to be included. One woman of Native American descent is part of this sample, but she was not raised within that heritage and her identification is Anglo. While there is a diversity of class and regional backgrounds, the racial representation is hardly more than token. The women most willing to be interviewed were those lesbians who knew me, trusted me, and shared many demographic characteristics with me. They were, therefore, Euro-American and non-New Mexico women.[4] These lesbians are survivors as well as resisters, in that they were willing to be interviewed and portrayed themselves as relatively successful and well adjusted.

The two groups of women are not perfectly comparable sets. I could make no precise matches, given the historical distance between them, the changes in sexual and gender norms, and the

varying positions of never-married women in our present culture. Furthermore, work options and educational opportunities
had changed significantly. The choice to limit the second group
to self-identified lesbians was an effort to avoid the types of
sexual silences Simon (1987) encountered among single women
who did not claim lesbian identities. Given the nature of my
research, it was important to be able to discuss women's sexual
choices when possible.

Another issue is the disparity of personal prominence between the two groups. While not all of the turn-of-the-century
women had national reputations, many of them did. As noted,
none of the contemporary lesbians included in this study has yet
gained such recognition. It is harder to locate private, personal
documents from "average" turn-of-the-century women just as it
is harder to gather oral history interviews of nationally known,
never-married lesbians born before 1951. As stated above,
sources guide our research. Because I was exploring unknown
territory, it was important to proceed with the best options
possible. With these findings, it is now possible to identify more
parallel samples for future studies.

Methods and Sources

In women's history and feminist research generally, scholars
have been concerned with the idea of placing women at the
center of the analysis, recognizing female subjectivity and
agency. Listening to women's voices either though oral histories
or their writings supports these goals (Smith-Rosenberg 1985;
Scott 1988). Nevertheless, all sources have their limitations. As
stated above, for the turn-of the-century women, I used private
papers and autobiogrpahical material. How women have chosen
to present themselves in their autobiographical writings reflects
not only the individual woman, but also her historical period
and her particular role within that era. Estelle C. Jelinek (1980,

1986) notes, for example, how Elizabeth Cady Stanton worked to present herself as an "average" woman in her autobiography. Jelinek analyzed this tactic as a political strategy on the part of Stanton to make her ideas on women's emancipation more palatable to the general public. Since I was looking at women who led somewhat exceptional lives, I had to consider the extent to which such women minimalized differences between themselves and their more traditional contemporaries. I had to consider if this perspective would be evident even if the materials studied were not written for publication.

The research method I used with the contemporary women was the oral history interview. Some similar and some unique issues are involved in oral histories, when compared to archival research. While little of the growing literature on oral history research focuses on the specific issues of lesbian research, feminists have made oral history central to their scholarship in many areas. The most extensive feminist discussion on oral history research and the overlapping method of enthographic interviews address situations in which various cultural, linguistic, and related status differences exist between the interviewer and the interviewee, and which are termed "insider/outsider" issues. Certain of the issues raised by other oral historians are important here. As discussed above, in the course of my research it became clear that only women who already trusted me and considered me an insider to their community agreed to participate. Several of these women had already participated in my research on the Albuquerque Lesbian Community (Franzen 1993) or on another smaller research project on women activists. Nevertheless, as a researcher I cannot assess how comfortable the women who participated in this research felt. The quality of the interviews is a result of what Elizabeth A. Meese (1985) calls a "collaborative event." What is produced, in her words, is both "a dialogue between them [the researcher and the informant] and . . . the dialogue between the informant and her own historical and cultural consciousness." This research is certainly a product of both types of dialogue.[5]

Records of the real lives, the whole lives of lesbians in the United States—studies that look at more than sexual choices and identities—are few, with our greatest resources still found in autobiographical writings and fiction.[6] Research is needed that centers on lesbian lives in their diversity and in their contexts. Because little research has been done on how sexuality systems function in individuals' lives, I had no guidelines to pinpoint specific factors or life stages as critical points for the influence of gender and sexuality norms. I therefore needed to hear these women's lives in their entirety to see continuities and changes in both what they did and how they perceived themselves. I also wanted to allow them the opportunity to introduce issues and describe processes they deemed important in their lives, an option that might be lost in an interview structured around predetermined topics.

This qualitative study of never-married turn-of-the-century women and contemporary lesbians is a pilot project. The method was designed to allow these women to speak for themselves and define their own issues, placing them at the center, so to speak. What these women have done and the rhetoric they used in describing their choices provide their own analyses of their lives, a glimpse into the consciousnesses of certain women who made nontraditional choices, and show us how the gender and sexuality systems of their lives functioned. Though one must be careful not to generalize from a small study, the stories of their lives, the questions these women pose, and the choices they made contribute more pieces to our dynamic and expanding scholarship.

Appendix

Tables

TABLE I.

Backgrounds of Turn-of-the-Century Women

DOB	Name	Hometown	Class
1867	Edith Hamilton	Ft. Wayne, IN	Upper
1869	Alice Hamilton	Ft. Wayne, IN	Upper
1870	Leonora O'Reilly	New York, NY	Working
1873	Mary Anderson	Chicago, IL	Working
1873	Sara "Jo" Baker	Poughkeepsie, NY	Middle
1873	Frances Kellor	Coldwater, MI	Working
1874	Molly Dewson	Quincy, MA	Middle
1875	Mary E. Dreier	New York, NY	Upper
1876	Mary E. Arnold	Sommerville, MA	Middle
1883	Connie Guion	Lincoln, NC	Middle
1887	Lura Beam	Marshfield, ME	Middle
1888	Edith Stedman	Cambridge, MA	Middle
1889	Frieda Miller	La Crosse, WI	Upper
1890	Pauline Newman	New York, NY	Working
1891	Martha May Eliot	Dorchester,MA	Middle

TABLE 2.
Backgrounds of Contemporary Lesbians

DOB	Name	Region	Race	Class
1936	Audrey Streig	Northeast	Euro-A	Upper
1936	Jo Martinez	New Mexico	Chicana	Working/Middle
1938	Jamie Henson	Northeast	Euro-A	Working
1941	Bobbi Denova	Northeast	Euro-A	Working
1943	Jean Labov	Northeast	Euro-A/J	Working
1943	Carrie Stern	New Mexico	Euro-A	Upper
1944	Paula Mitchell	Midwest	Euro-A	Middle
1945	Anne McConnell	South	Euro-A	Middle
1946	Amy Adams	West	Euro-A	Middle
1947	Gloria Whelan	Northeast	Euro-A	Working
1947	Robin Edwards	New Mexico	Euro-A	Working/Middle
1948	Yolanda Peña	New Mexico	Chicana	Working
1949	Trudy Hardin	Northeast	African-A	Working
1949	Lee Powell	South	African-A	Working
1951	Iris Miller	South	Euro-A/NA	Middle

TABLE 3.
Educations of Turn-of-the-Century Women

Name	Degree	Year	School	Field
Anderson				
Arnold			Drexel	Business
			Cornell	Agriculture
			Berkeley	
Baker	M.D.	1898	N.Y. Infirmary	Medicine
	Ph.D.	1917	NYU/Bellevue	Public Health
Beam	B.A.	1908	Barnard	
	M.A.	1917	Columbia	Education
Dewson	A.B.	1897	Wellesley	Economics
Dreier			School of Philanthropy	
Eliot	A.B.	1913	Radcliffe	
	M.D.	1918	Johns Hopkins	Medicine
Guion	B.A.	1906	Wellesley	Chemistry
	M.A.	1913	Cornell	Chemistry
	M.D.	1917	Cornell	Medicine

Name	Degree	Year	School	Field
A. Hamilton	M.D.	1893	Michigan	Medicine
		1896	Germany	
		1897	J. Hopkins	Pathology
E. Hamilton	A.B.	1892	Bryn Mawr	Classics
	A.M.	1894	Bryn Mawr	Classics
Kellor	LL.B	1897	Cornell	Law
			Chicago	Sociology
Miller	A.B.	1911	Milwaukee Downer	Liberal Arts
			Chicago	Economics
Newman			Socialist Literary Society	
O'Reilly	Cert.	1900	Pratt Institute	Domestic Arts
Stedman	B.A.	1910	Radcliffe	

TABLE 4.

Selected Professions of Turn-of-the-Century Women

Name	Work
Mary Anderson	Bootmaker
	Labor Leader
	Director, Women's Bureau
Mary Ellicott Arnold	Cafeteria Director
	Indian Matron
	Cooperative Administrator
Sara "Jo" Baker	Medical Doctor
	Director, N.Y. Dept. of Child Hygiene
Lura Beam	Educator
	Researcher
	Writer
Molly Dewson	Social Worker
	Farmer
	Political Leader
Mary Elisabeth Dreier	Labor Leader
Martha May Eliot	Medical Professor
	Director, Children's Bureau

TABLE 4. (*Continued*)

Name	Work
Connie Guion	Professor Medical/Clinical
Alice Hamilton	Professor Industrial Medicine Investigator
Edith Hamilton	Professor Educator/Administrator Classicist
Frances Kellor	Social Worker Researcher Arbitration Administrator
Frieda Segelke Miller	Labor Leader Director, Women's Bureau
Pauline Newman	Garment Worker Labor Leader
Leonora O'Reilly	Labor Leader Teacher
Edith Stedman	Social Worker Educational Administrator

TABLE 5.
Educations of Contemporary Lesbians

Name	Degree	Major	School
Audrey Streig	B.A.	Sociology	Private
	M.S.W.	Social Work	Private
Jo Martinez	B.A.	Education	Public
	M.A.	Education	Public
Jamie Henson	R.N.	Nursing	Private
	CERT.	Professional	Private
Bobbi Denova	R.N.	Nursing	Private
	CERT.	Professional	Public
Jean Labov	B.A.	English	Public
	CERT.	Paraprofessional	Public
Carrie Stern	B.A.	Religion	Private
Paula Mitchell	B.A.	Education	Public
	M.A.	Education	Public
Anne McConnell	B.A.	English	Private
	M.A.	Counseling	Public

Name	Degree	Major	School
Amy Adams	B.A.	Religion	Private
	M.A.	Education	Private
	C.P.A.	Accounting	Public
Gloria Whelan	B.A.	Education	Public
	M.A.	Education	Public
	Ph.D.	Education	Public
Robin Edwards	B.A.	Education	Public
Yolanda Peña	TECH.	Drafting	Public
	B.A.	Psychology	Public
Trudy Hardin	B.A.	English	Private
Lee Powell	B.A.	Arts	Private
	M.A.	Counseling	Public
Iris Miller			

TABLE 6.
Selected Professions of Contemporary Lesbians

Name	Work
Audrey Streig	Social Worker
	Rancher
	Sales
Jo Martinez	Teacher
	Educational Administrator
Jamie Henson	Nurse
	Health Care Professional
Bobbi Denova	Nurse
	Health Care Professional
Jean Labov	Social Services
	Teacher
	Para-Professional
Carrie Stern	Teacher
	Business Owner
	Sales
Paula Mitchell	Teacher
	Business
Anne McConnell	Educational Administrator
	Business Owner
	Writer
Amy Adams	Teacher
	Business Owner
	Accountant
Gloria Whelan	Teacher
	Educator

TABLE 6. (*Continued*)

Name	Work
Robin Edwards	Teacher
Yolanda Pena	Drafter
	Social Worker
Trudy Hardin	Teacher
	Planner
Lee Powell	Artist Educational Administrator
	Counselor
Iris Miller	Business

TABLE 7.
Ages When Partnerships Formed

1892	Mary Ellicott Arnold	16	Mabel Reed	17
1900	S. Josephine Baker	27	Florence Laighton	na
1911	Molly Dewson	37	Polly Porter	27
1905	M. Elisabeth Dreier	30	Frances Kellor	32
1918	Martha May Eliot	27	Ethel Durham	26
1919	Edith Hamilton	52	Doris Reid	24
1919	Frieda Miller	30	Pauline Newman	29

Notes

Notes to List of Progressive Era Spinsters

1. An "Indian Matron" was a woman working on American Indian reservations around the turn of the century. Her work was similar to the Americanization work carried out among immigrants: basic education, housekeeping, and cooking classes for the females. Mary Ellicott Arnold and Mabel Reed worked among the Klamath people in northern California. They described those years in *In the Land of the Grasshopper Song: The Story of Two Girls in Indian Country, 1908–09* (1957).

2. Pauline Newman's birth records were lost during immigration and she simply claimed an approximate date and year of birth.

Notes to the Introduction

1. Both Morantz-Sanchez (1985) and Gordon (1994) wrote excellent books in U.S. women's history and are among the best for including never-married women. Both acknowledge the importance and contributions of never-married women. Nevertheless, Morantz-Sanchez depicts her never-married women doctors as anachronisms once they were able to more easily have careers and marry. Implicitly, married is the preferred status for all women. Gordon presents a more complex

analysis but flattens all of the never-married women in the social welfare network she studied into socially conservative spinsters. I suspect that with more scholarly attention, regional and generational differences will emerge to produce a greater diversity of lifestyles and perspectives among always-single women.

2. The earliest of the contemporary feminists who theorized lesbianism shared an analysis of this sexual identity as involving economic, social/familial, as well as sexual challenges to systems of male dominance. See, for example, Radicalesbians 1971; Myron and Bunch 1975; Bunch 1975; Small 1975; Rubin 1975; and Valeska, 1981. Over the past two decades this discussion has expanded with the introduction of the terms, "homosocial," "romantic friendships," and "lesbian continuum"; with the lessons from academic and community-based sexuality debates; through more open discussions of intimate behaviors; and in studies of the diversity of lesbian history. Scholars and activists in this emerging field have broadly explored the centrality of sex, sexual desire, and sexual acts in the definitions, history, and identities of lesbians (Smith-Rosenberg 1975, 1985; Faderman 1978, 1981, 1984; Rich 1980; Ferguson, Zita, and Addelson 1981; Freedman 1984; Bullough and Bullough 1977; Simmons 1979; Katz 1976, 1983; Newton 1984; Nestle 1987; Rubin 1984; Kennedy and Davis 1993). This focus was argued as a necessary corrective by those who protested against a desexualizing of lesbian life, a continuing cultural taboo against female-defined sexual discourse, and an overemphasis on the lives of privileged, literate women. While these contributions and discussions have driven us to articulate fuller, clearer, yet more complex analyses of the variety of lesbian experiences and histories, the field of lesbian studies still has many unexplored areas. Sexual behavior does not function in a vacuum. We need to expand those studies which investigate what conditions must exist for us to act on our desires, what prices we pay when we do, and how such conditions and consequences have changed. We have much work to do, but, as Martha Vicinus (1992) has reminded us, lesbian history is still in its infancy and still suspect.

3. The two most important studies of independent women remain Vicinus's (1985) study of the first and second generation of independent, professional women in England, and Chambers-Schiller's (1984) *Liberty, A Better Husband,* a study of earlier generations of U.S. women.

4. See, for example, Sochen 1972; Freedman 1983; Newton 1984; and Smith-Rosenberg 1985 for discussions of "new women."

5. Meyerowitz (1988) provides the most complete study of single working-class women.

The limited scholarship on never-married turn-of-the-century women is white centered. It makes sense that it was a combination of race and class privilege which allowed most of these women to become self-supporting at a level of reasonable comfort, but we need also to consider if race-bound norms forced more white women to have to choose between work and family. African American women, married or not married, always worked at higher rates than white women (Jones 1985; Matthaei 1982). We are only beginning to hear the voices of never-married women of color, which may reveal a very different history. One of the recent best-selling nonfiction books, *Having Our Say: The Delany Sisters' First 100 Years,* is the story of never-married African American sisters close to the age of the youngest of this sample (Delany and Delany 1993). Gordon (1994) has identified a number of politically active, never-married African American women. Angelina Grimke's life deserves a fuller analysis.

6. It is important to note that there were also high proportions of never-married men. From census data, 1890–1920, men have had a consistently higher never-married rate than women, reflecting more men in the population than women. Throughout these years there are few regional cohorts in which there were more women than men. The northeastern states generally reported more women than men. For cohorts born after 1905, there were more women than men in the southern states. Ryan (1979) specifies the cohort born between 1865 and 1874 as the least marrying one. The reasons behind this are not clear. Chambers-Schiller (1984) suggests that there was a shortage of men, especially in the northeastern states, while Evans (1989) proposes that the depression of 1893–94 may have left many men without the economic prerequisites for marriage.

7. "Race suicide" was a term used by those distressed over the low birthrate of native-born, privileged, white women during this period, 1890–1920, especially when compared to the birth rates of immigrant women and African Americans. Male leaders were convinced that those of northern European descent would become the minority if "Yankee" women did not begin to have larger families (D'Emilio and Freedman 1988).

Notes to Chapter One

1. In none of the sources on these women have I found any of them claiming a lesbian identity or any equivalent term. So, officially they did not take on the identity or the stigma, but, as I will argue later, they may have internalized or struggled with their sexual/affectional choices as discussions of women's sexuality became more commonplace (Katz 1976; Vicinus 1992).

2. While "exceptional" women such as Elizabeth Cady Stanton may have "normalized" themselves in their autobiographies for political reasons, Jo Baker's position as one of those suspect "new women" suggests another use for this autobiographical frame (Jelinek 1980, 1986).

3. "Sex variant" is most often used sympathetically by those who urge either acceptance or therapeutic treatment of nonheterosexuals, and was used mostly by those studying or treating middle-class individuals (Terry 1990). The term "sex deviant" is most often used to label the poor or people of color by those who focused on the criminal aspect of nonconforming sexual behavior (Lunbeck 1987; Penn 1994).

4. West and Petrik's recent anthology, Small Worlds (1992) contains some of the best of the new research in this area. As with any developing area of scholarship, the beginning works focus more on building an overview. This anthology does begin to address issues of racial, class, and gender differences. Rosenzweig (1993) is an important addition to this scholarship.

5. Davis's sample included more never-married women (1,200) than married women (1,000). All her never-married women were college graduates. Davis sent requests for participation in this study to women who were on women's organizations' mailing lists. She very much wanted to have sexual information on "respectable" women (Davis 1929; Fitzpatrick 1990).

Notes to Chapter Two

1. See for example, May 1988; Ehrenreich 1989; Breines 1992; Crawford, Rouse, and Woods 1990; Halberstam 1993; Harvey 1993; Douglas 1994; and Meyerowitz 1994.

2. One of the questions to consider is if single, never-married

women could achieve national leadership positions during the post-World War II era. Very few powerful women were found in state or national politics. Margaret Mead was the best-known woman academic. Eleanor Roosevelt maintained an active life and high profile until her death. Both Mead and Roosevelt had earned their reputations for their own work, but both had been married. See Kaledin 1984; Meyerowitz 1994.

3. Issues of childhood traumas, including physical and sexual abuse, were not originally included in the oral history topics I developed. Among the first women I interviewed was a woman who had "come out" as an incest survivor in the Albuquerque community. I am grateful to this individual. If she had not been willing to speak publicly about her abuse I might not have added the space in my interviews for discussions of these taboo topics. After that interview I asked the informants if there had been any childhood traumas. To my introduction of the interviewing process I added the statement that my participants could refuse to answer any questions they chose, no questions asked.

4. The long-term effects of sexual abuse are not yet understood, nor are these findings integrated into theories of women's development. Judith Hermann (1981) posits that incest in childhood produces isolation especially from other women, low self-esteem, a sense of great sexual power over men, depression, and difficulties in forming trusting and loving relationships. Hermann's conclusions must be qualified because her small, all-Anglo sample was drawn totally from survivors currently in or seeking therapy.

5. Terry (1990) discusses how one of the recommendations George Henry made after his 1930s study of lesbians and gay men was for parents to monitor for gender-appropriate behavior, specifically mentioning that young women should be well practiced in domestic skills and boys in mechanics. He argued that enforcing these behaviors and removing taboos around heterosexual activities would prevent "sex variants." It would be interesting to study if this message was widely disseminated during the 1940s and 1950s.

6. Martha Vicinus (1992) uses a very similar quote from Rosa Bonheur in her article on the roots of modern lesbian identities.

7. Sarah Deutsch's study (1987) argues that Chicanas in the Southwest used the land as their economic base and source of autonomy once men began to leave the land for waged work.

8. There may be a difference in consciousness of lesbians between

the women raised in small towns and the women raised in urban areas such as New York City. Both Audrey and Jean knew about lesbians as teenagers, while others like Robin and Jamie didn't. Again, knowing about lesbians appears to be connected to living near a lesbian community.

Of course, another interpretation of this question is what do you do sexually with your attraction to women. Such ignorance would be less surprising if it were known that lesbians even today are less vocal about explicit sexual activities. See, for example, Loulan 1990; Frye 1990.

Notes to Chapter Three

1. This is the beginning of a longer quote from Leonora O'Reilly in which she responds in her diary to the news of "three marriages in the Socialist ranks" (O'Reilly Papers SL).

2. The Bryn Mawr Summer School for Women Workers was a special program arranged between this college, situated outside of Philadelphia, and women active in the labor movement. It started in 1921 and continued at different locations through the 1930s (Schneiderman and Goldwaite 1967; Evans 1989).

3. Most of the founders of women's colleges supported the idea that women needed a separate and "female" education. Alice Freeman Palmer, an early president of Wellesley College, was one of the best-known women supporting this position, while M. Carey Thomas was the most vocal of those believing that women deserved an education equal to that available to men. See Wein 1974; Frankfort 1977; Horowitz 1984; Dobkin 1979; Palmer 1908.

4. These early private women's colleges, all of which were located in the Northeast, are Barnard, Bryn Mawr, Radcliffe, Mt. Holyoke, Smith, Vassar, and Wellesley. A wonderful discussion of their foundings can be found in Horowitz 1984.

5. Smith-Rosenberg (1985) characterizes all the "new women" as having contested relationships with their mothers, such as M. Carey Thomas and Anna Howard Shaw did. This research suggests that the second generation of new women may have had fewer tensions with their mothers for two reasons. First, the childhoods of this second generation of women were during some very difficult times economically, and this may have changed their parents' views of their daughters' efforts for self-support. Furthermore, as the second generation,

they and their mothers may have had a set of female role models to emulate. Rosenzweig (1993) found similar relationships among the middle-class nineteenth-century women she studied.

6. These women's medical schools flourished during a period of significant flux in medical training in the United States. Few survived the formalization of medical training except for the Women's Medical College of Pennsylvania. The Woman's Medical College of New York Infirmary was founded in 1868 by sisters Elizabeth and Emily Blackwell. The New England Hospital for Women and Children was led by Marie Zakrzewska. See Morantz-Sanchez 1985; Moldow 1987; and Drachman 1984.

7. Morantz-Sanchez (1985) argues that this struggle as well as Alice Hamilton's treatment by Harvard foreshadowed women's marginalization in the fields they had founded and developed. This type of gender imperialism argues for the continuation of women-only institutions.

8. Sicherman (1984) suggests that none of the Hamilton cousins thought much of marriage in part because the Hamilton men were "difficult and demanding and did not encourage a high regard for their sex." Consequently, marriage was not a promising option for these independent and intellectual young women.

On the other side, the image of the gold digger who used her sexuality for money was a twentieth-century creation. See Meyerowitz 1988.

9. The "family claim" describes the nineteenth-century expectation that females had loyalty and duty toward their family of birth.

10. Alice Hamilton wrote of being pushed off sidewalks and lifted out of her seat at the opera. While she enjoyed the camaraderie in some of the laboratories, she was also barred from other facilities and procedures because of her sex. See Sicherman 1984.

11. See, for example, Frankfort 1977; Kessler-Harris 1982; Sahli 1979; Faderman 1978; and Simmons 1979.

12. While Frances Kellor came from a poor family, her education brought her into social welfare work via the middle-class path, one not open to the other women from working-class backgrounds.

13. Among these women, only Mary Elisabeth Dreier clearly never needed to work. While some references suggest that Frieda Miller inherited a significant sum of money, it is not clear if this amount would have been sufficient to live on for a lifetime. See Payne 1988; Montgomery 1980.

14. This is another point at which the second generation had

greater opportunities than the first. They knew they were going to work—the question was where. The first generation did not know what they could do after their education ended.

15. Geraldine Clifford (1989), in her study of women in coeducational institutions, did find women who achieved their positions through family connections. None of the women in this group appear to have benefited from family connections in their efforts. This may have been a deliberate decision to distance themselves from their birth families.

16. As discussed, while Frances Kellor's background was also working-class/poor, her path to independence was a unique combination of factors. Mary Elisabeth Dreier, her life partner, wrote after Kellor's death that Kellor had worked all her life without a salary. It makes sense that Dreier supported her. See O'Connell 1980; Filler 1977; Wooley 1903; and Fitzpatrick 1990.

17. The success and difficulties involved in the Women's Trade Union League's efforts to bridge class differences among women is discussed in Dye 1980. For a contemporaneous discussion, see Henry 1915.

18. Moldow (1987) provides the fullest discussion of the problems faced by African American women doctors. Hine (1989) gives a complementary description from her focus on African American nurses.

19. One of the issues I have not explored is sibling support or rivalry. Stedman's brother was not the only brother trying to control his sister (Stedman Papers SL). Pauline Newman's brother tried to bribe her to abandon her politics (Newman Papers SL).

20. Gordon (1991) found that African American welfare leaders demonstrated less classism in their welfare work than the Euro-American leaders. She also argues that African American women were more likely to accept that mothers worked and provide support in the form of day nurseries, while Euro-American women developed policies which assumed that mothers would not work.

21. Alice Hamilton appeared to have developed a class-based strategy, or she felt she did. Her method was to act the "lady." Hamilton was something of a class snob. While a medical student she felt superior to the other women medical students whom she referred to as "micky," a negative term for the Irish, and she was concerned that the faculty wives did not understand and appreciate her class background. See Sicherman 1984.

22. Smith-Rosenberg (1985) argues that Krafft-Ebbing linked "in-

version," cross-dressing, and feminist demands, while Havelock Ellis separated issues of personal appearance from sexual preference.

23. Leonora O'Reilly lived with her mother and they shared child-care responsibilities (O'Reilly Papers SL). Edith Hamilton and Doris Reid both assumed responsibilities for Reid's nieces and nephews, though Edith was in the home more than Doris (Reid 1967). Frieda Miller was the legal parent of Elisabeth. Though Pauline and Frieda were lifelong companions, both of them worked. It is unclear what their child-care arrangements were (Newman Papers SL).

24. Katherine Susan Anthony and Elisabeth Irwin, a lesbian couple who were both members of the Greenwich Village Heterodoxy Club, also raised several children. See Schwarz 1986.

25. Davis found that about one-third of the unmarried women in her study had no regrets, and a smaller number stated that they would never marry under any circumstances. "These one hundred and ninety-seven women include those who are in ill-health, most but not all of the women over fifty, some of those who have family obligations, some but not all of the homosexuals, and all those who dislike marriage as an institution" (Davis 1929).

26. On the idea that the major barriers to women's emancipation had been dismantled, see, for example, Irwin 1934; Breckinridge 1972; and Roosevelt 1933.

Notes to Chapter Four

1. Just as some women have stories about fathers and playing catch, several of the women say that their mothers rescued them from sewing, making their "home ec" aprons for them. They shared a hatred of this activity and were determinedly incompetent. Jo, an excellent student, failed "home ec." It seemed these young women could not help but reject this required girls-only class.

2. Barbara Solomon (1985) argued that women were deliberately made to feel out of place on campuses, especially in graduate and professional schools, as veterans supported by the G.I. Bill swept onto campus in record numbers. The 1950s were the low point for women in education and the professions. Women's numbers began to rise again only after the biggest influx of veterans left after 1956. The National Defense Education Act was passed in 1958 and somewhat equalized support for education.

3. In 1940, 77,000 women represented 41 percent of the students in higher education, while in 1950, 103,000 women students were only 24 percent. The most impressive numerical rise for women occurred between 1960 and 1970. In 1960, 136,000 women earned B.A. degrees, while in 1970, 343,000 did. During this same period the number of women earning both master's and doctorate degrees (or the equivalent) tripled (Department of Education 1981).

4. Newcomer's statistics appear to contradict Mira Komarovsky's (1964) conclusion that working-class families considered "college education for daughters . . . to be a dispensable luxury." Nevertheless, at all economic levels, fewer women than men were going to college in 1967. Among African Americans, more women than men attended college. This is a long-term trend, which was ending in 1967 (Carnegie Commission 1973).

5. By the end of the 1920s, 69 percent of the postsecondary educational institutions were coeducational. With women's colleges, this added up to 1,124 institutions open to women. As a percentage of students, women peaked at 47.3 percent in 1920. Horowitz (1984) argues that women's need for a different education gained support during this period and many schools began consciously to prepare women to be homemakers. New women's colleges, such as Sarah Lawrence, Bennington, and Scripps, were founded and financially backed by women and men who supported traditionally female interests in the arts, homemaking, and early-childhood education. See Solomon 1985; Newcomer 1959; and Brown 1987.

6. See, for example, Fox 1989; Theberge 1989; Association of American Colleges 1982; Frazier and Sadker 1973; and Stacey, Bereaud, and Daniels 1974.

7. In seven years this dropped to 10 percent (Carnegie Commission 1973).

8. Two of the other women who went into Physical Education made similar statements about this career path being the only way they could continue to "play." At first consideration this seemed to be an expression of not wanting to grow up. Through further discussion, these women clarified that they wanted to keep organized athletic activities in their lives. They had not seen any models of this in their childhoods except among their gym teachers.

Though women had carved a niche for themselves in anthropology since the turn of the century, they were usually in ethnology. Archeology remained a male-dominated and defined sub-field. In this area, Ellis was a pioneer. She was the only woman interviewed for the "Daughters of the Desert" project who felt she had been discriminated against on the basis of her gender (personal communication with Louise Lamphere; Babcock and Parezo 1988; Linda Cordell, unpublished manuscript).

9. Discussions of the continuation of this message can be found in Van Horn 1988 and Margolis 1984.

10. Audrey Streig was born and raised in New York City, but when her father retired the family moved back to their home state of Wisconsin.

Notes to Chapter Five

1. This is a strong characterization of single women to come from a leading feminist such as Charlotte Perkins Gilman. It speaks, in part, of some of the splits that would divide feminists between those who believed women were different and saw mothering as their destiny, and women who didn't share this view. See Rosenberg 1982.

2. Molly Dewson, for example, was asked by Frances Perkins to stand in as her family at FDR's inauguration (Ware 1987). For a fuller discussion of these communities and relationships, see Freedman 1979; Sklar 1985; and Cook 1979.

3. Schneiderman continued with the WTUL until its demise in the 1950s, while Newman returned to the ILGWU and was the long-time educational director of its health clinic. See Dye 1980; Schneiderman and Goldwaite 1967; and James 1981.

4. Morantz-Sanchez (1985) notes that Hamilton kept a distance from the Medical Women's National Association and did not take a particular interest in women physicians as a group. It appears as more than just a question of time and priorities. Alice Hamilton, though a modern scientist and individualist, often seemed like a nineteenth-century upper-class "lady." This is very different from Connie Guion; though she also attended a coeducational medical school, she was very much a supporter of women in medicine.

5. While I develop this idea further in my conclusion, I began considering these questions after reading Linda Gordon's (1991) work on women welfare activists. These single, Euro-American women were suspect on the basis of their unmarried state, sexuality, and their relationships with other women, which may have pushed them to promote

a defensively conservative position on issues such as working mothers and single mothers.

6. A significant subgroup of women leaders and pioneers were being publicly discredited in subtle and not so subtle ways, which had an impact on women's positions in all the professions. Nevertheless, many studies treat women's choices to be single or to partner with other women as personal choices only. See, for example, Morantz-Sanchez 1985. While Ware (1987) begins to connect Dewson's public and personal lives, she does not fully explore how her class, race, and sexuality influenced the policies she supported. The same is true in Fitzpatrick's (1990) discussion of Frances Kellor's career.

7. "Companionate marriage" was a term introduced by Ben Lindsey and Wainwright Evans (1927). They advocated a strong emotional bond between husband and wife in which sexual intimacy played an important role. See Fass 1977; Gordon 1976; Simmons 1979; Epstein 1983. While this became the new ideal, as always, theory does not translate easily to practice. Both Margaret Dreier Robins and Lucy Sprague Mitchell continued to have full extradomestic lives after their marriages, yet both were owning-class women of independent wealth. They were able to continue their work because of their economic situation. Both women, nevertheless, relocated to accommodate their husbands' careers. Both husbands demanded great emotional support from their wives. See Antler 1987 and Payne 1988. Marie Jenny Howe, a Unitarian minister, an important activist for suffrage and founder of Heterodoxy, did not have a career (Schwarz 1986). Even among the radicals of Greenwich Village, marriage most often led to a traditional economic arrangement with men as the primary breadwinners, leaving women with the domestic responsibilities.

8. But would these women be given credit as role models? One of the tenets of social and feminist history is to analyze the influence that "marginalized" groups have on the construction of hegemonic models. Often innovations that originate among those outside the power structure are only recognized when a more powerful and respectable source claims them. Feminist scholarship is not immune from this process either. Though we continue to give lip service to the connection between theory and practice, we do not have an adequate means for acknowledging the insights gained from practice or from activists.

9. It was only after she officially retired that Edith Hamilton began the work for which she is best known—her works on classical Greece and Rome. This second career allowed her to remain at home. See Reid 1967.

10. An interesting contrast is seen when Baker's (1939) and Anderson's (1951) published autobiographies are compared to Stedman's unpublished autobiography (Stedman Papers SL). The two published works hardly mention personal/private issues at all, while Stedman goes into detail on these. Stedman had tried unsuccessfully to publish her book. The question remains if the women who were published chose not to include discussions of their private lives, or if they were advised to limit themselves to their public activities.

11. Smith-Rosenberg (1985) reports that Jane Addams and Crystal Eastman differed over issues of sexuality and sexual freedom. This may be another difference between the first and second generations of new women, just as it may involve class, race, and area of domicile. Addams was born in 1860 and was a Euro-American, upper-class midwesterner. Eastman, also white and privileged, was twenty-one years her junior and lived mostly in the New York City area.

12. This weapon was what seems to have been available to U.S. women. Smith-Rosenberg (1985) does not cite any American women at this time who developed an alternative sexual language in their writings as Barnes and Woolf did. If there was as great a difference between male views of transgressive sexuality and female views, the social science methods of the time would have been inadequate to conceptualize and measure it.

13. Karin Lutzen (1987) and Myriam Everard (1987) both presented early arguments that class was a major factor in determining which women were labeled lesbian. They contrast treatment of lesbian inmates in prisons and mental hospitals with middle-class women who were their contemporaries, arguing that the poor women were diagnosed as mentally ill or labeled perverse, while middle-class women involved in similar behavior were not.

14. With the Comstock Law still being enforced, women such as Margaret Sanger and Mary Ware Dennett were not only legally prosecuted, but also vilified in the press. See D'Emilio and Freedman 1988.

Notes to Chapter Six

1. The issue of homophobia in women's sports and in the field of Physical Education was such a taboo that when Margaret Cruikshank edited *Lesbian Studies: Present and Future* (1982b), no one from within the field would write on the topic. Today more women are willing to address this issue. Because sports have always been a refuge

for lesbians and many other women who resisted the myths of womanly passivity or frailty, we can ask when a defensive, self-protective strategy becomes oppressive and a mechanism for social control. See Nelson 1991; Boutilier and SanGiovanni 1983; Twin 1979; Lenskyj 1986; Griffin 1990; and Woods and Harbeck 1991.

2. Kennedy and Davis (1993) found a change occurred between the 1950s and the earlier period, with lesbians not only defending their right to public space in the 1950s, but also reaching out to new or novice lesbians, incorporating them into the community and culture.

3. The absence of any information about woman-to-woman sexual practices is another area that needs to be integrated into the stories of this generation. Marilyn Frye, for example, wrote of participating in a long and heated discussion of S/M with lesbians in which no one explicitly defined which sexual practices they were referring to. See Frye 1990. Unfortunately, I did not include such questions in my oral history interviews.

4. Evidence suggests a different history for gays and lesbians within the African American communities in the United States; some argue that there was greater openness while others argue for greater homophobia. See Lorde 1984; Garber 1989; Kennedy and Davis 1993; Nestle 1993; and Faderman 1991. It is not yet clear if the visibility of lesbians and gays in Lee's home community was common.

5. All of these women except Lee first found lesbian bars in New Mexico. See Franzen 1993. Among African Americans, house parties and lesbian friendly clubs had been part of the New York and Buffalo communities. See Kennedy and Davis 1993; Garber 1989; Faderman 1991.

6. In my study of the Albuquerque lesbian community (1993), softball emerged as a social alternative to the bar, a place where closeted lesbians who would not go to the bar could meet with their friends. In other communities other women's teams served similar purposes.

7. These are certainly overlapping communities, ranging from feminist organizations that are anti-homophobic on principle but have never really dealt with sexual differences, through predominantly lesbian organizations with activities open to all.

8. Jonathan Katz (1976, 1983) identifies the Society for Human Rights, based in Chicago and founded in 1924, as the first documented homosexual emancipation organization in the United States. The Mattachine Society was founded in 1951, going public in 1953. The Daughters of Bilitis was founded in 1955 in California.

Notes to Chapter Seven

1. While the women of this generation may have used different words, none claimed a same-sex sexual identity.

2. This vicious image of ridiculous, man-hating matrons is evident in D. W. Griffith's 1916 film, *Intolerance*.

3. There was only one view of the family, and it must be considered that "family" then and now is a code for male dominance. See Simmons 1979; Wandersee 1981, 1988; Ware 1981.

4. A trend which has only increased since that time; children's "big wheels" now come in pastels for girls, primary colors for boys. Clothing, birthday cards, soaps, and deodorants are only a few items that have been so divided. Even the traditional christening gown worn by girl and boy infants alike is being replaced by christening suits for boys. Paoletti (1987) discusses some of the early gendering of clothes.

5. It is unclear if the suggestions Terry (1990) found in George Henry's prevention recommendations, which linked strict enforcement of gender-appropriate play with the prevention of sex variance, could have reached these parents.

6. Martha Vicinus (1982a, 1985) considers these issues with the British women she studied.

7. The Chinese Exclusion Act was passed in 1882, renewed in 1892, and made permanent in 1902. The alarm raised by Theodore Roosevelt and others about the immigrant birthrate finally led to immigration restrictions in 1924 with the Johnson-Reed Act. Race riots between 1898 and 1921, lynchings, and black migration before and after World War I attest to escalating race difficulties relating to African Americans. See Foner and Garraty 1991.

8. These were not uncomplicated positions. The Women's Trade Union League was the site of both class and racial struggles. See Foner 1979, 1980. Leonora O'Reilly was a founder of the National Association for the Advancement of Colored People; Beam taught in the South; and Kellor conducted most of her earliest research on African Americans and immigrants. Nevertheless, the efforts made by some women could not counter the stereotypes held by most. See O'Reilly Papers SL; Beam Papers SL; Fitzpatrick 1990.

9. The Chinese Exclusion Act of 1882 had forced a decline in the Chinese population. Most Mexican Americans remained in the

Southwest during this period, while Native Americans were restricted to reservations separated from urban centers.

10. See, for example, Simmons 1979; Newton 1984; Jeffreys 1985; Smith-Rosenberg 1985; D'Emilio and Freedman 1988.

11. Throughout the late nineteenth and early twentieth centuries, newspapers highlighted the movement's internal problems and public defeats, ignoring its successes and underplaying its strength. See Du-Bois 1987.

12. Davis (1929) argued as much in her study. Her liberal attitude on homosexuality and race was exceptional. See Fitzpatrick 1990.

13. The political repression of the post-World War I era cost the United States Emma Goldman's voice, one of a few to call same-sex love honorable. See Katz 1976.

14. Middle-class women who did not want children or were unhappy in their marriages were thought to have individual psychological problems, while sexually active working-class women were called hypersexual females. See Lunbeck 1987; Rothman 1978.

Notes to "On Methodology"

1. "Accessible" in this case meant that the private papers of most of these women were among the collections housed at the Schlesinger Library at Radcliffe College.

2. My original intention was to have a greater diversity among this turn-of-the-century sample, but my search for never-married African American women of this generation who left sufficient records was not productive. In her article on women's social welfare activism, Linda Gordon (1991) found that 85 percent of the African American national women's leaders were married, while only 34 percent of the Euro-Americans were. Additional research is needed to determine how racial differences in attitudes toward combining marriage and motherhood, as well as differing employment options and attitudes toward sexuality, contributed to such a differential.

3. Martha Vicinus (1985) examined the lives of independent women in Great Britain during the same period.

4. In her introduction to the lesbian issue of *Signs*, Estelle Freedman (1984) discussed the importance of trust in building contacts for lesbian research, and how the lack of diversity among much lesbian scholarship reflects a segregation within lesbian communities. Such segregation also

exists in the Albuquerque lesbian community (Franzen 1993). That reality, along with the fact that most lesbians still cannot be out on their jobs and many choose not to be out to their families, most probably contributed to the reluctance of women who don't know me to participate in this study.

5. See Hoffman and Culley 1985; Oakley 1981; Robertson 1983; Ladner 1971; Jameson 1982, for a more extensive discussion of these issues.

6. There is a wealth of material in this area. Rather than try to summarize this genre, I suggest looking at Faderman 1994, which includes selections from a diversity of lesbian writings plus suggestions for additional readings. Abelove, Barale, and Halperin (1993) list "contemporary testimony and memoirs" and "literary studies" under their "Suggestions for Further Reading."

References

Primary Sources

Archival Material

Mary Ellicott Arnold Papers, Schlesinger Library, Radcliffe College, Cambridge, Massachusetts.

Lura Ella Beam Papers, Schlesinger Library, Radcliffe College, Cambridge, Massachusetts.

Molly Dewson Papers, Schlesinger Library, Radcliffe College, Cambridge, Massachusetts.

Mary Elisabeth Dreier Papers, Schlesinger Library, Radcliffe College, Cambridge, Massachusetts (includes the correspondence and other documents of Frances Kellor).

Martha May Eliot Papers, Schlesinger Library, Radcliffe College, Cambridge, Massachusetts.

Hamilton Family Papers, Schlesinger Library, Radcliffe College, Cambridge, Massachusetts.

Frieda Segelke Miller Papers, Schlesinger Library, Radcliffe College, Cambridge, Massachusetts.

Pauline Newman Papers, Schlesinger Library, Radcliffe College, Cambridge, Massachusetts.

Leonora O'Reilly Papers, Schlesinger Library, Radcliffe College, Cambridge, Massachusetts.

Edith Gratia Stedman Papers, Schlesinger Library, Radcliffe College, Cambridge, Massachusetts.

Published Primary Sources

Anderson, Mary with Mary N. Winslow. 1951. *Woman at Work*. Minneapolis, Minnesota: University of Minnesota Press.

Arnold, Mary Ellicott, and Mabel Reed. 1957 *In the Land of the Grasshopper Song: The Story of Two Girls in Indian Country, 1908–09*. New York: Vantage Press.

Baker, Sara Josephine. 1939. *Fighting for Life*. Huntington, N.Y.: Robert E. Krieger.

Breckinridge, Sophonisba P. 1972 [1933]. *Women in the Twentieth Century: A Study of Their Political, Social and Economic Activities*. Reprint, New York: Arno Press.

Clarke, Edward. 1873. *Sex in Education; or a Fair Chance for the Girls*. Boston: J. R. Osgood.

Davis, Katherine B. 1929. *Factors in the Sex Life of Twenty-two Hundred Women*. New York: Harper and Row.

———. 1928. "Why They Failed to Marry." *Harpers Magazine* 156 (March): 460–69.

Delany, Sarah, and A. Elizabeth Delany, with Amy Hill Hearth. 1993. *Having Our Say: The Delany Sisters' First 100 Years*. New York: Kodanska International.

Dickinson, Robert Latou, and Lura Beam. 1934. *The Single Woman: A Medical Study in Sex Education*. Baltimore: Williams and Wilkins.

Gilman, Charlotte Perkins. 1903. *The Home: Its Work and Influence*. New York: McClure, Philips.

———. 1906. "The Passing of Matrimony." *Harper's Bazar* 40 (June): 498.

Guion, Connie. 1958, 1972. "The Reminiscences of Connie Guion." Columbia Oral History Collection, Columbia University.

Hamilton, Alice. 1934. *Exploring the Dangers Trades*. Boston: Little, Brown.

Irwin, Inez Haynes. 1934. *Angels and Amazons: A Hundred Years of American Women*. Garden City, N.Y.: Doubleday, Doran.

Kellor, Frances A. 1915. *Out of Work: A Study of Unemployment*. New York: G. P. Putnam.

Lindsey, Ben, and Wainwright Evans. 1927. *Companionate Marriage*. New York: Boni and Liveright.

Newcomer, Mabel. 1959. *A Century of Higher Education for Women.* New York: Harper and Brothers.

Newman, Pauline. 1980. Interview with Pauline Newman in *American Mosaic: The Immigrant Experience in the Words of Those Who Lived It,* by Joan Morrison and Charlotte Fox Zabusky, 8–14. New York: E. P. Dutton.

Ostlund, Leonard. 1957. "Occupational Choice Patterns in Negro College Women." *Journal of Negro Education* 26 (Winter): 86–91.

Palmer, George Herbert. 1908. *The Life of Alice Freeman Palmer.* Boston: Houghton Mifflin.

"The Private Life of Gwyned Filling." 1948. *Life* (May 3): 36–38.

Reid, Doris Fielding. 1967. *Edith Hamilton: An Intimate Portrait.* New York: W. W. Norton.

Roosevelt, Anna Eleanor. 1933. *It's Up to the Women.* New York: Frederick A. Stokes.

Schneiderman, Rose, and Lucy Goldwaite. 1967. *All for One.* New York: Paul S. Erikson.

Spock, Benjamin. 1946. *Baby and Child Care.* New York: Basic Books.

Wooley, Celia Parker. 1903. *The Western Slope.* Evanston, Ill.: William S. Lord.

Wylie, Philip. 1942. *A Generation of Vipers.* New York: Reinhardt.

Secondary Sources

Abelove, Henry, Michele Aina Barale, and David M. Halperin. 1993. *The Lesbian and Gay Studies Reader.* New York: Routledge.

Antler, Joyce. 1980. " 'After College, What?' New Graduates and the Family Claim." *American Quarterly* 32, no. 4 (Fall): 409–34.

———. *Lucy Sprague Mitchell: The Making of a Modern Woman.* 1987. New Haven, Conn.: Yale University Press.

Association of American Colleges, Project on the Status and Education of Women. 1982. "The Classroom Climate: A Chilly One for Women?"

Babcock, Barbara, and Nancy J. Parezo. 1988. *Daughters of the Desert.* Albuquerque: University of New Mexico Press.

Bacon, Helen. 1980. "Edith Hamilton." In *Notable American Women: The Modern Period,* ed. Barbara Sicherman and Carol Hurd Green, 306–8. Cambridge, Mass.: Belknap Press.

Bass, Ellen, and Louise Thorton, eds. 1984. *I Never Told Any One:*

Writings by Women Survivors of Child Sexual Abuse. New York: Harper and Row.

Baumgartner, Leona. 1971. "Sara Josephine Baker." In *Notable American Women: A Biographical Dictionary,* ed. Edward T. James, 85–86. Cambridge, Mass.: Belknap Press.

Benstock, Shari. 1989. "Paris Lesbianism and the Politics of Reaction, 1900–1940." In *Hidden from History: Reclaiming the Gay and Lesbian Past,* ed. Martin B. Duberman, Martha Vicinus, and George Chauncey, Jr., 332–46. New York: New American Library.

Berube, Allan. 1990. *Coming Out under Fire: The History of Gay Men and Women in World War Two.* New York: Free Press, 1990.

Bloch, Ruth H. 1978. "American Feminine Ideals in Transition: The Rise of the Moral Mother, 1785–1815." *Feminist Studies* 4 (2): 101–26.

Boutilier, Mary A., and Lucinda SanGiovanni. 1983. *The Sporting Woman.* Champaign, Ill.: Human Kinetics Publishers, 1983.

Breines, Wini. 1992. *Young, White, and Miserable: Growing Up Female in the Fifties.* Boston: Beacon Press.

Brown, Dorothy. 1987. *Setting the Course: Women in the 1920s.* Boston: Twayne.

Brown, Helen Gurley. 1962. *Sex and the Single Girl.* New York: Bernard Geis Associates.

Bullough, Vern, and Bonnie Bullough. 1977. "Lesbianism in the 1920s and 1930s: A New Found Study." *Signs* 2, no. 4 (Summer): 895–905.

Bunch, Charlotte. 1975. "Not for Lesbians Only." *Quest: A Feminist Quarterly* 2, no. 2 (Fall): 50–56.

Carnegie Commission on Higher Education. 1973. *Opportunities for Women in Higher Education.* New York: McGraw-Hill, 1973.

Chambers-Schiller, Lee V. 1984. *Liberty, A Better Husband.* New Haven, Conn.: Yale University Press.

Chauncey, George, Jr. 1989. "From Sexual Inversion to Homosexuality: The Changing Medical Conceptualization of Female 'Deviance.' " In *Passion and Power: Sexuality in History,* ed. Kathy Peiss and Christina Simmons, 87–117. Philadelphia: Temple University Press.

Chodorow, Nancy. 1978. *The Reproduction of Mothering.* Berkeley: University of California Press.

Clifford, Geraldine Joncich, ed., 1989. *Lone Voyagers: Academic*

Women in Coeducational Institutions, 1870–1937. New York: Feminist Press.

Cook, Blanche Wiesen. 1979. "Female Support Networks and Political Activism: Lillian Wald, Crystal Eastman, Emma Goldman." In *A Heritage of Her Own*, ed. Nancy F. Cott and Elizabeth H. Pleck, 412–44. New York: Simon and Schuster, Touchstone.

Cooke, Joanne, Charlotte Bunch-Weeks, and Robin Morgan, eds. 1970. *The New Women*. Greenwich, Connecticut: Fawcett.

Cookingham, Mary E. 1984. "Combining Marriage, Motherhood, and Jobs before World War II: Women College Graduates, Classes of 1905–1935." *Journal of Family History* (Summer): 178–195.

Cordell, Linda. "Women Archaeologists in the Southwest" (unpublished paper).

Costin, Lela B. 1983. *Two Sisters for Social Justice: A Biography of Grace and Edith Abbott*. Urbana: University of Illinois Press.

Cott, Nancy F. 1987. *The Grounding of Modern Feminism*. New Haven, Conn.: Yale University Press.

Crawford, Vicki L., Jacqueline Anne Rouse, and Barbara Woods. 1990. *Women in the Civil Rights Movement: Trailblazers and Torchbearers, 1941–1965*. Bloomington: Indiana University Press.

Cruikshank, Margaret. 1982a. "Notes on Recent Lesbian Autobiographical Writing." *Journal of Homosexuality* 8, no. 1 (Fall): 19–26.

———, ed. 1985. *The Lesbian Path*. San Francisco: Grey Fox Press.

———. 1982b. *Lesbian Studies: Present and Future*. Old Westbury, N.Y.: Feminist Press.

Davis, Madeline, and Elizabeth Lapovsky Kennedy. 1986. "Oral History and the Study of Sexuality in the Lesbian Community: Buffalo, New York, 1940–1960." *Feminist Studies* 12 (Spring): 7–26.

D'Emilio, John. 1983. *Sexual Politics, Sexual Communities: The Making of a Homosexual Minority in the United States, 1940–1970*. Chicago: University of Chicago Press.

———. 1989. "The Homosexual Menace: The Politics of Sexuality in Cold War America." In *Passion and Power: Sexuality in History*, ed. Kathy Peiss and Christina Simmons. Philadelphia: Temple University Press.

D'Emilio, John, and Estelle B. Freedman. 1988. *Intimate Matters: A History of Sexuality in America*. New York: Harper and Row.

Department of Education. 1981. *Digest of Education Statistics*. National Center for Educational Statistics. Washington, D.C.: Government Printing Office.

Deutsch, Sarah. 1987. *No Separate Refuge: Culture, Class and Gender on an Anglo-Hispanic Frontier in the American Southwest, 1880–1940.* New York: Oxford University Press.

Dobkin, Marjorie Housepian, ed. 1979. *The Making of a Feminist: Early Journals and Letters of M. Carey Thomas.* Kent State, Ohio: Kent State University Press.

Douglas, Susan J. 1994. *Where the Girls Are: Growing Up Female with the Mass Media.* New York: Random House, 1994.

Drachman, Virginia G. 1984. *Hospital with a Heart: Women Doctors and the Paradox of Separatism at the New England Hospital, 1862–1969.* Ithaca, N.Y.: Cornell University Press.

DuBois, Ellen C. 1987. "Working Women, Class Relations, and Suffrage Militance: Harriot Stanton Blatch and the New York Woman Suffrage Movement, 1894–1909." *The Journal of American History* 74 (June).

Dye, Nancy Schrom. 1980. *As Equals and as Sisters: Feminism, the Labor Movement, and the Women's Trade Union League of New York.* Columbia: University of Missouri Press.

Ehrenreich, Barbara. 1989. *Fear of Falling: The Inner Life of the Middle Class.* New York: Pantheon Books.

———. 1983. *The Hearts of Men: American Dreams and Flight from Commitment.* Garden City, N.Y.: Anchor/Doubleday.

Elsasser, Nan, Kyle MacKenzie, and Yvonne Tixier y Vigil, eds. 1980. *Las Mujeres: Conversations from an Hispanic Community.* Old Westbury, N.Y.: Feminist Press.

Epstein, Barbara. 1983. "Family, Sexual Morality, and Popular Movements in Turn-of-the-Century America." In *Powers of Desire: The Politics of Sexuality,* ed. Ann Snitow, Christine Stansell, and Sharon Thompson, 117–30. New York: Monthly Review Press.

Espin, Olivia M. 1984. "Cultural and Historical Influences on Sexuality in Hispanic/Latin Women: Implications for Psychotherapy." In *Pleasure and Danger: Exploring Female Sexuality,* ed. Carole Vance. Boston: Routledge and Kegan Paul.

Evans, Sara. 1989. *Born for Liberty: A History of Women in America.* New York: Free Press.

Everard, Myriam H. M. 1986. "Lesbian History: A History of Change and Disparity." *Journal of Homosexuality,* 123–37.

———. 1987. "Lesbianism and Medical Practice in the Netherlands,

1880–1940." Paper given at the Seventh Berkshire Conference on the History of Women, Wellesley College, June 1987.

Ewen, Elizabeth. 1980. "City Lights: Immigrant Women and the Rise of Movies." *Signs* 5, no. 3 (Spring): 45–65.

Faderman, Lillian, ed. 1994. *Chloe plus Olivia: An Anthology of Lesbian Literature from the 17th Century to the Present.* New York: Viking.

———. 1978. "The Morbidification of Love Between Women by Nineteenth-Century Sexologists." *Journal of Homosexuality* 4, no. 1 (Fall): 73–90.

———. 1984. "The 'New Gay' Lesbians." *Journal of Homosexuality* 10, no. 3/4 (Winter): 85–95.

———. 1988. "A Response to Myriam Everard's 'Lesbian History: A History of Change and Disparity.' " *Journal of Homosexuality* 15 (3/4): 137–41.

———. 1981. *Surpassing the Love of Men: Romantic Friendships and Love between Women from the Renaissance to the Present.* New York: William Morrow.

———. 1991. *Odd Girls and Twilight Lovers: A History of Lesbian Life in Twentieth-Century America.* New York: Columbia University Press.

Fass, Paula S. 1977. *The Damned and the Beautiful: American Youth in the 1920s.* New York: Oxford University Press.

Ferguson, Ann. 1985. "Lesbian Identity: Beauvoir and History." *Women's Studies International Forum* 8 (3): 203–8.

Ferguson, Ann, Jacquelyn Zita, and Kathryn Pyne Addelson. 1981. "On 'Compulsory Heterosexuality and Lesbian Existence': Defining the Issues." *Signs* 7, no. 1.

Filler, Louis. 1977. "Frances Kellor." In *Dictionary of American Biography,* 380–81.

Fitzpatrick, Ellen F. 1990. *Endless Crusade: Women Social Scientists and Progressive Reform.* New York: Oxford University Press.

———. 1987. *Katherine Bement Davis, Early Twentieth-Century American Women, and the Study of Sex Behavior.* New York: Garland.

Foner, Eric, and John A. Garraty, eds. 1991. *The Readers Companion to American History.* Boston: Houghton Mifflin.

Foner, Philip S. 1979. *Women and the American Labor Movement: From Colonial Times to the Eve of World War I.* New York: Free Press.

Foner, Philip S. 1980. *Women and the American Labor Movement: From World War I to the Present.* New York: Free Press.

Fox, Mary Frank. 1989. "Women and Higher Education: Gender Differences in the Status of Students and Scholars." In *Women: A Feminist Perspective,* ed. Jo Freeman, 217–35. Mountain View, Calif.: Mayfield.

Frankfort, Roberta. 1977. *Collegiate Women: Domesticity and Career in Turn-of-the Century America.* New York: New York University Press.

Franzen, Trisha. 1993. "Differences and Identities: Feminism and the Albuquerque Lesbian Community." *Signs* 18, no. 4 (Summer): 891–906.

Frazier, Nancy, and Myra Sadker. 1973. *Sexism in School and Society.* New York: Harper and Row.

Freedman, Estelle. 1984. "Editorial." *Signs* 9, no. 4 (Summer): 551–54.

———. 1983. "The New Woman: Changing Views of Women in the 1920s." In *Decades of Discontent: The Women's Movement, 1920–1940,* ed. Lois Scharf and Joan Jensen. Westport, Conn.: Greenwood Press, 1983: 21–44.

———. 1982. "Sexuality in Nineteenth-Century America: Behavior, Ideology, and Politics." *Reviews in American History* 10 (December): 196–215.

———. 1979. "Separatism as Strategy: Female Institution Building and American Feminism, 1870–1930." *Feminist Studies* 5, no. 3 (Fall): 512–29.

———. 1981. *Their Sisters' Keepers: Women's Prison Reform in America, 1830–1930.* Ann Arbor: University of Michigan Press.

———. 1989. " 'Uncontrolled Desires': The Response to the Sexual Psychopath, 1920–1960." In *Passion and Power: Sexuality in History,* ed. Kathy Peiss and Christina Simmons, 199–225. Philadelphia: Temple University Press.

Freedman, Estelle, and John D'Emilio. 1990. "Problems Encountered in Writing the History of Sexuality: Sources, Theory and Interpretation." *Journal of Sex Research* 27, no. 4 (November): 481–95.

Freeman, Ruth, and Patricia Klaus. 1984. "Blessed or Not? The New Spinster in England and the United States in the Late Nineteenth and Early Twentieth Centuries." *Journal of Family History* (Winter): 394–414.

"Frieda Segelke Miller." *The National Cyclopedia of American Biography* 61: 163–64.

Frye, Marilyn. 1990. "Lesbian 'Sex'." In *Lesbian Philosophies and Culture,* ed. Jeffner Allen, 305–56. Albany: State University of New York Press.

Gans, Herbert. 1967. *The Levittowners.* New York: Vintage Books.

Garber, Eric. 1989. "A Spectacle in Color: The Lesbian and Gay Subculture of Jazz Age Harlem." In *Hidden from History: Reclaiming the Gay and Lesbian Past,* ed. Martin B. Duberman, Martha Vicinus, and George Chauncey, Jr., 318–31. New York: New American Library.

Giddings, Paula. 1984. *When and Where I Enter: The Impact of Black Women on Race and Sex in America.* New York: William Morrow.

Gordon, Linda. 1976. *Woman's Body, Women's Right: A Social History of Birth Control in America.* New York: Grossman.

———. 1994. *Pitied but Not Entitled: The History of Single Mothers and Welfare.* New York: Free Press.

———. 1991. "Black and White Visions of Welfare: Women's Welfare Activism, 1890–1945." *Journal of American History* 78 (September): 559–91.

Griffin, Pat. 1991. "From Hiding Out to Coming Out: Empowering Lesbian and Gay Educators." *Journal of Homosexuality: Coming Out of the Classroom Closet* 22 (3/4): 167–96.

Griswold, Robert L. 1993. *Fatherhood in America: A History.* New York: Basic Books.

Halberstam, David. 1993. *The Fifties.* New York: Villard Books.

Hartmann, Susan M. 1982. *The Home Front and Beyond: American Women in the 1940s.* Boston: Twayne.

Harvey, Brett. 1993. *The Fifties: A Women's Oral History.* New York: HarperCollins.

Henry, Alice. 1915. *The Trade Union Woman.* New York: D. Appleton.

———. 1923. *Women and the Labor Movement.* New York: George H. Doran.

Hermann, Judith Lewis. 1981. *Father-Daughter Incest.* Cambridge, Mass.: Harvard University Press.

Higginbotham, Evelyn Brooks. 1993. *Righteous Discontents: The Women's Movement in the Black Baptist Church.* Cambridge, Mass.: Harvard University Press.

218 • References

Hine, Darlene Clark. 1989. *Black Women in White: Racial Conflict and Cooperation in the Nursing Profession, 1890–1950*. Bloomington: Indiana University Press.

Hoffman, Leonore, and Margo Culley, eds. 1985. *Women's Personal Narratives: Essays in Criticism and Pedagogy*. New York: Modern Language Association of America.

Horowitz, Helen Lefkowitz. 1984. *Alma Mater: Design and Experience in the Women's Colleges from Their Nineteenth-Century Beginnings to the 1930s*. New York: Alfred A. Knopf.

James, Edward T. 1980. "Mary Anderson." In *Notable American Women: The Modern Era*, ed. Barbara Sicherman and Carol Hurd Green, 23–25. Cambridge, Mass: Belknap Press.

———, ed. 1981. *Papers of the Women's Trade Union League and Its Principal Leaders*. Woodbridge, Conn.: Research Publications.

Jameson, Elizabeth. 1982. "May and Me: Relationships with Informants and the Community." Insider/Outsider Relationships with Informants. SIROW Working Paper No. 13, 3–13.

Jeffreys, Sheila. 1985. *The Spinster and Her Enemies: Feminism and Sexuality, 1880–1930*. London: Pandora.

Jelinek, Estelle C. 1986. *The Tradition of Women's Autobiography: From Antiquity to the Present*. Boston: Twayne.

———, ed. 1980. *Women's Autobiography: Essays in Criticism*. Bloomington: University of Indiana Press.

Jones, Jacqueline. 1985. *Labor of Love, Labor of Sorrow: Black Women, Work, and the Family from Slavery to the Present*. New York: Basic Books.

Kaledin, Eugenia. 1984. *Mothers and More: American Women in the 1950s*. Boston: Twayne.

Katz, Jonathan, ed. 1976. *Gay American History: Lesbians and Gay Men in the U.S.A.* New York: Thomas Crowell.

———, ed. 1983. *Gay/Lesbian Almanac: A New Documentary*. New York: Harper and Row.

Kennedy, Elizabeth Lapovsky, and Madeline Davis. 1993. *Boots of Leather, Slippers of Gold: The History of a Lesbian Community*. London: Routledge.

———. 1989. "The Reproduction of Butch-Fem Roles: A Social Constructionist Approach." In *Passion and Power: Sexuality in History*, ed. Kathy Peiss and Christina Simmons, 241–56. Philadelphia: Temple University Press.

Kessler-Harris, Alice. 1986. "Independence and Virtue in the Lives of

Wage-Earning Women: The United States, 1870–1930." In *Women in Culture and Politics: A Century of Change*, ed. Judith Friedlander, Blanche Weisen Cook, Alice Kessler-Harris, and Carroll Smith-Rosenberg, 3–13. Bloomington: Indiana University Press.

———. 1982. *Out to Work: A History of Wage-Earning Women in the United States*. New York: Oxford University Press.

Kinsey, Alfred, et al. 1953. *Sexual Behavior in the Human Female*. Philadelphia: W. B. Saunders.

———. 1948. *Sexual Behavior in the Human Male*. Philadelphia: W. B. Saunders.

Komarovsky, Mira. 1964. *Blue-Collar Marriage*. New York: Random House.

Ladner, Joyce. 1971. *Tomorrow's Tomorrow*. Garden City, N.Y.: Doubleday.

Lenskyj, Helen. 1986. *Out of Bounds: Women, Sport, and Sexuality*. Toronto: Women's Press.

Lorde, Audre. 1984. "Scratching the Surface: Some Barriers to Women and Loving." In *Sister Outsider*. Trumansburg, N.Y.: Crossing Press.

Loulan, Joanne. 1990. *The Lesbian Erotic Dance: Butch, Femme, Androgyny and Other Rhythms*. San Francisco: Spinsters Book Company.

Lunbeck, Elizabeth. 1987. " 'A New Generation of Women': Progressive Psychiatrists and the Hypersexual Female." *Feminist Studies* 13, no. 3 (Fall): 513–43.

Lutzen, Karin. 1987. "Women-Loving Women in Denmark, 1880–1915." Paper given at the Seventh Berkshire Conference on the History of Women, Wellesley College, June.

Margolis, Maxine L. 1984. *Mothers and Such: Views of American Women and Why They Changed*. Berkeley: University of California Press.

Matthaei, Julie A. 1982. *An Economic History of Women in America: Women's Work, the Sexual Division of Labor, and the Development of Capitalism*. New York: Schocken Books.

Maxwell, William Joseph. 1968. "Frances Kellor in the Progressive Era: A Case Study in the Professionalization of Reform." Unpublished dissertation, Teachers College, Columbia University.

May, Elaine Tyler. 1988. *Homeward Bound: American Families in the Cold War Era*. New York: Basic Books.

McGovern, James R. 1986. "The American Woman's Pre-World War I

Freedom in Manners and Morals." *Journal of American History* 55, no. 2 (September): 315–33.

Meese, Elizabeth A. 1985. "The Languages of Oral Testimony and Women's Literature." In *Women's Personal Narratives: Essays in Criticism and Pedagogy,* ed. Leonore Hoffman and Margo Culley, 24–25. New York: Modern Language Association of America.

Meyerowitz, Joanne M., ed. 1994. *Not June Cleaver: Women and Gender in Postwar America, 1945–1960.* Philadelphia: Temple University Press.

————. 1988. *Women Adrift: Independent Wage Earners in Chicago, 1880–1930.* Chicago: University of Chicago Press.

Moldow, Gloria. 1987. *Women Doctors in Gilded-Age Washington: Race, Gender, and Professionalization.* Urbana: University of Illinois Press.

Montgomery, Dee Ann. 1980. "Frieda Segelke Miller." In *Notable American Women: The Modern Period,* ed. Barbara Sicherman and Carol Hurd Green, 478–79. Cambridge, Mass.: Belknap Press.

Moore, Elizabeth Payne. 1980. "Mary Elisabeth Dreier." In *Notable American Women: The Modern Period,* ed. Barbara Sicherman and Carol Hurd Green, 204–6. Cambridge, Mass.: Belknap Press.

Morantz-Sanchez, Regina Markell. 1985. *Sympathy and Science: Women Physicians in American Medicine.* New York: Oxford University Press.

Mosse, George L. 1982. "Nationalism and Respectability: Normal and Abnormal Sexuality in the Nineteenth Century." *Journal of Contemporary History* 17: 221–46.

Myron, Nancy, and Charlotte Bunch, eds. 1975. *Lesbianism and the Women's Movement.* Baltimore: Diana Press.

Nelson, Mariah Burton. 1991. *Are We Winning Yet? How Women Are Changing Sports and Sports Are Changing Women.* New York: Random House.

Nestle, Joan. 1993. "Excerpts from the Oral History of Mabel Hampton." *Signs* 18, no. 4 (Summer): 925–35

————. 1987. *A Restricted Country.* Ithaca, N.Y.: Firebrand Books.

Newton, Esther. 1984. "The Mythic Mannish Lesbian: Radclyffe Hall and the New Woman." *Signs* 9, no. 4 (Summer).

Oakley, Ann. 1981. "Interviewing Women: A Contradiction in Terms." In *Doing Feminist Research,* ed. Helen Roberts, 30–61. London: Routledge and Kegan Paul.

O'Brien, Sharon. 1987. *Willa Cather: The Emerging Voice.* New York: Oxford University Press.

O'Connell, Lucille. 1980. "Frances Kellor." In *Notable American Women: The Modern Period*, ed. Barbara Sicherman and Carol Hurd Green. Cambridge, Mass.: Belknap Press.

Palmieri, Patricia A. 1981. "In Adamless Eden: A Social Portrait of the Academic Community at Wellesley College, 1875–1920." Unpublished dissertation, Harvard University, Cambridge, Massachusetts.

———. 1980. "Patterns of Achievement of Single Academic Women at Wellesley College, 1880–1920." *Frontiers* 5, no. 1 (Spring): 63–67.

———. 1983. "Here Was Fellowship: A Social Portrait of Academic Women at Wellesley College, 1895–1920." *History of Education Quarterly* 23, no. 2 (Summer): 198–203.

Paoletti, Jo B. 1987. "Clothing and Gender in America, 1890–1920." *Signs* 13, no. 1 (Autumn): 136–44.

Payne, Elizabeth Anne. 1988. *Reform, Labor, and Feminism: Margaret Dreier Robins and the Women's Trade Union League*. Urbana: University of Illinois Press, 1988.

Peiss, Kathy. 1986. *Cheap Amusements: Working Women and Leisure in Turn-of-the-Century New York*. Philadelphia: Temple University Press.

Penn, Donna. 1994. "The Sexualized Woman: The Lesbian, the Prostitute, and the Containment of Female Sexuality in Post-War America." In *Not June Cleaver: Woman and Gender in Post-War America*, ed. Joanne M. Meyerowitz. Philadelphia: Temple University Press.

Radicalesbians. 1971. "Women-Identified Woman." In *Liberation Now!*, ed. Deborah Babcox and Madeline Belkin. New York: Laurel Books.

Rich, Adrienne. 1980. "Compulsory Heterosexuality and Lesbian Existence." *Signs* 5, no. 4 (Spring): 631–660.

Robertson, Claire. 1983. "In Pursuit of Life Histories: The Problem of Bias." *Frontiers* 7 (2): 63–69.

Rosenberg, Rosalind. 1982. *Beyond Separate Spheres: The Intellectual Roots of Modern Feminism*. New Haven, Conn.: Yale University Press.

Rosenzweig, Linda. 1993. *The Anchor of My Life*. New York: New York University Press.

Rothman, Ellen K. 1984. *Hands and Hearts: A History of Courtship in America*. New York: Basic Books.

Rothman, Sheila M. 1978. *Women's Proper Place: A History of Changing Ideals and Practices, 1870 to the Present*. New York: Basic Books.

Rubin, Gayle. 1984. "Thinking Sex: Notes for a Radical Theory of the Politics of Sexuality." In *Pleasure and Danger: Exploring Female Sexuality*, ed. Carole Vance. Boston: Routledge and Kegan Paul.

———. 1975. " 'Traffic in Women:' Towards a Political Economy of Sex." In *Towards an Anthropology of Women*, ed. Rayna Reiter. New York: Monthly Review Press.

Rubin, Lillian. 1976. *Worlds of Pain: Life in the Working-Class Family*. New York: Basic Books.

Rush, Florence. 1980. *The Best Kept Secret: Sexual Abuse of Children*. New York: McGraw-Hill.

Ryan, Mary. 1979. *Womanhood in America: From Colonial Times to the Present*. 2d ed. New York: New Viewpoints.

Sahli, Nancy. 1979. "Smashing: Women's Relationships before the Fall." *Chrysalis* 8 (Summer): 17–27.

———. 1984. *Women and Sexuality in America: A Bibliography*. G. K. Hall.

"Sara Josephine Baker." *National Cyclopedia of American Biography* 34: 91–92.

Schwarz, Judith. 1986. *Radical Feminists of Heterodoxy: Greenwich Village, 1912–1940*. Norwich, Vt.: New Victoria Publishers.

Scott, Joan W. 1988. "Deconstructing Equality-Versus-Difference: Or, the Uses of Post-Structuralist Theory for Feminism." *Feminist Studies* 14, no. 1 (Spring): 33–50.

———. 1988. *Gender and the Politics of History*. New York: Columbia University Press.

Shively, Charles. 1971. "Leonora O'Reilly." In *Notable American Women: A Biographical Dictionary*, ed. Edward James, 651–53. Cambridge, Mass.: Belknap Press.

Sicherman, Barbara. 1980. "Alice Hamilton." In *Notable American Women: The Modern Period*, ed. Barbara Sicherman and Carol Hurd Green, 303–6. Cambridge, Mass.: Belknap Press.

———. 1984. *Alice Hamilton: A Life in Letters*. Cambridge, Mass.: Harvard University Press.

Simmons, Christina. 1979. "Companionate Marriage and the Lesbian Threat." *Frontiers* 4, no. 3 (Fall): 54–59.

Simon, Barbara Levy. 1987. *Never Married Women*. Philadelphia: Temple University Press.

Sklar, Kathryn Kish. 1985. "Hull House in the 1890s: A Community of Women Reformers." *Signs* 10, no. 4 (Summer): 658–77.

Small, Margaret. 1975. "Lesbianism and the Class Position of Women." In *Lesbianism and the Women's Movement*, ed. Nancy Myron and Charlotte Bunch, 49–55. Baltimore: Diana Press.

Smith-Rosenberg, Carroll. 1985. *Disorderly Conduct: Visions of Gender in Victorian America*. New York: Alfred A. Knopf.

———. 1975. "The Female World of Love and Ritual: Relations between Women in Nineteenth-Century America." *Signs* 1, no. 1 (Autumn): 1–30.

Sochen, June. 1972. *The New Woman: Feminism in Greenwich Village, 1910–1920*. New York: Quadrangle Books.

Solomon, Barbara Miller. 1985. *In the Company of Educated Women: A History of Women and Higher Education in America*. New Haven, Conn.: Yale University Press.

Stacey, J., S. Bereaud, and J. Daniels. 1974. *And Jill Came Tumbling After*. New York: Dell.

Terry, Jennifer. 1990. "Lesbians under the Medical Gaze: Scientists Search for Remarkable Differences." *Journal of Sex Research* 27, no. 3 (August): 317–39.

Theberge, Nancy. 1989. "Women's Athletics and the Myth of Female Frailty." In *Women: A Feminist Perspective*, ed. Jo Freeman, 507–22. Mountain View, Calif.: Mayfield.

Twin, Stephanie L. 1979. *Out of the Bleachers: Writings on Women and Sport*. Old Westbury, N.Y.: Feminist Press.

Valeska, Lucia. 1981. "The Future of Female Separatism." In *Building Feminist Theory: Essays from Quest: A Feminist Quarterly*, 20–31. New York, Longman.

Van Horn, Susan Householder. 1988. *Women, Work, and Fertility, 1900–1986*. New York: New York University Press.

Vicinus, Martha. 1985. *Independent Women: Work and Community for Single Women, 1850–1920*. Chicago: University of Chicago Press.

———. 1982a. " 'One Life to Stand Beside Me': Emotional Conflicts in First-Generation College Women in England." *Feminist Studies* 8, no. 3 (Fall): 603–28.

———. 1982b. "Sexuality and Power: A Review of Current Work in the History of Sexuality." *Feminist Studies* 8, no. 1 (Spring): 135–56.

———. 1992. " 'They Wonder to Which Sex I Belong': The Historical Roots of the Modern Lesbian Identity." *Feminist Studies* 18, no. 4 (Fall): 467–497.

224 • References

Wandersee, Winifred. 1988. *On the Move: American Women in the 1970s.* Boston, Twayne.

———. 1981. *Women's Work and Family Values, 1920–1940.* Cambridge, Mass.: Harvard University Press.

Ware, Susan. 1981. *Beyond Suffrage: Women and the New Deal.* Cambridge, Mass.: Harvard University Press.

———. 1987. *Partner and I: Molly Dewson, Feminism, and New Deal Politics.* New Haven, Conn.: Yale University Press.

Wein, Roberta. 1974. "Women's Colleges and Domesticity, 1875–1918." *History of Education Quarterly* 14, no. 1 (Spring): 31–48.

Welter, Barbara. 1978. "The Cult of True Womanhood." In *The American Family in Social-Historical Perspective* (2d ed.), ed. Michael Gordon, 313–33. New York: St. Martins Press.

West, Elliott and Paula Petrik, eds. 1992. *Small Worlds: Children and Adolescents in America, 1850–1950.* Lawrence: University Press of Kansas.

Wickes, George. 1976. *The Amazon of Letters: The Life and Loves of Natalie Clifford Barney.* New York: G. P. Putnam's Sons.

Wiebe, Robert H. 1967. *The Search for Order, 1877–1920.* New York: Hill and Wang.

Woods, Sherry E., and Karen M. Harbeck. 1991. "Living in Two Worlds: The Identity Management Strategies Used by Lesbian Physical Educators." *Journal of Homosexuality* 22 (3/4): 141–65.

Index

Abuse, physical or sexual, 9, 27, 28, 31, 32, 37, 165

Adams, Amy, xxvi, 35, 38, 40, 43, 84, 90, 91, 96, 102, 137, 138, 141, 142, 144, 145, 149, 152, 158

African Americans, xxii, xxiii, xxvii, 28, 66, 90, 170, 171, 180; African-American gays, 148, 152, 169, 170; African-American women workers, 33

Anderson, Mary, xxii, 14, 18, 20, 21, 48, 62, 63, 64, 66, 74, 100, 108, 109, 110, 113, 115, 168

Arnold, Mary Ellicott, xxiii, 15, 21, 49, 52, 67, 109, 118, 119, 120, 121

Athletics, sports, among contemporary lesbians, 21, 34, 35, 38, 44, 82, 93, 137, 144, 152

Baker, Sara Josephine "Jo," xxii, 11, 12, 13, 15, 17, 20, 21, 23, 35, 39, 49, 50, 51, 52, 53, 54, 55, 56, 57, 63, 64, 65, 66, 69, 70, 71, 99, 109, 110, 116, 118, 119, 121, 125, 159, 160, 162, 173

Barnard College, xxiii, 22, 51

Beam, Lura, xxiii, 16, 20, 21, 51, 55, 109, 128, 129

Boys, 23, 36, 165; boys'clothes, 36; playing with, 20, 23, 34, 35, 39, 40; wanting to be, 35, 37, 39

Bryn Mawr College, xxi, 49, 51, 52, 54, 109

Bryn Mawr School, xxi, 118, 125

Bureau of Child Hygiene, xxii

Chicanas, xxv, xxvii, 26, 181

Childhoods, 179; nineteenth-century ideals, 19; of Post WW II Era lesbians, 9, 26, 27, 28, 33, 34, 38, 39, 45, 81, 98, 156, 165, 166; of Progressive Era women, xxiv, 9, 11, 13, 19, 21, 22, 23, 48, 58, 112, 121, 159, 162, 163; theories, 98, 162; working-class women, 14

Children's Bureau, xxiv, 71

Communities, 98, 104, 152, 161, 168, 169, 177; working-class, 113, 180
Communities of color, 33, 38, 148, 153, 169
Communities, lesbian/gay, 10, 26, 28, 40, 105, 133, 136, 137, 141, 142, 145–49, 151–54, 156–58, 167, 181, 183; lesbian-feminist, 136; working-class, 41, 142, 145, 160
Communities, women's, 4, 9, 11, 44, 45, 77, 95, 100, 107–9, 111–13, 116–18, 131, 132, 153, 161, 163, 177
Community activists, 152
Competence, among contemporary lesbians, 33, 38, 39, 45, 81, 106, 165; among nineteenth-century mothers, 17, 18, 60; among Progressive Era women, 12, 17, 21, 23, 48, 79, 115, 120
Cornell University, xxii, xxiii, 49, 53, 67

Davis, Katherine B., 22, 76, 123, 128, 131, 159, 173, 181
Denova, Bobbi, xxv, 30, 32, 37, 78, 79, 81, 90, 95, 99, 101, 103, 138, 139, 150, 151, 152, 156
Depression/New Deal era, 132, 164, 175
Depressions, nineteenth-century, 5, 13, 14, 19
Dewson, Mary "Molly," xxii, 16, 17, 21, 39, 51, 54, 55, 57, 70, 75, 76, 108, 110, 115, 117, 118, 120, 121, 168
Dickinson, Dr. Robert Latou, xxiii
Dreier, Mary Elisabeth, xxii, xxiii, 13, 26, 50, 107, 108, 109, 113, 117, 121, 122, 168
Dress, among contemporary lesbians, 36, 37, 101, 137; among Progres-

sive Era women, 69, 70, 71, 173
Durham, Ethel, xxiv, 117, 119

Education, 4; of Post WW II Era lesbians, 81–85, 169; of Progressive Era women, 15, 47–50; racism in, 82
Education, college/post-secondary, 129; changing options, 80, 163, 182; class differences among contemporary group in education, 85; historians' discussion of, 88; homophobia in, 138–40; of Post WW II Era lesbians, 78–81, 83, 84, 86–90, 93, 94, 96, 99, 101, 106, 154–56, 166, 169; of Progressive Era women, 51–58, 60–62, 64, 66, 73, 75, 108, 111–13, 117, 120, 161, 162; parental expectations of women's, 89; in Progressive Era, 50–51; rates in twentieth century, 89
Edwards, Robin, xxvii, 3, 25, 32, 35, 40, 42, 46, 86, 87, 97, 100, 101, 103, 109, 110, 137, 140, 143, 149, 152, 169
Eliot, Martha May, xxiv, 52, 53, 54, 55, 64, 67, 68, 75, 117, 119, 120
Employment, careers, 6, 8, 54, 57; African-American, 73; among contemporary lesbians, xxv–xxvii, 6, 9, 37, 42, 78, 80, 81–90, 94–96, 99–103, 108, 141, 148, 152, 154, 157, 169, 174; among mothers, 28–29; among Progressive Era women, xxi–xxv, 4, 14, 15, 18, 21, 47–49, 55–63, 65–70, 74, 75, 77, 80, 108–27, 132, 133, 163; changing options, 6, 131, 163, 164, 182; class differences among contemporary group, 91, 93, 103; historians' discussion of, 118; homophobia in, 135, 157; modern norms, 94, 105; parental expectations of women's,

102, 103; parents', 82, 88, 89, 103; rates among African-American women, 33; working-class, 14, 73; working-class lesbians, 148; World War II, 146, 147

Faderman, Lillian, 126
Fathers, 88, 98; modern norms, 16, 27, 29; of Post WW II Era lesbians, xxvi, xxvii, 28–32, 34, 37, 42, 81, 82, 84, 85, 87, 95, 103; of Progressive Era women, xxii–xxiv, 11, 14–17, 21, 24, 29, 48, 55, 60, 72, 126, 162, 168; Progressive Era ideals, 62
Freud, Sigmund, 6, 7, 40, 134, 162, 172

Gender systems/norms, 45, 159, 181, 184; and contemporary lesbians, 3, 9, 34, 39, 156; and Progressive Era women, 108, 112, 114, 170, 173; and clothes, 70; modern norms, 4, 7, 10, 41, 43, 45, 54, 71, 80, 81, 84, 87, 93, 98, 102, 104, 106, 123, 129, 130, 131, 132, 153, 154, 158, 163, 164, 165, 166, 167, 169, 172, 175; nineteenth-century, 18, 19, 23, 24, 39, 60, 69, 71, 77, 160, 162
Guion, Connie, xxiii, 14, 15, 17, 21, 51, 53, 54, 55, 56, 57, 64, 109, 115

Hall, Radclyffe, 159, 174
Hamilton, Alice, xxi, 17, 18, 22, 39, 50, 52, 53, 54, 55, 56, 57, 59, 64, 65, 66, 70, 72, 73, 74, 99, 108, 110, 111, 114, 115, 123, 125, 126, 168, 181
Hamilton, Edith, xxi, 17, 18, 22, 50, 51, 52, 54, 57, 59, 72, 76, 109, 118, 120, 123, 124, 125, 126

Hardin, Trudy, xxvii, 28, 29, 31, 37, 83, 87, 100, 101, 144
Harvard University, xxi, 53, 115, 164
Henson, Jamie, xxv, xxvi, 27, 39, 40, 42, 79, 85, 89, 90, 91, 95, 99, 101, 103, 145, 150, 151, 152, 156
Homosexuality, 7, 71, 128, 129, 135, 143, 147, 166, 171, 174
Homosocial networks, 51, 109, 113, 116, 131, 132, 139, 164, 166
Hull House, xxi, 108, 109, 111, 113, 115, 126, 153

Industrial medicine, xxi
International Ladies Garment Workers' Union (ILGWU), xxiv, 114, 115

Johns Hopkins University, xxiv, 53

Kellor, Frances, xxii, 18, 48, 49, 54, 57, 107, 108, 109, 110, 117, 121, 171
Kennedy, Elizabeth L., and Madeline Davis, 106, 146, 148, 180

Labov, Jean, xxvi, 31, 32, 34, 37, 40, 42, 87, 95, 97, 103, 104
Lesbian history, 2, 105, 118, 157, 167, 177, 180
Lesbians, 1–4, 7–10, 26, 34, 39, 40, 41, 45, 80, 81, 95, 96, 98, 101, 105, 134, 135, 137, 140, 142, 143, 146, 147; closeted lesbians, 140, 152–54, 157–61, 169, 175–77, 179, 181, 182, 184; working-class lesbians, 105, 106, 117, 129, 130, 157; World War II, 134, 147, 148, 152

Marriage, 4, 77, 108, 118, 126, 128, 130, 131, 134, 145, 170, 171, 175; class differences among contempo-

Marriage *(Cont.)*
  rary group, 73, 74; companionate,
  6, 119; critiques by Progressive Era
  women, 75; expectations for, 43,
  79; modern norms, 6, 9, 41, 44,
  45; Progressive Era, 68; rates in
  twentieth century, 8; rejection of,
  2, 12, 25, 41, 42, 46; role of, 94;
  views about, 24, 42, 43, 74, 75, 80,
  103, 104, 125, 154
Martinez, Jo, xxv, 28, 29, 31, 38, 82,
  93, 101, 103, 133, 144, 152, 153,
  157
McConnell, Anne, xxvi, 27, 28, 31,
  35, 37, 40, 44, 82, 83, 86, 87, 90,
  97, 103, 139, 140, 141, 143, 152,
  157
Miller, Frieda, xxiv, 15, 52, 67, 68,
  76, 107, 109, 110, 117, 121, 127
Miller, Iris, xxvii, 28, 36, 40, 84, 87,
  95, 96, 99, 101, 136, 142
Mitchell, Paula, xxvi, 27, 30, 34, 39,
  42, 43, 91, 101, 136, 139, 144,
  145, 148, 152
Mothers, 5, 98, 116, 164; African-
  American, 69; historians' discussion of, 51; lesbians as, xxv, 154;
  of Post WW II Era lesbians, xxvii,
  25, 27, 28, 29, 32, 36, 37, 40, 84,
  85, 86, 95, 98, 169; of Progressive
  Era women, xxiv, 11, 14, 15, 16,
  17, 18, 28, 48, 49, 55, 57, 60, 72,
  73, 123, 162, 163; Progressive Era
  women as, 76; role of, 7, 9, 25, 26,
  27, 43, 108, 155, 168; single,
  176; views about, 74, 75, 76, 82,
  132

New England Hospital for Women
  and Children, 52, 110
Newman, Pauline, xxiv, 14, 16, 21,
  49, 62, 64, 76, 107, 109, 113, 114,
  115, 117, 121, 127, 128
New Woman, 8, 162, 173

New York Infirmary for Women and
  Children, xxii, 52, 109, 110

O'Reilly, Leonora, xxi, 13, 14, 18,
  57, 62, 64, 76, 109, 113, 168

Partners/relationships, 32, 177;
  among contemporary lesbians, 40,
  96, 103, 133–34, 136, 138–45,
  148–51, 155–57, 160, 167, 168;
  among Progressive Era women,
  xxiii, 2, 4, 9, 74, 77, 107, 116–30,
  160, 163, 180; historians' discussion of, 118, 131, 134; sexuality in,
  122
Peña, Yolanda, xxvii, 28, 31, 38, 82,
  85, 87, 89, 90, 95, 96, 97, 100,
  101, 140
Physical Education (P.E.), 43, 84, 85,
  93, 137; homophobia in, 136, 137,
  141
Powell, Lee, xxvii, 28, 29, 37, 38, 40,
  42, 83, 91, 95, 101, 144, 148, 149,
  152, 153
Progressive Era, 1, 3, 4, 8, 9, 10, 11,
  32, 41, 44, 47, 87, 93, 95, 98, 107,
  108, 142, 152, 161, 163, 164; Progressive Era women, xxi, 55, 59,
  60, 62, 69, 80, 163, 166, 167, 170,
  171, 179, 180

Race, 93, 96, 101, 105, 161, 167,
  168, 169, 170, 171, 174, 176, 177,
  181; race privilege, 66, 68, 180;
  race suicide, 5; and racism, 9, 27,
  66, 82, 83, 90, 144, 165, 166, 167,
  170
Radcliffe College, xxiii, xxiv, 47, 50,
  51, 53, 68, 111, 180
Reed, Mabel, xxiii, 21, 67, 118, 120
Reid, Doris, xxi, 76, 118, 120, 123,
  124, 125, 126

Sexologists, 6, 41, 98, 105, 126, 129, 135, 162, 173, 174, 176
Sicherman, Barbara, 54, 123, 125, 126
Smith-Rosenberg, Carroll, 51, 77, 174
Spinsters, xxi, 1–4, 6, 9, 10, 68, 159
Stedman, Edith, xxiii, 15, 16, 20, 21, 47, 50, 52, 68, 100, 109, 111
Stern, Carrie, xxvi, 28, 36, 43, 84, 90, 97, 102, 104, 139, 152
Streig, Audrey, xxv, 28, 40, 84, 89, 90, 91, 95, 96, 99, 102, 105, 136, 138, 154, 157, 166, 169

Tomboys, 11, 30, 35
Travel, xxiii, 155, 163; among contemporary lesbians, 9, 80, 81, 94, 95, 97, 99; among Progressive Era women, 21, 22, 23, 48, 56, 59, 68, 127
Triangle Shirtwaist Factory, xxiv

University of Chicago, xxii
University of Michigan, xxi, 52

Vassar College, 12, 17, 49, 51, 52, 56

Ware, Susan, 16, 70, 118, 121
Wellesley College, xxii, xxiii, 16, 19, 51, 53, 54, 56, 75, 117, 130
Whelan, Gloria, xxvii, 32, 35, 36, 37, 40, 81, 85, 86, 90, 93, 101, 136, 141, 152, 158
Women in Industry Service, xxii, 63
Women's Bureau, xxii, xxiv, 60, 63, 64, 67, 110, 115
Women's history, 1, 2, 3, 118, 176, 177, 180, 182
Women's Trade Union League (WTUL), xxii, xxiii, xxiv, 61, 63, 109, 110, 113, 114, 153, 170
Working-class women; among contemporary lesbians, xxv, 85, 87, 89, 93, 99, 101, 103; among Progressive Era women, 5, 14, 18, 48, 58, 60, 62, 63, 64, 66, 73, 74, 75, 113, 114, 117, 162, 163, 164, 174, 180
World War I, xxii, 47, 68, 109, 163, 170, 175
World War II, 134, 140, 146

Yale University, xxiv